A Good Time Coming

A Good Time Coming

Mormon Letters to Scotland

edited by
Frederick Stewart Buchanan

with a Foreword by
Charles S. Peterson

For Laurel Thatcher Ulrich: Congratulations on your many accomplishments and thanks for creating uncommon history from the lives and artifacts of "common" folk. Yours aye, Fred S Buchanan

University of Utah Press
Salt Lake City
1988

Volume 4
in the Utah Centennial Series
Charles S. Peterson, Series Editor

Copyright © 1988 by the University of Utah Press
Printed in the United States of America
ISBN 0-87480-294-6

Library of Congress Cataloging-in-Publication Data

A Good time coming : Mormon letters to Scotland / edited by
Frederick Stewart Buchanan : with a foreword by Charles S. Peterson.
    p.   cm. — (Utah centennial series : v. 4)
    Bibliography: p.
    Includes index.
    1. Converts, Mormon–United States–Correspondence. 2. Scots–
Correspondence. 3. McNeil family. I. Buchanan, Frederick
Stewart. II. Series.
BX8693.G63 1988
289.3'092'2 — dc19
[B]   88–17150
                                              CIP

To My Sons
Richard Malcolm, Brian John, Glenn Stewart,
Alan Don, and Scott Reid
That they might remember their Scottish-Mormon heritage

Contents

ILLUSTRATIONS

Foreword

In *A Good Time Coming*, editor Frederick Buchanan continues a long-time interest in immigration. Covering experiences from the coal mines of Illinois and Wyoming to Arizona's Gila River, but focused in Utah, the MacNeil-Thompson letters of this volume are remarkable for what they show about the complexity of the American experience as well as what they reflect about life in Utah. The MacNeils and their kin emigrated from the coal mines of Scotland. Yet they never broke entirely from them. Four died violently—three in mining accidents, one of a related drowning. Their mindset was controlled largely by their experience in the collieries. Their actions were the actions of wage earners and laborers. Hoping for a better life they left Scotland. Once in Utah they misunderstood efforts to get them involved in Mormon rural community life and took recourse to day labor. Ill at ease with church authority and status arrangements, they remembered Scotland, or, roving at will, they became American immigrants in the large sense. They were not Marxist or given to class conflict, yet at least one of them viewed slavery as a flaw in the world's best "goviment" and for humanity's sake was willing to get involved in the Civil War. Their failure to embrace the vision of the Mormon kingdom was a testament to the resilience of mining's claims—claims Brigham Young feared as he warned against "scattering" on the mining frontier. These are elements that reach deeply into our national experience as editor Buchanan has rightly recognized.

An associate professor in the Department of Educational Studies at the University of Utah, Frederick Buchanan has specialized in the history of education, participating widely in that field. Born in Scotland himself, he has written several articles on the role of Scottish immigrants in Utah and contributed an excellent chapter to *The Peoples of Utah* ("Imperial Zion: the British Occupation of Utah"), ed. by Helen Papanikolas (1976). In *A Good Time Coming* he adds a significant new title to the literature of Utah and western immigration.

Permanent Euro/American settlement began in Utah with the Mormons in the years after 1847. Later, when the territory was opened by railroads and mining, others of American and northern European stock came in response to economic opportunities. Arriving during the turn-of-the-century decades were southeastern Europeans, including the Greeks, whose role was recognized in Helen Papanikolas's *Emilia—Emily; Yoryis—George*, an earlier volume in this series. During the last fifty years Utah has participated in the movement of peoples that has characterized the recent West including tourism and recreation, natural resource management, military mobilization, defense production, urban growth, occupational mobility, and the new Asian migration.

A Good Time Coming is part of a rich documentation that deals with the Mormon gathering. Basic to this body of literature are the revering accounts of church and family histories. Often these are the documentation of success. The human costs of migration are accepted as noble sacrifices, but, in the main, it was the person who was successfully absorbed into the Mormon community whose story is told.

The story of the Mormon gathering was also the account of the physical process of migration. Remarkable among contemporary travel descriptions was Frederick Hawkins Piercy's illustrated *Route from Liverpool to Great Salt Lake Valley* (1855). Written as a journal and offering "the best pictorial record of" Mormon migration from Britain, *Route from Liverpool* was published by the church as an aid to migration.

Scholarly works also examine the Mormon contribution to the peopling of Utah. They not only describe migration itself but also examine the "astonishing force" of the Mormon missionary system and the efficiency of the church as a travel agency, as well as the demographic impact of migration upon Utah's population. Three of these stand out. Wallace Stegner's popular *The Gathering of Zion*, which appeared in 1964 as a volume in the American Trails Series, deals primarily with the "exodus," or flight from

Illinois, in the years after 1846. Basically a trails account, it offers only the most general analysis of migration's implications for Utah's population. William Mulder's well-conceived *Homeward to Zion: The Mormon Migration from Scandinavia* (1957) goes far beyond travel aspects. It analyzes the dynamics behind the decision to emigrate, the role of the church in organizing migration, and the process by which Scandinavians became Utahns. Another careful study is P. A. M. Taylor's *Expectations Westward* (1965), a statistical analysis of the process by which converts were made in Britain and of subsequent migration.

To some degree these writers have joined the writers of Mormon memoirs in celebrating a success story. In the broader history of American immigration some attention has been paid to the costs of the move. Well-known works that address this fuller dimension include John Higham's *Strangers in the Land* (1955) and Oscar Handlin's *The Uprooted* (1973) which look at the difficulties involved in leaving one's native land, the terrors of the voyage, and opposition in a new country. Focusing on the problems of specific nationalities are Carey McWilliams's *North from Mexico* (1949) and Andrew Rolle's *The Immigrant Upraised: Italian Adventure and Colonists in an Expanding America* (1968), both of which have implications for western states. O. E. Rolvaag's superb novel, *Giants in the Earth* (1927) examines the psychic costs of emigration from Norway to a Great Plains homestead.

Helen Papanikolas's work on Greek immigrants and Robert Goldberg's 1986 *Back to the Soil: The Jewish Farmers of Clarion, Utah, and Their World,* also published in this series, bring strong elements of realism to bear on the Utah story. Yet no approach to Utah migration has allowed for a more realistic view of its costs than does Frederick Buchanan's *A Good Time Coming.*

Scottish immigrants have made major contributions to Utah. This fact is borne out in biographies of famous figures such as Leonard Arrington's *David Eccles* (1974) and novels like Claire Noall's *Surely the Night* (1972), and in the present volume by Frederick Buchanan's sensitive and informed treatment of background, meaning, and context. Their presence is also seen in the existence of the Utah-Scottish Association, in the celebration of Scottish traditions and culture in Utah's four pipe bands, and in the three yearly Scottish Highland gatherings. But the letters of the MacNeil-Thompson family members as they worked to fit sensitive temperaments and values formed during the industrialization of Scotland into the visions and austerity of pioneer Utah go beyond the celebration of a single ethnic group. They reflect the universal challenges of uprooting that beset all newcomers to the United States. They also characterize and foreshadow the tensions of modern America's mobile society. Pathos, tragedy, frustration, impatience, anger, poverty, and betimes perception that allows the limits of reality to fit with soaring vision — of such are the letters in *A Good Time Coming*. Ultimately it is the stuff of which a state's relation to the nation and the region around it is made. It is in that sense that this book is presented as Volume 4 in the University of Utah Press's Centennial of Utah Statehood Series.

Charles S. Peterson   July 24, 1988
Utah State University

Preface

In order to become acquainted with an age or a people we must also know something of its second-rate and obscure men. It is in the beliefs, sentiments and lot of unimportant and unknown families that the lot, sentiments, and the beliefs of the country are to be found. — François Guizot, cited in Andrew L. Drummond and James Bulloch, *The Church in Victorian Scotland 1843–1874*, p. vii.

After James McNeill died at his home in Ayr, Scotland, in 1964, his son Ruari began the ritual of clearing out the loft. In the process he uncovered a Victorian gentleman's traveling writing desk wrapped in brown paper. The writing desk had apparently belonged to Ruari's grandfather, David MacNeil, Jr., who died in 1922 at Glasgow. Its existence was a surprise to the family. Even more surprising was the discovery that it contained 180 letters written between 1847 and 1917 to members of the MacNeil clan by friends and relatives in England, Scotland, the United States, Australia, Canada, and Burma. Of these letters, 140 were from two friends and three sons of David and Ann MacNeil who had emigrated to Utah and elsewhere in the United States between 1853 and 1872, when Mormon converts were flocking to the "promised land."

Eventually Professor Christopher Smout of the Department of Scottish History at the University of St. Andrews saw the letters, recognized their significance, and suggested that they be deposited in the archives of the University of St. Andrews and that attempts be made to have them published. Inquiries to Professors

Richard Tompson and Davis Bitton of the Department of History at the University of Utah eventually led to my being invited to edit and prepare the letters for publication.

These letters are only a small sampling of the letters which the thousands of Scots who became Mormons must have written during the nineteenth century. No claim is made that they are representative; however, these particular communications tend to defy common stereotypes that have portrayed all Mormons as alike in their responses to their church, their environment, or even to their kith and kin. The various attitudes of the writers offer insight into the variety of personalities that made up Mormon pioneer society—ranging from the volatility of John MacNeil as he contends with economic and religious challenges, to the peaceful, almost resigned contentment of John Thompson as he puts spiritual goals above material ones. There is the sometimes naive moralizing of the new convert, James MacNeil, as he tries to convince his family to commit to Mormonism, coupled with the earthy, pragmatic approach of John Marshall who does the same thing, but with no pretense of being perfect himself. Here and there are touches of wry Scots' humor.

Unfortunately, almost no letters from Scotland have survived in Utah, and we must read between the lines to get a sense of what was happening to the MacNeil-Thompson family in Scotland between 1853 and 1904, the period covered by the letters selected for this volume. The tensions of challenges to their faith, and their desire to emigrate (which shifts with their changing fortunes), are obvious concerns of the MacNeils in Lanarkshire. In addition, the questions they asked about Mormon practices and doctrines or about what life was like in Utah for women give us a sense of their feelings about Mormonism.

These first-hand accounts, devoid of artifice and pretense, clearly demonstrate that the convert's experience has many facets—joy in the good news of Mormonism's claim to be the "Restored Gospel" or in North America as the "promised land" was certainly only one part of that experience. For the MacNeils, life in America also included conflicts with other Mormons, as well as the challenge of adapting to their new land. Never totally absent is the need to face growing doubt and cynicism in themselves and others when their aspirations remained unrealized. These then are not "faith-promoting" letters of unwavering optimism in the face of adversity. They are unvarnished testimonials of struggling mortals. Some of these immigrants grew in their faith while others shrank, but all of them had something to say about their times. America, to these letter writers, was envisioned as a land of opportunity and hope. It was also eventually seen as an arena where the forces of nature and human conflicts could prevent newcomers from ever achieving the "good times coming."

Of course, collections of letters based on the lives of successful Scots such as Robert L. Campbell, Territorial Superintendent of Common Schools from 1862 to 1874; Eilley Orrum, the "Queen of the Comstock Lode" silver bonanza in Nevada in the 1860s; David Eccles, Utah's first millionaire entrepreneur; David O. Calder, business manager of the Mormon Church's *Deseret News*; or Charles W. Nibley, who served as a member of the First Presidency of the Mormon Church from 1925 to 1931, would communicate a tale of success and achievement quite at odds with the tale of woe and disappointment apparent in many of the letters found in James MacNeil's attic. These letters are honest, sometimes painfully so. Because of this, they may help us to arrive at a more balanced historical picture of the rhythms and routines that made up the lives, not only of Scottish immigrants in Utah, but of the great mass of individuals who sought a better life in America. Many never quite met their goals and expectations, and the biggest miracle in the lives of these ordinary strivers lies in the fact that so many survived against sometimes overwhelming odds.

Mourning is a major motif of these letters as the deaths of four out of the five letter writers are encountered (three in the prime of their lives, and in accidents related to mining). The pessimism that permeates the letters of John MacNeil, for example, is due in some measure to the fact that hope was crushed out of him by the realities of life in western America in the nineteenth century. But even John Thompson in Illinois and James MacNeil in Arizona, for all their optimism and faith, fail to reach the "good times" they were hoping for.

The pathos of these family tragedies is summed up by David MacNeil's brief final note to his daughter, Ann, in Scotland: "I can't write. Four times I have undergone this kind of calamity, hand shakes so much. God preserve you."

Acknowledgments

To Ruari McNeill of Edinburgh (great-grandson of David MacNeil), Gladys Henkel Thorne of Murray, Utah (granddaughter of John MacNeil), Juanita May Thompson Juenger of Belleville, Illinois (great-granddaughter of John Thompson), Cleone Marshall Wayment of North Ogden, Utah, and Dean L. Marshall of Modesto, California (great-grandchildren of John Marshall), I owe a special debt of gratitude. Without their willingness to share their family's personal letters and to permit their publication, this collection would never have appeared. Mrs. Thorne has been most helpful in sharing with me data from her personal genealogical files and in giving me insights into the life of her grandfather, John MacNeil.

I am indebted to the Research Committee at the University of Utah for their generosity in enabling me to spend time at the University of St. Andrews during the summer of 1982, during which I examined the original letters. A grant from the Utah-Scottish Association provided the means for photocopying the collection for use in Utah. The Research Committee also granted a Faculty Fellow Award for the winter of 1985, thus allowing me to concentrate on this project. During the period I have worked on this manuscript, three chairs of the Department of Educational Studies at The University of Utah, Michael Parsons, Flo Krall, and Ralph Reynolds, have been very generous in the material and psychological support they have given to see that the project was completed. My colleagues in the Graduate School of Education have borne my Scottishness and my bagpipes with good humor and a large measure of tolerance!

Leonard Arrington, Roald Campbell, Joyce Kinkead, Gary Knowles, Tom Loveridge, Dale LeCheminant, Louis A. Moench, Charles Peterson, Suzanne Stauffer, Malcolm Thorp, Richard Tompson and Ronald Walker have given me the benefit of their insights. I deeply appreciate their comments and suggestions on my introductions and notes. I, of course, am responsible for the final interpretation placed on the letters. From its inception, the staff of the University of Utah Press has been a consistent and enthusiastic supporter of this project. I am grateful to them for encouragement and professional assistance. I have also benefited from Ron Bitton's and Patricia Degges's editorial expertise in sharpening and focusing my commentary and notes.

Courtesies extended to me as a visiting scholar at the University of St. Andrews by the Keeper of the Muniments, Robert N. Smart, and Professor Christopher Smout during the summer of 1982 are deeply appreciated. Dr. John McCaffrey and Dr. Bernard Aspinwall of the Department of Modern History, University of Glasgow, provided me with valuable insights into the pertinent literature on the history of nineteenth-century Scotland. The staffs of the Historical Department and the Family History Library of the Church of Jesus Christ of Latter-day Saints in Salt Lake City and the Special Collections Division of the University of Utah have helped me locate materials related to the letters. Their professional expertise made it a pleasure to do research in Mormon history.

Madelon Brunson, Archivist of the Reorganized Church of Jesus Christ of Latter Day Saints (RLDS) in Independence, Missouri, assisted me in tracing John Thompson's descendents in Illinois and in supplying me with information about Scots who had joined the RLDS Church. The staff of the Mitchell Library in Glasgow were very generous in responding to numerous inquiries by mail and in giving me valuable insights on Scottish words sprinkled throughout the letters. A special word of thanks is due Gillian Fraser, of the University of St. Andrews, whom I have never met, but who prepared a superb hand-list of the original letters which has been of inestimable value to me in preparing the letters for publication.

France Rimli painstakingly transferred the complete manuscript to disks and transformed all of the letters into a readable document. Cathleen Stewart transcribed a number of the manuscript letters in the early stages of this project. She and Paige Rallison on numerous occasions saved me from losing the manuscript in the labyrinth of word-processing technology. To each of these proficient secretaries I am deeply indebted for their professional assistance. My son Alan typed the final bibliography.

My wife, Rama Richards Buchanan, spent many hours in transcribing the original, often almost unreadable, letters. Her task was more than simple typing — she helped give meaning to the project as together we "translated" the faded letters and unraveled the history contained in these Mormon documents. For her patience with my long absences from home while I completed this work, for her expertise and gentle criticisms and for her loyal support, I am deeply grateful.

Frederick S. Buchanan
University of Utah
St. Andrew's Day
30 November 1987

A NOTE ON TRANSCRIPTION

For the most part the letters have been reproduced as written. However, for ease in reading, some punctuation, capitalization, and paragraphing have been added. Original spelling has been retained throughout, except where the letter writer has apparently made an inadvertent slip in the placement of letters in a word. For ease of reference, dates have been standardized in the day/month/year format. Formalized greetings such as "Hope this finds you well as it finds us likewise" have been in most instances deleted, as have portions of letters which do not add to our understanding of the writer's situation as an emigrant. Such deletions are indicated by the use of ellipses. Words added to improve clarity or meaning have been placed in brackets.

A word about the spelling of the names Thomson and MacNeil: the first is spelled in the Scottish manner — Thomson — on all original Scottish documents (e.g., census returns and Mormon Church records) relating to this family. However, John Thomson added a "p" to his name in signing his letters. To avoid confusion, I have chosen to use John's spelling of the family name — Thompson — throughout my commentary and notes. The MacNeils changed the spelling of their name from time to time in signing their letters — McNeill, McNeil, McNeal, and MacNeil. These idiosyncrasies have been preserved in the letters, but references to the family in the text appear as MacNeil — the form used latterly by John.

Because the letters in this collection deal primarily with only two generations, a detailed genealogical pedigree chart has not been included. Instead, two family group sheets show the relationships dealt with in the letters.

The Thomson-Boggie family group sheet shows the family of John Thomson, Sr., and Ann Beaton Boggie. Their son John Thomson wrote most of the letters in Chapter 2 to his mother, his step-father David MacNeil, Sr., and his sister Elizabeth.

The MacNeil-Boggie family group sheet shows the family of David MacNeil, Sr., and Ann Beaton Boggie Thomson. John and James MacNeil wrote most of the letters in Chapters 3 through 6 to their parents and to their sister Ann and brother David.

Throughout the correspondence there are references to Margaret and Janet Thomson (and their spouses Robert Paterson and John McLean), to William Forbes Thomson and to David MacNeil, Jr.

The information on these family group sheets was obtained from records in the possession of Mrs. Gladys H. Thorne, the Family History Library of the Church of Jesus Christ of Latter-day Saints in Salt Lake City, the National Archives in Washington, D.C., and New Register House in Edinburgh.

HUSBAND: JOHN THOMSON, Cotton Handloom Weaver and Mineral Laborer
Born: c. 1811, Scotland
Married: c. 1832
Died: c. 1846
Father: Not known
Mother: Not known

WIFE: ANN BEATON BOGGIE
Born: 17 July 1811, Stromness, Orkney Islands, Scotland
Died: 8 July 1887, Wishaw, Lanarkshire, Scotland
Second husband: David MacNeil
Father: James Boggie, Soldier and Shoemaker, 1791–1866
Mother: Margaret Clouston, 1787–1835

	CHILDREN	BORN	MARRIED	DIED
1	James Thomson	c. 1833		c. 1841–51
2	"Son" Thomson	c. 1835		before 1841
3	John Thomson	27 Dec. 1837 Pollockshaws, Renfrewshire	Elizabeth Haig 28 April 1865 Alton, Ill.	30 Aug. 1875 Belleville, Ill.
4	Margaret Thomson	c. 1839 Pollockshaws, Renfrewshire	Robert Paterson 5 June 1860 Dalmellington, Ayrshire	
5	William Forbes Thomson	c. 1841 Pollockshaws, Renfrewshire	Jessie Paton Wilson 24 April 1860 Old Monkland, Lanarkshire	8 Sept. 1863 Kirkintilloch, Dumbarton-shire
6	Elizabeth Thomson	c. 1843 Pollockshaws, Renfrewshire	Unmarried	9 Oct. 1906 Wishaw, Lanarkshire
7	Janet Thomson	c. 1845 Old Monkland, Lanarkshire	John McLean 1 June 1870 Old Monkland, Lanarkshire	

MACNEIL-BOGGIE FAMILY

HUSBAND: DAVID MACNEIL, Miner, Draper, and Clerk
Born: 13 June 1829, Edinburgh, Scotland
Married: 1 Feb. 1847, Edinburgh, Scotland
Died: 29 Oct. 1904, Salt Lake City, Utah
Father: John MacNeil, Spirit Merchant and Grocer, 1801–41
Mother: Margaret McKinlay, 1799–1833

WIFE: ANN BEATON BOGGIE THOMSON
Born: 17 July 1811, Stromness, Orkney Islands, Scotland
Died: 8 July 1887, Wishaw, Lanarkshire, Scotland
First husband: John Thomson
Father: James Boggie, Soldier and Shoemaker, 1791–1866
Mother: Margaret Clouston, 1787–1835

	CHILDREN	BORN	MARRIED	DIED
1	John MacNeil	5 Dec. 1847 Carnbroe, Lanarkshire	Annie Cooper Warrilow 2 Feb. 1874 Salt Lake City, Utah	8 Nov. 1903 Park City, Utah
2	David MacNeil	7 April 1850 Rosehall, Lanarkshire	Mary Murray 16 July 1872 Glasgow, Scotland	26 Dec. 1922 Glasgow, Scotland
3	Ann MacNeil	22 Feb. 1852 Rosehall, Lanarkshire	Unmarried	12 May 1917 Wishaw, Lanarkshire
4	James Boggie Brady MacNeil	29 Jan. 1855 Cairnhill, Lanarkshire	Unmarried	18 March 1884 Pima, Ariz.

A Good Time Coming

1

"Is not Scotland as near to heaven as Amarica?"

After Mary Murdoch Mair of Auchenleck, Ayrshire, converted to Mormonism in 1851, her desire was to go to Utah where her younger children could be raised among Mormons. In 1866 she secretly abandoned her husband and her twenty-one-year-old son Allan and obeyed the call of "gathering to Zion," taking with her two daughters and her youngest son. Twenty-nine years later Allan queried his mother about why she had left them and asked: "Is not Scotland as near to heaven as Amarica?" For those Scottish converts who believed in the "doctrine of the gathering," the answer to the question would have been a resounding "No." To gather was every bit as important as being baptized or obeying any other of the laws of God.[1] In terms of its influence on the church and on the lives of thousands of individuals, this doctrine was perhaps Mormonism's most prominent feature in the nineteenth century. It was the initial and sustaining impetus for the far-flung prose-lyting activity of the church from 1837 to the close of the century.

The letters in this volume reflect the lives and fortunes of a small group of young coal and iron miners who left Lanarkshire, Scotland, as Mormon converts to seek their fortunes in America. Mining shaped their lives and their destinies in the United States

---

[1] Allan Faulds Mair to Mary Murdoch Mair McMillan, 7 November 1897, cited in Nicol, ed., *The James and Mary Murray Murdoch Family History*, 90–91. Kelly Finnegan drew my attention to this publication. For the doctrinal basis of the gathering see Doctrine and Covenants Sections 28:7–8, 63:36, 84:2–4; see also Mulder, *Homeward to Zion*, 18, 134.

CENTRAL SCOTLAND

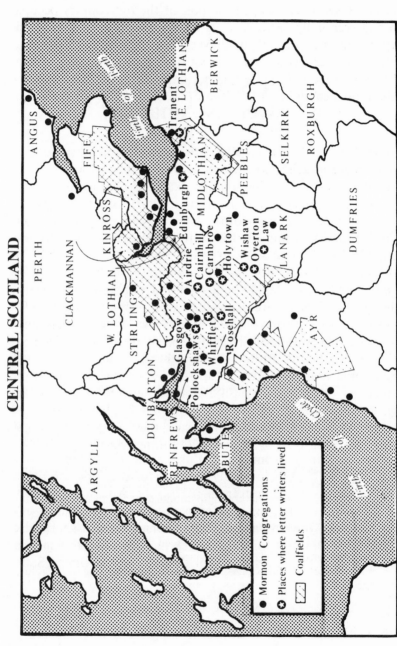

Note proximity of Mormon congregations to coalfields in 1850.

Virginia B. Hoefler

as it did in Scotland, just as surely as did their conversion to Mormonism. They never escaped the pull of the old-country occupation and eventually partook of its ultimate hazards as well. Their story begins, not with their conversion to the Church of Jesus Christ of Latter-day Saints, but with the transformation of central Scotland from a tightly knit region of rural pastures into one of the most heavily industrialized areas on the face of the earth.

ON THE INDUSTRIAL FRONTIER

Until the end of the eighteenth century, Scottish miners and their families were attached to their mine owners as de facto serfs or slaves. The stigma of being a miner extended even to some being refused burial in consecrated ground. Partly on humanitarian grounds and partly because of the difficulty owners had in attracting new recruits to mining, the serfdom of Scottish miners was finally abolished by an Act of the British Parliament in 1799. In the decades following their emancipation the former slavelike miners developed into a highly respected and well-paid work force. Although Scotland's developing industrial economy was becoming more dependent on coal, the miners were able to maintain a way of life that was generally unaffected by the growth of urbanization and industrialization. The miners in Lanarkshire enjoyed a traditional and respected occupation in a rural environment. Each collier was in large measure an independent operator whose work entailed a large range of technical skills, besides physical strength. Many had small holdings and their work in the mines was in part a seasonal occupation. The miner was in fact

> proud of his status as a craftsman and possibly anxious for respectability after more than a century of serfdom. The scarcity of his skills provided a relatively high standard of living and, as a kind of contractor, he enjoyed considerable freedom and autonomy in his work. Often living in a rural environment, the collier escaped the worst rigours of urban life faced by other sections of the working class. . . . The early years of the nineteenth century were remembered by old colliers in the 1840s as something of a "golden age."[2]

However, this "golden age" of the Scottish miners came to an end in the 1830s as the emerging iron industry demanded larger and

---

[2] Alan B. Campbell, *The Lanarkshire Miners*, 44. See also 9–43.

more efficient coal-mining operations. In the process of large-scale industrialization a once proud, almost hereditary class of semi-independent miners was reduced to an industrial laboring class. The new coal and iron masters also undermined the traditional culture of the miners by imposing rigid work schedules, and the miners' bargaining power was seriously impaired by the extensive use of Irish immigrant labor.

By the late 1840s the rural area of Lanarkshire had been transformed. Smokestacks, furnaces, and "bings" of waste from the newer, efficient coal mines replaced the small holdings and rolling pastures. A society based on close-knit family relationships evolved into one composed of emigrants from Ireland, the Highlands, and other areas of Scotland, essentially strangers whose main task was basic survival. The emergent era was characterized by overcrowding, substandard housing, and a breakdown in established social institutions. The *North British Review* for November 1847 noted with alarm the rapid social changes that were occurring and warned its readers that Lanarkshire's newly industrialized towns such as Airdrie and Coatbridge were ripe for a violent confrontation between workers and authorities.[3] The destruction of the semi-independent Scottish miner and his rural roots and the "hectic growth" of the Scottish iron industry created in a few years an

> explosion of frontier towns east of Glasgow like Airdrie, Coatbridge and Motherwell; in such places, murk, brutalization, and social incoherence produced fearful drunkenness and violence, against which struggled Chief Constables and their police forces.[4]

Contrary to the popular, romantic image of Scotland as the land of thistle, heather, and kilt, the Scots were in fact the "shock troops of modernization.[5] An assault on traditional social and economic arrangements took place in the squalid, "reekin' " industrial villages of "fire, smoke and soot" that ringed Glasgow by mid-century. Christopher Smout's description of life in Scotland during this era as "competitive, unprotected, brutal and, for many,

---

[3] Ibid., 104.
[4] Checkland, *Industry and Ethos*, 25.
[5] See Aspinwall, *Portable Utopia*, 2; see also the description of the new towns that encircled Glasgow in *The Ordinance Gazetteer of Scotland*, 1:273.

vile" succinctly puts the popular, romantic image into perspective.[6] It was a situation that many people wanted to change.
Responding to this social deterioration, the *Glasgow Herald* in
1849 published an article entitled "Social and Moral Conditions
of the Population in Glasgow" in which a correspondent argued
that a main cause of the breakdown in law and order was the lack
of effective religious institutions for dealing with the new problems created by industrialization. Failure of the establishment to
respond was leading to the production of

> a degraded, a discontented, and a dangerous population; and
> while many praiseworthy efforts are made to bestow the blessings
> of the Gospel on the pagans of India, Africa, and America, we
> have, in our own streets, wynds, and closes, more than one hun-
> dred thousand practical heathens, many of whom are "steeped to
> the very lips" in misery and crime, and who are left to rush head-
> long to destruction without any man to "care for their souls.[7]

Unless the tendency toward lawlessness were checked, the writer
saw only "a vast and a ruinous social convulsion." To counteract
this he suggested that in the city of Glasgow, thirty "philanthropic
Christian labourers" be appointed by the church to visit, instruct,
and bestow "Christian charity" on the residents living within the
confines of the city's 100 evangelical Christian congregations. One
"visitor" would then be familiar with the temporal and moral wel-
fare of the eighteen families nearest his home. In this way 270,000
persons would be brought into contact with the edifying influence
of the church and would thereby be saved from the brutalizing
influence of impersonal, urban life. Not only would "decent families be saved from ruin," but such personal intervention would
end impositions on the Parochial Boards, increase church attendance, and promote day schools, Sunday schools, and savings
banks. Perhaps most importantly in a time when revolution was
almost the order of the day in Europe, such a scheme would reduce
the distance between the higher and the lower classes and thus
promote kindly feelings between the two estranged segments of
society.

It is doubtful that this plan could have made more than a
dent in the new industrial order of society even if it had actually

[6] Smout, *A Century of the Scottish People*, 7-8, 31.
[7] *Glasgow Herald*, 5 February 1849.

been initiated. However, the proposal underscored one of the social realities of the period: large segments of Scotland's working class, at least in the crowded industrial centers, had lost contact with the established church — the Church of Scotland. In the words of one Presbyterian leader, the Rev. Thomas Chalmers (who may indeed have been the writer of the foregoing proposal), the most important challenge facing the "Kirk" was that of "excavating the heathen" in the heartland of industrial Scotland.[8] The central belt of Scotland had by the late 1840s become "one of the most intensely industrialized regions on the face of the earth" and it is little wonder that Dr. Chalmers viewed it as a foreign mission field — it was indeed *terra incognita* for the middle-class establishment of church and state.[9]

The Church of Scotland was facing new and bewildering social and economic conditions in the rapidly growing cities. Compounding the difficulties, it was also suffering from the effects of a split in its own ranks. Known as "The Disruption," this dispute grew out of disagreements within the Kirk over the proper relationship betwen church and state. In 1843, Thomas Chalmers and a third (470) of the Church of Scotland ministers seceded and formed the Free Church of Scotland — free from restrictions imposed by Acts of Parliament on the officially supported state church. In the long term, the competition resulting from the disruption of the church promoted a "reinvigoration of Scottish religious life" at the local parish level. But in the short term, "The Disruption" split Presbyterianism into "a three cornered affair" — the official Church of Scotland, the Free Church of Scotland, and the United Presbyterian Church — "a weak institutional basis on which to meet the new theological and cultural challenges" presented by Biblical criticism, secularism, scientific thought, and the new industrial era.[10]

Scotland's urban working classes did not, however, wait for the Kirk to lead them to the promised land of social and economic justice. Many asserted themselves through the activities of Scottish Chartism, which by 1840 had become the most vocal and articulate advocate of the working man's place in society. Scottish

---

[8]Checkland, *Industry and Ethos*, 6.
[9]Smout, *A Century of the Scottish People*, 86.
[10]Checkland, *Industry and Ethos*, 122-23.

Chartism championed reform through education and moral persuasion rather than through violence and social disruption. The religious dimension in the Scottish experience also came to the fore in the Scottish interpretation of Chartist principles. Generally seen as a secular movement elsewhere in Great Britain, in Scotland one of the striking things about Chartism was its use of religious idiom to promote reform. By 1841 there were twenty Christian Chartist churches in the industrialized area of central Scotland and from the pulpit itinerant Chartist preachers were expounding Chartist principles as consistent with Christianity. One enthusiast went so far as to say that the "man who is not a Chartist is not a Christian. . . . Practical Christianity can never be reconciled to narrow systems of politics."[11]

In addition to the idealism expressed by the organized Chartist movement, there was considerable popular hope that things would eventually improve for the working classes — perhaps not miraculously, but through concerted political and social action. The Scottish-born writer Charles MacKay gave expression to this secular hope of a new order in such verses as "The Good Time Coming" — an expression that occurs frequently in the MacNeil letters. Probably many working-class families were familiar with the poems that expressed this secular prophet's vision of a peaceful world, social justice, and social harmony. They were written around 1845–46 and appeared in a collection of verses entitled "Voices from the Crowd" during a "time of social and political agitation." MacKay said that his verses were meant to express the "general sentiments of the toiling classes" as they sought a more equitable society:

> There's a good time coming, boys,
> A good time coming:
> Hateful rivalries of creed
> Shall not make their martyrs bleed
> In the good time coming.
> Religion shall be shorn of pride,
> And flourish all the stronger;
> And Charity shall trim her lamp;
> Wait a little longer.

[11] Wilson, *The Chartist Movement in Scotland*, 138.

There's a good time coming, boys,
  A good time coming:
And a poor man's family
Shall not be his misery
  In the good time coming.
Every child shall be a help,
  To make his right hand stronger;
The happier he the more he has;
  Wait a little longer.

There's a good time coming, boys,
  A good time coming:
Little children shall not toil,
Under or above the soil,
  In the good time coming;
But shall play in healthful fields
  Till limbs and minds grow stronger;
And everyone shall read and write;
  Wait a little longer.[12]

The hope for a better age was persistent throughout much of Scotland in these years. However, the Kirk as an institution was slow to respond to the needs of the working classes, although the times were seemingly ripe for change.

Within the Kirk there also appeared a charismatic note of dissent between 1827 and 1830. In this period a religious "restorationist" awakening involving spiritual manifestations swept through "western Scotland (much as it was sweeping through the area of upstate New York that gave rise to the Mormon Church in the same period). "Quite ordinary folk," men, women, and children, were reported to be receiving direct responses to their prayers, and healings and speech in unknown tongues were manifest in the spring of 1830. About this time, the Rev. Edward Irving, with his teachings about the imminence of Christ's second coming and his emphasis upon healings, speaking in tongues, and other "manifestations of the Spirit," drew vast crowds, especially among the poor. His activities and his unorthodox beliefs about Christ's human nature also drew the ire of the Kirk, and he was expelled from the Church of Scotland in 1832. During this time Irving was a member of a group of concerned churchmen in London which eventually organized the Catholic Apostolic Church c. 1832 as an expres-

---

[12] MacKay, *Poetical Works*, 209–10.

sion of their belief that Christianity had strayed from the teachings and practices of the primitive church. It should be noted that Joseph Smith, the founder of Mormonism, claimed that he had been chosen to restore the "primitive" church. Smith was also aware of Irving and his teachings. Indeed, although he regarded "Irvingite" authority as counterfeit, in his estimation their beliefs were "perhaps the nearest of the modern sectarians" to the ancient Christian church, at least as he perceived it.[13]

Bernard Aspinwall views the "dynamic millennialism" of Irving as an expression of the notion held by many Scots that their nation, like the United States, was a chosen redemptive nation with a divine mission to prepare mankind for the second coming. Two of Irving's Glasgow contemporaries, Dr. David Bogue and the Rev. David Brown, wrote books dealing with the establishment of the Kingdom of God on earth that were widely read in the United States. For some the secular development leading to improved social and economic conditions was an expression of the divine will being worked out in human affairs. In Brown's view, "Individual failings might persist but all lands and nations would be united in one faith and one lord: the process was already underway."[14] Such millennial hopes were also shared by the Mormons.

The social and religious conditions in Scotland in the 1830s promoted discontent, the emergence of the charismatic "Irvingites," and a sense that better times lay ahead for the working classes. Combined with Scottish religious idealism, democratic theory, and educational practice, and their symbiotic and reciprocal development in the United States, these conditions helped prepare a fertile seedbed in Scotland for the teachings of the Church of Jesus Christ of Latter-day Saints.

THE GATHERING FROM SCOTLAND

The first Mormon missionaries to the Scots were Alexander Wright and Samuel Mulliner. They accepted Mormonism in Canada and

---

[13] Davenport, *Albury Apostles*, 21–47; Joseph Fielding Smith, ed., *Teachings of the Prophet Joseph Smith*, 210.

[14] Aspinwall, *Portable Utopia*, xi–xiv, 185. For a discussion of the "common culture" that Scotland and the United States shared, see 1–42. See also Aspinwall, "A Fertile Field."

then returned to their native land with the message that Christianity had indeed apostatized and that the "true church" had been restored to Joseph Smith, the prophet of the "new dispensation." In May 1840 the first Scottish congregation of the Mormon Church was organized at Paisley by Mormon Apostle Orson Pratt. At a church conference in Manchester, England, in July 1840, Samuel Mulliner reported that there were 193 Latter-day Saints in the vicinity of Glasgow. On 8 August 1840 the Glasgow Branch was officially organized at the home of John Wardrobe, and Walter Crane was called to be an elder in the new church.[15] Less than a month later, Walter Crane, his wife, and Isabel Begg of Paisley sailed from the Clyde on the *Achilles* en route to Nauvoo, the Mormon community in Illinois founded by Mormon Church President Joseph Smith the previous year. Until Brigham Young and the pioneers arrived in the Great Salt Lake valley in 1847, Nauvoo was the principal gathering place and attracted thousands of emigrants from the United Kingdom.

This pattern of conversion, baptism, and emigration was repeated many times. Some five thousand Scots left for America during the 19th century as part of the Mormon doctrine of the gathering. Not that going to America was a uniquely Mormon-inspired venture. For many years before the 1840s there had been a well-established pattern of Scots leaving their homeland. Sometimes they were pushed by political conflicts and economic hard times; at other times they were pulled by the lure of the new world and its promise of "a good time coming." Often emigration was the only alternative when people were caught in the "age-old shifts in land use which recur in all human history."[16] In the aftermath

---

[15]For an overview of Mormon beginnings in Scotland see Buchanan, "The Ebb and Flow of the Mormon Church in Scotland." A "branch" in the LDS Church is a local congregation presided over by a branch president or presiding elder; it is distinguished from a ward, which is presided over by a bishop. There are two divisions of priesthood in the LDS Church—the Melchizedek Priesthood and the Aaronic Priesthood. The former deals with spiritual matters and contains the offices of elder, seventy, and high priest. The latter deals with the temporal affairs of the church and consists of the offices of deacon, teacher, and priest. See Doctrine and Covenants 20:38–67, 107:1–25.

[16]Richards, *A History of the Highland Clearances*, 9. For a discussion of the overall emigration of Scots to the United States see Lehman, *Scottish and Scotch-Irish Contributions*; Brander, *The Emigrant Scots*, 55–72, 89–112; Aspinwall, "The Scots in the United States," 80–110.

of the "Highland Clearances," for example, thousands of Highlanders left their native glens for North America when their traditional crofting way of life was disrupted as landlords cleared the land of its people in order to make it more profitable for sheep raising. The Mormon appearance in Scotland in the 1840s happened to coincide with the socioeconomic circumstances of the mid-century, giving the Mormon message of gathering a compelling appeal and adding a religious dimension to the traditional reasons for crossing the Atlantic. As one Fifeshire Mormon, Henry Hamilton, expressed it in commenting on the commitment of a new member: "I could see he had some faith in the principles of the Gospel, he desired to go to America."[17]

Even if the British Mission of the Mormon Church was meeting the practical needs of the church by infusing it with loyal blood at a crucial time in the church's history (namely the financial and political crisis that erupted in Kirtland in 1837), the basic religious motivation of the converts cannot be ignored. For Mormons, God had commanded his people to come out of Babylon and gather with the "chosen people" — and they did that in droves. As one observer has noted, "Such converts accepted a body of doctrine which included the concept of 'gathering' to build up a perfect society, and which regarded as a 'mission' even the most material labours to that end."[18]

The success of Mormon proselyting activity in the British Isles and the subsequent "gathering" of Mormons to the United States has sometimes been explained as simply the desire of the poor and dispossessed for material improvement. However, this explanation has generally been derived from studies in England and may not altogether fit the Scottish condition. Of course, Scotland shared with England many features of industrialization, but as E. P. Thompson points out, Scotland and England had significantly different popular cultures until at least 1820 and English Methodism was certainly *not* the same as Scottish Calvinism.[19] More intensive studies of the background of Scottish Mormons in the 1840s will be necessary before we can determine precisely the

[17] Hamilton, Journal, 28 November 1855.
[18] Taylor, "Why Did British Mormons Emigrate?" 251.
[19] See Thompson, *The Making of the English Working Class*, 390, 801–2; also Armytage, *Heaven Below*, 260.

extent to which Mormon conversions in Scotland might be linked to the peculiar idiosyncracies of Scottish cultural, economic, social and religious conditions. Until such studies are undertaken, perhaps the most accurate generalization is that Scots became Mormons for a variety of reasons, including religious, social and economic factors. The social and economic conditions in Scotland (as elsewhere) helped shape an environment which gave the Mormon religious message a compelling appeal.

A contemporary commentator explained the general success of Mormon missionaries in Great Britain as a combination of the claims of receiving continuous divine inspiration, mass psychology, prevalence of discontent, and the appeal to social equality. With promises of a new millennial day dawning the Mormons were able to gratify the "aspirations after 'a good time coming,' which fill the dreams of their democratic converts." William Gibson, a miner and former Chartist, addressed this issue of "a good time coming" when he spoke to a group of striking miners in Oakley, Fifeshire, in the 1840s. His friends had criticized him for being disloyal to Scotland in planning to emigrate, but he told them that it was poverty, not disloyalty, that forced his hand. Gibson stated that he was leaving so that he could eventually own a piece of land "and own no master but our God." After this impassioned speech, those who had criticized Gibson lifted him on their shoulders and carried him through the town. They apparently understood his message.[20]

The religious and spiritual commitment of a man like Gibson is obvious as he expresses himself in his journal and in his lifelong involvement in Mormon affairs. He was converted, no doubt. But this former political activist was just as fervent in his statement that he was motivated to leave Scotland by economic and social problems. It may be that his reformist bias is one factor that shaped his view of Mormonism as a means of escaping the adverse conditions in Scotland. For Gibson, as for many Mormon converts, it was apparently God's will that he emigrate and be twice blessed—materially *and* spiritually.

The personal religious issues involved in the conversion process are pointed out in Malcolm R. Thorpe's analysis of 198 case

---

[20] [Coneybeare], "Mormonism," 378–80; Gibson, Journal, 150:113; 151B:130.

studies of British converts (including twenty-one Scots) between 1837 and 1852. According to Thorpe, the factors that seemed to loom large in the conversion process (as revealed in the journals kept by these British converts) were (a) a perception of the established churches as being weak and in retreat against the problems of the day; (b) the search for a religion that agreed with a Christian fundamentalist perception of the "New Testament Church"; (c) dissatisfaction with sectarian conflicts; (d) concern over the issue of "eternal damnation" as preached by traditional churches; (e) personal crises brought about by illness or social dislocation; and (f) a degree of anticlericalism. The Mormon notion of a restoration of primitive Christianity made a great deal of sense to those who had become disaffected with their religion, particularly those with fundamentalist beliefs. At the same time, it should be noted that the Mormons made little headway where people were satisfied with their religious tradition, as in Ireland or the Highlands of Scotland.[21]

Of the twenty-one Scottish converts he studied, Thorpe identified seventeen as belonging to the working class, two as lower middle class, and two from the middle class. An examination of 588 Scottish Mormon males who emigrated between 1855 and 1870 reinforces Thorpe's conclusions and shows that 40 percent were miners, 11 percent were from the textile industry, and 15 percent were general laborers and metal workers.[22] If these cases are typical, Mormon converts in Scotland in the early years were decidedly working class—not at all surprising when one considers that the vast majority of Mormon branches were situated in the industrial areas surrounding Glasgow. Working-class Scots were also more likely to become affiliated with other dissenting religious groups, at least in the 1840s and 1850s.

The Mormon presence in Scotland, however, must be kept in perspective since membership was small. Even at the peak of proselyting success in 1850 there were only 3,257 members of the church in Scotland out of a population of 2.9 million. A major

---

[21] Thorpe, "The Religious Background of Mormon Converts in Britain," 51–66; for a perceptive discussion of the religious and social conditions in Scotland which may have contributed to the success of Mormon and other dissenting groups in the 1840s and 50s see Brown, *The Social History of Religion*, 44–54, 72–74.

[22] Buchanan, "The Emigration of Scottish Mormons," 55–57.

reason for the small numbers, of course, was the policy of continually sending members to the United States. Another was the fact that obedience and discipline were essential requirements of the faithful "Saint," and while there were 1,308 baptisms between 1852 and 1856, over 1,400 persons were excommunicated for failure to adhere to church standards, ranging from failure to attend meetings, to criticism of leaders, to serious moral infractions. It is easy to see why membership in the Mormon Church fell from a total of 3,257 in 1850 to 1,224 in 1859. Only for a few years (1848–56) were total baptisms able to keep pace with the tide of emigration and excommunication. Excommunication accounted for some 11 percent of the loss during the period 1860 to 1900, but the major loss sustained by Mormon congregations in Scotland continued to be emigration (see Table 1).

Table 1[23]

Years	Baptisms	Emigration	Emigration as % of Baptisms
1850–59	3,477	1,871	54%
1860–69	1,864	1,559	83%
1870–79	767	956	125%
1880–89	874	772	88%
1890–99	546	171	31%
Total 1850–99	7,528	5,329	70%

In 1890, there were only 203 baptized members, the lowest church membership since the beginning of Mormon proselyting in 1840. But even then, of the twenty-two new converts added that year, 90% (twenty) were lost through emigration.

The emigration of Scottish Mormons was part of a general movement of populations that occurred during the latter half of the nineteenth century when three to four million persons were admitted to the United States as new residents each decade. Mormon immigrants to the United States numbered some 80,000 souls, a relatively small number among the millions who crossed the Atlantic on their way to new homes. However, the Mormon migra-

---

[23] See statistical account of the Edinburgh Conference, 1840–68; Glasgow Conference, 1840–80; Scottish Conference, 1880–99. Although there may be some discrepancies in the total figures because of the absence of some Dundee and Kilmarnock statistics, these figures appear to give an accurate account of the overall trends.

tion was perhaps the largest movement to be stimulated by a religious belief. Between 1840 and 1900 British Mormons accounted for 67 percent of the European Mormon emigration; the Scottish Mormons accounted for about 10% of the British total.[24] The extent of the British contribution to populating Utah can be seen by realizing that between 1860 and 1880 the British-born population in Utah averaged some 22 percent of the total population and comprised over 67 percent of the total foreign-born population. Of the total British-born population, some 11 percent came from Scotland, an accurate reflection of the Scottish proportion of the total population of the United Kingdom. The Scottish Mormons accounted for only 1.5 percent of the total Scottish emigration to the United States, but most of this small number (approximately 5,000) made their way to Utah, where they made up almost 8 percent of the foreign-born population between 1850 and 1900.

When the two sons of David and Ann MacNeil, John and James, arrived in Utah in the early 1870s, there were 2,391 Scottish-born residents in the territory, ranking as the third largest immigrant group after the English-Welsh and the Danes. Nevertheless, Scots made up less than 3 percent of the total population, and by 1900 this had been reduced to 1.1 percent.[25] As a statistical entity, then, the Scots may seem hardly worth considering, but the history of immigrants is more than an account of how many came and how they compare to other groups. Qualitative dimensions in the lives of immigrants cannot easily be reduced to numbers. It is to those dimensions that the letters in this volume speak.

LETTERS OF A MORMON FAMILY

The story of the MacNeil family could be taken back to the beginning of Scottish history when their reputed ancestor, Neill of the Nine Hostages, was high King of Ireland. Or an attempt could be made to connect them to the MacNeils who dwelt on the rocky islands of Barra and Gigha in the Hebrides. One of their chieftains, known as *the* MacNeil, is said to have felt that he was just a

[24] On European (including British) emigration, see Taylor, *The Distant Magnet*. The same author has done a detailed analysis of British Mormon emigration in his *Expectations Westward*.

[25] For examples of the ways in which British immigrants contributed to the development of Utah, see Buchanan, "Imperial Zion," 61-113.

little above the ordinary. Each evening, after dinner, he would go to the battlements of Kisimul Castle overlooking the Atlantic. There he would "wipe his lips, sound a trumpet, and shout into the Atlantic winds, 'Hear, O ye people! And listen, O ye nations! The MacNeil of Barra has eaten! The princes of the earth may now dine!' "[26] There may be just a wee bit of the same attitude in the MacNeils of Lanarkshire, but no attempt will be made to prove the connection.

Originally a Highland clan, the MacNeils who settled in the Scottish Lowlands during the eighteenth century may have come there as a result of involvement in the Jacobite rebellions of 1715 and 1745. The ancestors of the Utah MacNeils were in Tranent, East Lothian, by the 1760s at least, most of them working in the coal mines. Their story—and that of their kin, the Thompsons—calls to mind Guizot's comment that in the lives of apparently "second-rate and obscure men" (and women) lies a key to understanding "the lot, sentiments, and beliefs of the country."

These letters had their beginning when a young Scottish miner, David MacNeil, and his wife, Ann Boggie Thompson, joined the Mormon Church at Airdrie, Lanarkshire, in February 1848.

David MacNeil was born in Edinburgh on 13 June 1829, the son of John MacNeil, a prosperous grocer and spirit merchant (he had three shops), and his wife, Margaret McKinlay. David was apparently the only one of their seven sons who survived to maturity. In 1833 David's mother died and his father married her sister, Euphemia McKinlay. Young David is reported to have ridden his own pony to a private school in Edinburgh. Eventually this rather well-to-do family seems to have made its way back to the ancestral home of John MacNeil in Tranent, nine and a half miles from Edinburgh. By 1841, when David was twelve, both his father and his stepmother were dead and he was left in the care of his uncle, George MacNeil. George is reported to have misused the trust—young David was put into the Tranent coal pits and the money that was intended for his education was appropriated by his Uncle George.[27]

---

[26] McPhee, *The Crofter and the Laird*, 12.

[27] Information on David MacNeil's early life was derived from a letter sent by his daughter, Ann MacNeil, to her niece, Ann MacNeil Henkel, Salt Lake City, c. 1908. Special Collections, University of Utah.

Details of his life as a miner in Tranent do not exist, but we can be sure that the work was hard and demanded great physical exertion. When a representative of a Royal Commission inquired into the practice of employing children and women in the mines in 1840, he interviewed nine-year-old David Neill of Tranent. The boy reported that he had worked for four pence a day since he was six, left home every day at 6 A.M. and returned at 4 P.M.: "Am very sick at times, as the work is hard, and gets naething but bits o'bread." Another lad, by the name of David M'Neill, also of Tranent, reported that he also had worked since he was six:

> Faither at first carried me doon. Faither is dead. Mother gets my weekly wages (3s.). I get my licks when I no like work. Mother gi'es me porridge an' sour milk when am no weel to work. Am no vera strong.

A thirty-eight-year-old woman named Elizabeth M'Neill recounted that she had been "sent below before ten years old" and had seven children, "three of whom work below." Then she added:

> I must confess that children are sent down too early, but it is better for them than running wild about, there being no teacher here till last week. Women think little of working below when with child; have wrought myself til the last hour, and returned again twelve or fourteen days after. I knew a woman who came up, and the child was born in the field next to the coalhill.

The official report on conditions in the Scottish mines in the early 1840s expressed disbelief that

> human beings can submit to such employment, crawling on hands and knees, harnessed like horses, over soft slushy floors, more difficult than dragging the same weight through our lowest common sewers, and more difficult in consequence of the inclination, which is frequently 1 in 3, to 1 in 6 inches.[28]

With working conditions like this it is no wonder that life in the pits was described as "severe, slavish, and oppressive in the highest degree." The reports of these MacNeils in Tranent (who might very well have been kin of the David of our story) reflect the kind of childhood young David MacNeil probably had after his parents

---

[28] Citations are from M'Neill, *Tranent and Its Surroundings*, 28–35. See also Smout, *History of the Scottish People*, 95. There are numerous MacNeils in Tranent and probably they are all related to some degree. Even those who have dropped the "Mac" and become "Neils" may be kin.

died. They also help explain why he and his children seemed to be continually seeking other kinds of work. David himself was in turn a miner, draper, and colliery clerk. The irony is that his children were so inured to life in the mines that they had difficulty leaving them. As a consequence of the inquiry into conditions in the coal industry, the British Parliament passed the Mines Act of 1842 which prohibited the employment of females and young children in the mines of the United Kingdom, although the employment of young children continued for some years in other industries.

Sometime in the 1840s, David MacNeil, who was still a teenager, met a thirty-six-year-old widow, Ann Beaton Boggie Thompson, the daughter of James Boggie of Edinburgh. Ann was born in Stromness, Orkney Islands, in 1811, where her father was stationed as a drummer with "Captain McNeils Company of the 9th Royal Veteran Battalion." By 1830 the family had returned to the Edinburgh area, and about 1831 Ann married John Thompson, a cotton handloom weaver, by whom she had seven children. Handloom weavers were facing stiff competition from the factory system, and about 1836 the Thompsons moved west to Pollockshaws in Renfrewshire, probably in search of employment. In addition to a son, James, born c. 1831, John and Ann had four more children who survived beyond 1841: John, Margaret, William Forbes, and Elizabeth. After a move to Old Monkland, Lanarkshire, Janet was born c. 1845. Shortly after her birth, John Thompson died and his widow returned to her widower father's home near Edinburgh.

There is a family tradition that Ann Thompson worked in the mines and that she was respected for her gift of "second sight," whereby she was able to warn her fellow miners of impending disasters. Given the date (1843) when women and children were no longer allowed to work in the mines and David MacNeil's employment there after 1841, it is unlikely that she worked with David MacNeil at Tranent. However, when she returned to her father's home around 1845, she became acquainted with the young miner from Tranent. Indeed, David was actually lodging in her father's home at Little Jack's Close in Edinburgh's Cannongate in February 1847. At that time, seventeen-year-old David MacNeil married the thirty-six-year-old widow Ann Thompson in Edinburgh's Cannongate Parish, and so the family that helped produce these Mormon letters from Utah came into being. The nineteen-year difference in age between David and Ann may help explain some of the difficulties the family experienced in later years as Ann became an "old woman" while David was still "middle-aged."

Lack of records precludes a detailed description of the family life of David and Ann MacNeil, but we do know that shortly after their marriage they moved thirty-six miles west from the Edinburgh area to the vicinity of Whifflet and Carnbroe in north Lanarkshire. Here both David MacNeil and John Thompson, Jr., Ann's oldest son, were apparently employed in the ironstone mines. On 22 February 1848, a year after their marriage, both David and Ann MacNeil were baptized into the Mormon Church and joined the LDS congregation at Airdrie. David may have become familiar with the Mormons during his stay in Tranent, where in 1850 the Mormons had a branch of 55 members. According to a local historian, Peter M'Neill, the Latter-day Saints in Tranent

> flourished to an extraordinary degree. So rapidly did their numbers increase in the village, that they actually established an instrumental brass band for their own amusement, and upheld it for a considerable time.[29]

The MacNeils may have been encouraged to come to the Lanarkshire area by Archibald MacNeil, who was also from Tranent and had joined the Mormon Church in December 1847. From comments in the letters it appears that he was regarded as an "uncle" of David MacNeil, although he was more likely one of the family's numerous "Scotch cousins."[30]

Shortly after her own baptism in February 1848, Ann's oldest son, John Thompson, age twelve, was baptized by "Uncle" Archibald MacNeil. Between 1848 and 1852 all of John's and Ann's children with the exception of William Thompson, had been "blessed" and given a name in the Mormon Church (the equivalent of christening), making them all, nominally at least, unbaptized members of the church.[31]

---

[29] M'Neill, *Tranent*, 79–80.

[30] The *Oxford English Dictionary* defines a "Scotch cousin" as a distant relative — so named because of the Scottish trait of tracing relationships to the uttermost degree.

[31] Airdrie Branch Record of Members. Mormons do not believe in infant baptism; children are usually baptized by immersion when they are eight years old.

There is, unfortunately, no account of what attracted David and Ann MacNeil to Mormonism, but it is clear from their sons' letters that they at one time believed the Mormon claim that it was the Restored Gospel and that they transmitted some of their beliefs (and perhaps some of their misgivings) to their children. We do know that he and his wife were committed enough to be instrumental in the 1850 conversion of an old friend, John Marshall, who later tried to get the MacNeils to come to Utah.[32] Perhaps they had within them the utopian expectation and millennialist fervor that seemed to grip many early Mormons.

The persistent theme that runs through these letters is that in time things will improve. It is not too much to think that such hopes were involved in the initial decision to join the church. David also exhibited traits of the restlessness that characterized much of his sons' experience in the United States. Very early in his experience as a Mormon, David rebelled in some way against the church and three months after having been ordained a priest by Elder Matthew Rowan, he was "cut off" or excommunicated. Whatever the reason, David's having been "cut off" did not cause the MacNeils to sever their ties with the church, because when a second son, David, was born in April 1850 he was also blessed in the Airdrie Branch the following month. Ten months later, David MacNeil, Sr., was baptized for the second time, followed by a second ordination as a priest, in January 1852.

We do not know exactly what Matthew Rowan or Henry Baxter said to David MacNeil when they ordained him a priest, but in accord with other blessings given at this time, it is possible that the ordination included words of encouragement for David to live faithfully so that he could be gathered home to Zion. We do know that Rowan was himself filled with the "spirit of gathering." In 1850 he wrote (to the tune of "My Native Highland Home") words which communicate the deep-seated desire to gather:

> Call not this place of birth my home,
> 'Tis false, I feel exiled;
> I claim some other spot to roam
> Where all around looks wild;

---

[32] See Life History of John Marshall in Appendix.

Where Joseph's remnants draw the bow
Their Buffalo meal to kill.
To there! O there, I fain would Go,
And bid this land farewell.[33]

Emigration to the United States had been suspended by the church during the movement to Utah, but it was revived in the early 1850s after the pioneers had become established. Rowan once again gave expression to the gathering by composing a song to be sung to the popular tune "The Campbells Are Coming":

O heard ye what news from the valley has come?
O heard ye what news from the valley has come?
All we, who are faithful, are soon to go home;
O 'tis glorious news, from the valley, that's Come.

Long, Long we have cried for the help of the Lord
A day of deliverance, the true Saint's reward,
But his word through the prophet, has open'd the way,
So, gladly and promptly his voice we'll obey.

The gentiles may lie and the Devil may roar
They may threaten and plunder, and Murder still More
Yet we'll build up our Zion, and dwell in it too,
Despite all that Devil or Gentiles can do![34]

Desire, enthusiasm, and religious commitment were not, however, enough to transport a family to Zion. By 1851 David MacNeil, at the age of twenty-two, was the principal breadwinner for a family of eight. In these circumstances, his wages as an iron miner could not have provided much surplus to make immediate emigration a reality. He was probably earning about fifteen shillings per week (£38 per year) in the early 1850s, and the cost of Mormon-subsidized passage to Utah has been calculated at about £60 for a family with three children. Based on David's earnings, the MacNeil-Thompson family would have needed a reserve of almost three years' wages to enable them to make the move.[35] For the next three decades the MacNeils seem to have had emigration on their

---

[33] Rowan, Poetry Book, 22. Reference to Joseph's remnant reflects the Mormon belief that the Native Americans are descendants of Joseph the son of the Patriarch Jacob.

[34] Ibid., 12.

[35] On wages in the Glasgow area see Slaven, *Development of the West of Scotland,* 156; on cost of passage see Taylor, *Expectations Westward,* 123.

minds, but they were never quite able to make the move as a family. Close friends left, sons left, and tickets were even sent from the United States to bring the family to America, but for a variety of reasons — economic, personal, and even religious — the family kept its roots in Lanarkshire. Often when things were going well in Scotland it did not seem sensible to move; similarly, when depressions struck the United States economy, the family was less inclined to go. In addition it appears that the strong religious motivation to leave may have shriveled as the years went by. As far as can be determined from the letters, the MacNeil family, or at least David, remained believers in the 1850s. When Ann's son John Thompson wrote from America that he was abandoning the faith because it was "humbug," there are indications that David expressed displeasure at his action.

David MacNeil, Sr., appears to have been very mercurial — at one time waxing enthusiastic and faithful and at another expressing doubt and misgivings. His friend John Marshall expressed the hope in the late 1860s that he had rejoined the "fold of Christ," indicating that David may have been "cut off" a second time. From the letters that John Marshall and John and James MacNeil wrote in the 1870s, one gets the distinct impression that David was still a believer and a member of the LDS Church, although neither he nor his family appear in any of the surviving records of branches such as Wishaw or Holytown, where he might have been a member after leaving the vicinity of Airdrie. Nor is there a record of any of the six children being baptized in Scotland after John Thompson in 1848, although the general Mormon practice was to baptize children as soon as they reached eight years of age.

In spite of this, missionaries such as the intrepid pioneer Lot Smith and Brigham Young's business manager, Hamilton G. Park, continued to visit them. One can imagine the stories the red-haired, volatile Lot Smith might have told the family as he recounted his burning of the U.S. Army's wagons during the Utah War of 1858 or his contacts with Indians or his assignment from President Abraham Lincoln to guard the railroad and telegraph lines during the Civil War. Hamilton Park may also have given the family a sense of the possible prosperity they could have in Utah. After all, he was personally acquainted with the "Prophet Brigham" and had become highly successful — and so too could they.[36] Both men showed a distinct interest in the family for many years and offered to help John and James get established in Utah. Of course, what they talked about on their visits to the MacNeil home in the late 1860s is all conjecture. However, probably as a result of the contacts with Elders Lot Smith and Park, on 9 July 1870 the MacNeils' oldest son, John MacNeil, was baptized and confirmed by Elder Park. Only four days later he sailed from Liverpool with a group of emigrants on the *Manhattan*—bound Zionward. Significantly, James, who was born in 1855, was not baptized until 1874, after he had been in Utah two or more years. In the absence of details, all that can be said about MacNeil family involvement with the Mormon Church is that until the late 1860s there was still some spark of commitment in David MacNeil, Sr., but the children of the MacNeil-Thompson family seem to have been in the process of going their own way and disassociating themselves from the church their parents had joined in 1848. Certainly Ann seems to have been less interested in emigrating than her husband. None of the letters mention her views on religion, although they do deal with David's. At one point James even suggests that his mother was wrong when she refused to emigrate to Utah, because every faithful wife should obey her husband. Not to be discounted either is the fact that the age gap between David and Ann may have produced its own kind of tensions.

In addition to Ann's reluctance, David set up his own stumbling block when he went into business for himself as a draper in 1868 at Whifflet, a village near Coatbridge. He also attempted a similar enterprise in Overtown, near Wishaw, about nine miles southeast of Coatbridge. His first venture in business in 1868 apparently motivated David to turn down John Thompson's offer of aid in that year. John Thompson had actually sent tickets for the whole family to travel to the United States. David's second venture led to his bankruptcy, and the stock of his draper's store was auctioned off at a public roup.[37] Shortly after this financial disas-

---

[36] For an insightful treatment of the character of Lot Smith, see Peterson, "A Mighty Man was Brother Lot," 393–414. On Hamilton G. Park, see Jenson, *Latter-day Saint Biographical Encyclopedia*, 1:668–69.

[37] Among the letters was a broadside dated 15 April 1878, advertising a "Great Sale of Bankrupt Stock" from D. MacNeil's store.

ter, David left his wife of thirty-one years; apparently he went off with another woman. He was then forty-nine and Ann was sixty-seven.

If David had been at all disposed to maintain a semblance of his former religious commitment up to this time (and the hints in the letters suggest otherwise), certainly this act of infidelity to his wife demolished whatever commitment remained. It certainly did nothing to increase the chance that some of his children would remain in or join the church. In fact only one did — James. In the next decade John would tell his family in Scotland that he was no longer a Mormon. David (Jr.) contemplated emigration but hesitated because he was not a Mormon and neither apparently were any of the other children. Eventually, in 1889, David (Sr.) did make the trip to Utah. By then he was very much alone — one stepson, William, was killed in 1863 and another, John Thompson, in Illinois in 1875, and his son James had drowned in Arizona in 1884. In 1887 Ann Boggie MacNeil died at the age of seventy-six in Scotland. Two years later and almost forty years after he had first been exposed to the doctrine of gathering, David MacNeil, Sr., arrived in Salt Lake City. Ironically, he seemed to come at the personal behest of his son John MacNeil, not as a religious pilgrim.

The letters that were stored in the attic of the MacNeil home in Ayr for so many years give a series of impressions from the perspective of two friends of David and Ann MacNeil, James S. Brady and John Marshall, whom they had befriended during their early years in the Mormon Church; and from that of three of their sons, John Thompson, John MacNeil, and James Brady MacNeil. David MacNeil, Sr., himself added a few fragmentary impressions after he came to Utah in 1889 and communicated with his daughter and son, Ann and David, in Scotland.

Very few letters written from Scotland to the MacNeils in Utah have survived; these were written by David and Ann's only daughter, Ann, Jr., to her niece Ann MacNeil Henkel, between 1905 and 1914. The letters from David, Sr., as well as those written by other family members from 1904 to 1922, form a sort of diminuendo to the MacNeils' encounter with the gathering to Zion and have not been included in the present collection. It was Ann MacNeil, Jr., who seems to have assumed the role of family archivist and it was likely she who initially preserved the letters that were discovered in her nephew's home in Ayr in 1964. In a letter to her niece (Ann MacNeil Henkel) in 1908, Ann MacNeil, Jr., told her to keep the letter she had written about the family: "seeing this is history you will have to take care of it & lay it past." From the content of her letter it seems that Ann, Jr., did have a notion of the importance of family history, and the letters we do have are hers in a very real sense. She apparently preserved them, kept the correspondence going in a rather fractious family, and kept asking many of the questions which produced these Mormon letters from America.

IN MORMON COUNTRY

Leonard Arrington has suggested that Utah's development in the nineteenth century can be divided into four periods that reflect the major themes and issues of the times. The first period may be characterized as the initial colonization and settlement that took place essentially from 1847 to 1858 and saw the Mormons firmly in charge of the Great Basin and founding colonies from northern Idaho to San Bernardino in California; the second may be characterized as the era of consolidation, which ran from 1859 to 1869. Although toward the end of this period the federal government asserted its control over the area, in actual fact the Mormon Church dominated the economic and social life of the region. The church's encouragement of the immigration of Mormon converts made the Mormons a decided majority. It discouraged the settlement of non-Mormons and tried to keep the "Gentile" or non-Mormon influence at bay by discouraging trade and socializing between Gentiles and the local "Saints." The third period, 1869 to 1887, may be described as the period of conflict and challenge, symbolized by the coming of the railroad to Utah in 1869. During this period the non-Mormon presence increased to some 20 percent of the population. A period of struggle for political, economic, and social power ensued, in which non-Mormons fought against what they perceived to be the autocratic and un-American power of the Mormon Church. The struggle also reflected the intention of the national Congress to abolish the Mormon practice of polygyny, which the Mormons defended as an expression of freedom of religion. The conflict came to an end in 1890 after the federal government had enacted legislation that outlawed the practice of plural marriage and disincorporated the Mormon Church. The decades following 1890 may be termed the period of compromise and accommodation, as the church officially abandoned plural marriage and Utah attained statehood. By the turn of the century the Mormon Church was integrating itself more fully into the American political and economic mainstream.[38]

The MacNeil-Thompson letters dating from 1852 through 1904 are like snapshots taken at particular times during these eras, giving a series of impressions rather than a panoramic view. The first letters from James S. Brady belong to the period of "colonization and settlement" and reflect the problems that immigrants had as they made their way to Utah. In Utah Brady gave a keen sense of how a typical immigrant responded to the everyday problems of making a living while keeping his religious commitment.

The letters from John Thompson, written between 1857 and 1874, were not written from Utah, and they represent a little-known genre of emigrants: those who left the homeland intending to settle in Utah but either never made it or decided that Utah was not the place for them. As a member of the Union Army, John Thompson became more involved with the conflict over slavery and spent three years fighting for the "best govermint on the face of god's Earth"—a far cry indeed from the Mormon perception of the government as being more a hindrance than a liberator. John Thompson's letters are in a very real sense part of the Utah story since, after renouncing Mormonism as "humbug," he converted to the Reorganized Church of Jesus Christ of Latter Day Saints, which was founded on 6 April 1860 at Amboy, Illinois. He accepted Joseph Smith's son Joseph III as his religious leader, as did many emigrants who were unwilling to accept Brigham Young's leadership.

Most of the MacNeil letters were written during the third period of Utah's historical development, and they clearly reflect that period's characterization as one of "conflict and challenge." In a few letters written in the early 1870s, John Marshall gives a no-holds-barred account of the Mormon-Gentile conflict, acknowl-

---

[38] The literature on the history of Utah in the nineteenth century is extensive and no attempt is made here to cover all aspects of the subject. Some useful general sources are Arrington, *Great Basin Kingdom*; Larson, *The "Americanization" of Utah for Statehood*; Mulder and Mortensen, eds., *Among the Mormons*; Peterson, *Utah: A Bicentennial History*. For treatment of Utah themes within the context of Mormon history, see Allen and Leonard, *The Story of the Latter-day Saints*, and Alexander, *Mormonism in Transition*.

edges that Zion is made up of human beings, "saints and sinners," and gives an earthy appraisal of "Josephite" (Reorganized LDS) attempts to challenge the authority of Utah Mormons, which they did by sending Joseph Smith's son David to Utah as a missionary. In spite of all this, Marshall still encouraged the MacNeils to come to Utah. Of all the letter writers, John Marshall appears to have been the most successful economically. He also seems to have had the most balanced perspective on life. His success reflects the success that a few Mormons experienced in this period as mining began to influence the Utah economy. However, Marshall apparently heeded the warnings of Brigham Young and other leaders about mining for precious metals. They believed that mining camps were not conducive to the building of stable communities. He was not involved in mining directly, but limited himself to smelting the ore, which did not take him away from the central influence of the church community and his family.

The majority of the letters written from Utah during this period were written by the two brothers, John and James MacNeil. Their responses to life in Utah give a vivid impression of the extent to which mining came into conflict with the competing values of church community and an agrarian life style. Try as they might, neither one was able (or willing?) to give up his traditional means of earning a living and depend entirely on farming. Their letters reveal the personal dimension of the struggle and conflict of this period; the brothers said they wanted to do something else (i.e., farm), but their wish was never fully realized.

At another level, the letters (especially John's) reveal the dissatisfaction many immigrants must have felt as they found their original commitment to Mormonism waning. Under these circumstances, life in Utah became less a pioneer epic of conquering the desert for God and more a matter of making a living to support a growing family. Obviously, even the pioneers had to work to support their families, but there was also a religious motivation, which gave a sense of being involved in more than just earning one's bread. For many, the day-to-day rhythms of work and toil were accomplishing a divine purpose. There is no evidence of this attitude in the letters that John wrote to Scotland. The intertwining of economics, politics, and religion repelled some people (including John MacNeil), but others (including James MacNeil) viewed Brigham Young's efforts to make the Mormon cooperative economy succeed as a manifestation of the divine will in human affairs. During this period the Mormon leadership colonized other parts of the West, including the Salt River Valley area of Arizona, and James MacNeil was drawn to that region in the late 1870s. Once again, the need to mine intrudes on the call to settle. He spent his first few years employed in a copper mine — an environment that he conceded was not conducive to the kind of life he wanted. He felt the call of the land, though, and used the resources earned in mining to begin a more stable occupation as a pioneer farmer in the Thatcher area of Arizona. Ironically, his involvement in a more desirable occupation led to his death at the age of twenty-nine.

Running like a thread through the experience of the MacNeil brothers are their individualistic responses to the Mormon Church, with John becoming more and more bitter and cynical as time went on and James becoming more and more optimistic and faithful. They communicated these perspectives to their parents, and in so doing probably contributed in no small way to the failure of the MacNeils to come to Utah during the 1870s. Here is none of the idealistic, utopian perspective of proselyting missionaries that undoubtedly drew some people to Utah as converts. Instead, the brothers offered a hard-nosed, practical emphasis. It revealed the extent to which the Mormon Zion had to contend with the humanness of its inhabitants as well as unemployment, unpredictable weather, and the vagaries of eastern capitalists and unstable markets.

Only a dozen letters survive (or perhaps were ever written) in the final decade of the nineteenth century. Even the absence of letters may tell us something about the times. The big concern of the letters during this period of compromise and accommodation was not Mormon doctrine or practice, but simply how to make a living.

The sense of community that marked the first letters of James Brady is totally absent as talk of strikes, falling markets, and the concerns of the modern world crowd in on the land of promise. The letters effectively come to a close with the death of John MacNeil in a Park City mine in 1904.

From 1853 through 1903, these letters of Scottish Mormon settlers give a series of snapshot impressions of life among the Mormons. They are not always complimentary to the twentieth-century image of Mormonism or its proponents, yet they are an honest expression of the rhythms and routines, the concerns and conflicts which characterized the lives of ordinary pioneers and immigrants. From their correspondence comes an image of how lives were shaped and molded by the forces of religion, occupation, and economics. From them we can get a realistic assessment of what it was like to be a worker in nineteenth-century Utah. For all the religious idealism of building the Kingdom of God that permeates so many accounts of life in Utah, it was in fact a hard, grueling task, very often unrelieved by final success. The hoped-for good times never materialized for a large number of immigrants. In spite of the promise of America as a new Zion, the harsh reality is that while "some found a better life [and] a few achieved success[,] others had their hopes destroyed by unemployment and crop failure." Even in Utah with its emphasis on cooperation and helpfulness, the existence of widespread poverty in the nineteenth century added a quality of "precariousness for common folk.³⁹ Indeed, if Mormonism holds to the dictum that "man is that he might have joy," these particular Mormon letters tend to underscore the aphorism that "man was made to mourn."⁴⁰

---

³⁹From a display on the Atlantic migration in the Merseyside Maritime Museum, Liverpool; for commentary on poverty in pioneer Utah see Hartley, "Edward Hunter," 290.

⁴⁰Book of Mormon 2 Nephi 2:25; Burns, "Man Was Made to Mourn: A Dirge."

Descendents of John MacNeil have assumed this picture, taken at Coatbridge, Scotland, to be of Ann Boggie and her first husband John Thompson in the 1840s. However, analysis of the clothing by historic costume consultant Carma deJong Anderson of Provo, Utah, has suggested that it is more likely of Ann Boggie Thompson and her second husband, David MacNeil, Sr., c. 1850s or 60s. *Courtesy of Mrs. Gladys Henkel Thorne.*

This picture, taken at Edinburgh, has been presumed to be of seventeen-year-old David MacNeil, Sr., and his thirty-six-year-old wife, Ann Boggie Thompson MacNeil. On the basis of Carma deJong Anderson's analysis, it is probably Ann MacNeil and one of her sons by David MacNeil, perhaps her youngest, James, c. late 1860s. Note the traditional Tam o' Shanter bonnet in the boy's hand. *Courtesy of Mrs. Gladys Henkel Thorne.*

John MacNeil, eldest son of David and Ann MacNeil, and his wife
Annie Cooper Warrilow MacNeil. *Courtesy of Mrs. Gladys Henkel
Thorne.*

Presumably David MacNeil, Jr., second son of David and Ann MacNeil and the only son to remain in Scotland. *Courtesy of Mrs. Gladys Henkel Thorne.*

Ann MacNeil, only daughter of David and Ann MacNeil, and her step-sister Elizabeth Thompson, daughter of John and Ann Thompson. *Courtesy of Mrs. Gladys Henkel Thorne.*

James Brady MacNeil, youngest son of David and Ann MacNeil. *Courtesy of Mrs. Gladys Henkel Thorne.*

John Marshall, converted to the Mormon Church by David and Ann MacNeil. *Courtesy of Dean L. Marshall.*

Elizabeth Robson Marshall, second wife of John Marshall. *Courtesy of Dean L. Marshall.*

The Millizer Robinson Cooper cabin in Bountiful, Utah where John and James MacNeil lived during their early years in Utah and where John met Annie Cooper Warrilow. *Courtesy of Mrs. Gladys Henkel Thorne.*

Letter of David MacNeil, Sr., in Salt Lake City, to his daughter Ann MacNeil, 9 November 1903.

Alton Coalbranch
Sept. 24 1864

Dear father and brothers
I take the present opportunity
of writing you a few lines to
let you know that I am well
and in good health hoping this
may find you and family
injoying the same great blessing.
I have got through soldiering all
right and don't know that I
had last the march my time
was up on the 15th of August
but as there was so much thrown
behind at the time that we
could not get our papers made
out till about the last of this
thought when we was sent back
to Chattanooga where we was about
a week before we got mustered
out of the united States service

to have the hole family hear But I
think it will be best for you to do
as what you can till I find
Missing But I will end say time
so hope you think would be best
I should write an account of what
I have been through since I last
I sat go on But I guess it will
that be of much interest we had
tous months of a campaign and then
some hard fair during that time
I was wounded on the 27th of June
at [Kennesaw] mountain [Georgia] on the
in the arm with a piece of shell
But it did that break any bones
and only cut and [ ]
[ ] and I think it is
as good as ever that I will labor fine
Any recollection matters and all the
family and all in jusing friends
yours affectionetly John Thompson

Letter of John Thompson, in Alton, Illinois, to his stepfather, David MacNeil, and his mother, Ann Thompson MacNeil, 26 September 1864 (not in text).

Evenstone Friday April 28th 1871

Dear Father And Mother I take up My pen Once More to Let You know how Getting Along I Am Digging Coal Again You See And I think I Am doing pretty well I think I Am Making 5 Dollars Per day I Am Living With A Family of the Name of Livingstone who Crossed the Sea with Me they Are Ayrshire people And very kind people It was them that got Me work here they wrote to Me in Cash Valley and told Me to Come here I had A Letter from John Marshall on the 23rd And he has been Sick A few days but he is Getting better Me And John has Bought 160 Acres of Land in Rodgers Valley And he intends Moving there in the fall And Build him A house on it and Make improvements on on it till we Come to it he tells Me You have been Sick well I Am Very Sorrow to hear that You have Such poor health But keep up Your Spirits All of you

Letter of John MacNeil in Evanston, Wyoming, to his parents, David

I Am paying 5 Dollers A week for
Board But we get plenty of Good Grub
we do not work so hard as we did in the
Old Country we Come home every day at 12 Ocᶜᵏ
And take Dinner the Coal is 27 Feet in
hight they Only work Abought ten or eleven
feet of it at first it resembles Kirkwood
Main Coal very much if Daved was
here now Me And him Could in One fall
As Sett Us All up if David would Like
to Come here, And You Can Get Along
without for A Little while I would Like
You to Let Me know And if You have not
Money to Send him I will be Able to
furnish it in A very Short time John
Marshall is very Ancious that you Could
Come here I had the fever & Ague before
I Left Smithfield But Got over it All
wright I Stayed over Night with Tom Gray
Brother to Walter Grant on My way from
Cash he Lives in Wellsville I will finish up
by wishing You All health Give My Love to My Brothers &
Sisters Also John Hendry & wife And All inquiring friends
Your Loving Son John Mc Neil

and Ann MacNeil, 28 April 1871.

10-2

Pinal City
" " Co "
" " May 3 "
81

( ) Mr. Neils jun Dear Brother

I suppose you will have thought by this time that your Brother James has forsaken if or not by my not writing to you Sooner I will tell you my reasons for not doing so - is the Place that I was in when you wrote me last - I thought I would have steady employment for a few months & I knew that I could send money enough to bring you out if I could get the work work for 6 Months but just since I went out of work & I had to travel so I

concluded not to work to you until I got to my Distination 558 Miles from Utah when I got here I waited thinking that I would get into work so that I could give good Runs when I did work but it is up hill work when you aint aquainted I have been here 2 Months doing Nothing. so you may judge how I am fixed. if I dont get into work I will not be able to bring you & family out this season but if I get work I want be long untill I send for you. there is one thing you can depend on that is that

I will Devote my time &
Energys to that object. it is
not so very much the sum
but I look to against you..
Keep up your heart David
I will yet you out never
fear for that then I am
coming...
my mother I am Poorly
she to be home next year
some time. I have been
Longing to see my family
I Hate very much..
Your old age your children
the five from Liverpool
to Salt Lake City is $135.00
to one person
I wrote to my sister
Ann a long time ago.
but have received no
answer as yet I Hope
my folks are well as this
leaves me at present

give my best love to
long mother with kind
rehumbrances to all as iver
your faithfull Brother
Jas. B. McNeil

P.S. Let me know all
you can about Brother
Will's Boys John & Tom
See if they would not Like
to come out to America

Letter of James Brady MacNeil in Pinal, Arizona, to his brother David MacNeil, Jr.,
3 May 1881.

Interior of Daly West Mine, Park City, Utah, in which John MacNeil was killed in 1903. The miner in this picture, C. P. Saderup, also lost his life in this mine in 1902. *Courtesy of Utah State Historical Society.*

Alta City, Utah, 1873, where John and James MacNeil worked as silver miners. *Courtesy of Utah State Historical Society.*

2

"The Freist Countery in the Woreld"

Letters of James Brady, John Thompson,
and John Marshall
1853–67

The earliest letters written from the United States to the MacNeil family were written by their Irish friend James S. Brady. Brady was born on 16 March 1832 in Drung, County Cavan, the southernmost county in the province of Ulster, Ireland. He lived in Ireland until 1845 when, along with thousands of Irish who were being forced out of Ireland by the potato famine, he made his way to Scotland. On his sixteenth birthday, James Brady was baptized into the Mormon Church at Airdrie by James Burnett and became a member of the Airdrie Branch of the church. As a member of the Mormon community in the vicinity of Airdrie and Coatbridge, he no doubt became familiar with the newly converted MacNeil family. David and Ann MacNeil had joined the church a few weeks before Brady's baptism. At this time the family consisted of David and Ann MacNeil and the five children she had brought into the marriage, ranging in age from eleven to three. The relationship between young Brady and the MacNeils must have been quite close, because in 1855 David and Ann MacNeil named their last son James Brady Boggie MacNeil.

In February 1853 Brady obeyed the command to "gather" home to Zion. By May 1853 he was in Saint Louis, Missouri, and in June of the same year he was on his way to Salt Lake City. In Utah he was employed in the rock quarry in Red Butte Canyon a few miles east of Salt Lake City and on 6 January 1854 he was ordained to the office of a Seventy in the Thirty-ninth Quorum of Seventy. His contribution to Utah (as a keen observer of

50

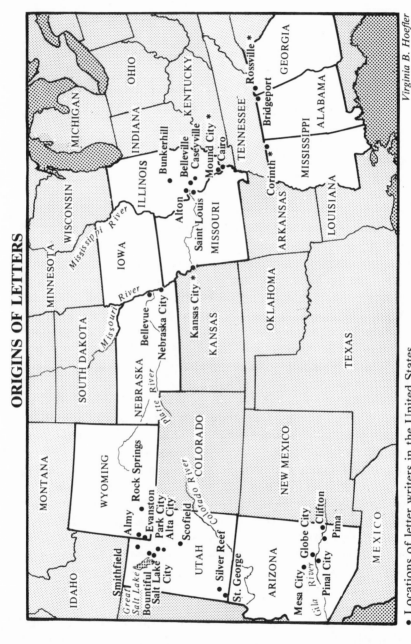

ORIGINS OF LETTERS

Virginia B. Hoefler

• Locations of letter writers in the United States

* Letters from these locations not included in this volume

the local scene) and his own aspirations to serve in the church were cut short by a fall of rock at Red Butte Canyon on 29 July 1854.

Apart from the three letters from James S. Brady and the one from their friend John Marshall (whose background will be given in the introductory materials to chapter 3), all of the other letters to the MacNeil home between 1852 and 1868 were written by John Thompson. He was ten years old when his mother, Ann MacNeil, and his stepfather, David MacNeil, joined the Mormon Church. John was the oldest of the five Thompson children who grew to maturity. At the time of his mother's marriage to David MacNeil he was only nine years younger than his stepfather. On 31 March, 1848, about two months after his parents had been baptized, John also became a Latter-day Saint. He was probably active in the affairs of the Mormon congregation in Airdrie, and he was ordained to the priesthood on 17 November 1855.

According to the Census of Bothwell Parish, Lanarkshire, in 1851 John was working as a miner at age fourteen, and it is this occupation he claimed when he shipped out from Liverpool on 4 May 1856. He was one of 700 passengers on the *Thornton*, including 117 Mormons from Scotland, who intended to make the pilgrimage to Utah.[1]

Unlike James Brady, John Thompson delayed his departure for Utah, and his letters indicate that he worked or looked for work in coal mines in Iowa, Nebraska, and Illinois. In 1857 he talked of helping bring his family "out of Babylon" to America and said that he "knew Mormonism is true and of God." However, he admitted that he had not been able to attend any meetings and had heard very little about the church since he came to America. By January 1859 he appears to have become disillusioned and regretted having contributed so much money to the church. He was apparently much influenced by the news coming out of Utah. In 1857 President James Buchanan sent the United States Army to Utah to quell the so-called Mormon Rebellion,

---

[1] Information on the MacNeil-Thompson family and their early church experience was obtained from the genealogical files of Mrs. Gladys Henkel Thorne of Murray, Utah, the Record of Members of the Airdrie Branch, and the Liverpool Emigration Records.

and newspapers of the time were filled with information and misinformation about events in Utah.[2]

In 1861 John Thompson volunteered for service in the Union Army and in the next few years he makes no mention of Mormonism in his letters, but he did give details of some of the military action he was involved in from the fall of 1861 to the winter of 1864. (Because these particular letters do not deal with his religious development or give any insight into Utah affairs they are not included in this volume.)

Not until he left the army did John mention religion again, this time to announce to his family that he had joined the Reorganized Church of Jesus Christ of Latter Day Saints in Illinois. John Thompson was one of numerous emigrants who rejected the authority and practices of the Mormon Church in Utah and eventually joined the Reorganized Church in the Midwest.[3]

In addition to the information about events in the family and among friends in Airdrie and in America, the letters of James Brady and John Thompson tell us a great deal about the writers' perceptions of American Mormonism. In James Brady's case he seemed to be able to separate Mormon ideals from practice. Although he said that the actions of some Saints in America had almost shocked Mormonism out of him, Brady did not allow the particular situation to influence his basic commitment to Mormonism. On the other hand, John Thompson displayed very little sympathy for Mormonism in his letters. At least immediately after he disavowed his allegiance to the church he seemed mainly concerned with making a living in Illinois. In the absence of an explicit rationale for becoming disillusioned, it is probable that contacts with Mormon apostates reinforced some doubts he was having about

---

[2] This conflict was viewed by the Mormons as a continuation of the persecution that had dogged their footsteps in Missouri and Illinois. The Buchanan administration, however, saw the Mormon hegemony in Utah as a challenge to federal authority. According to Furniss, "Not much blood was spilled during this war . . ." and to many participants "the whole affair was a farce from beginning to end." Furniss, *The Mormon Conflict*, vii. Among the Mormons the conflict was known as "Buchanan's Blunder"; it cost the federal government some fifteen million dollars.

[3] The Reorganized Church of Jesus Christ of Latter Day Saints was organized 6 April 1860 at Amboy, Illinois, as a result of the controversy over who should succeed Joseph Smith as leader of the church after Smith's death in 1844. For background see Quinn, "The Mormon Succession Crisis," 187–233; Launius, "Joseph Smith III and the Mormon Succession Crisis," 5–22.

the wisdom of continuing on to Utah. His reasons for staying in Illinois were, however, probably a mixture of economic, social, personal, and religious factors.

The letters from Brady and Thompson during the period 1852 to 1868 foreshadow the tensions which become so pronounced in the later letters from John Marshall and the two brothers, John and James MacNeil. These revelations of the less than ideal side of the Mormon story must have been the basis for much discussion in the MacNeil home.

While the letters from Scotland have not survived, given the persistence with which the question of emigration is pursued in the letters to Scotland, it is obvious that the MacNeils were very seriously considering it. One can only conjecture that Ann MacNeil may have resisted the idea — her father did not die until 1866 and her other children by John Thompson do not seem to have been involved in the Mormon Church after the 1860s. In addition it should be remembered that at this time Ann was in her 50s, while David was only in his 30s. The age difference may have been a factor in her decision to stay at home. Many of the Mormon families who emigrated to Utah during this period were deeply committed to "gathering" in Zion. The MacNeils wavered in this commitment. The criticisms of Mormonism in the letters from John Thompson probably did little to enhance whatever religious fervor they may have felt. In the late 1860s John Marshall hinted that David MacNeil, Sr., had not been faithful to the "sheepfold of Christ." It is likely that a cooling of religious ardor had something to do with the failure to gather home to Zion and follow the trail blazed by James Brady and John Thompson.

On a more practical level, however, the failure to emigrate during the 1850s could be accounted for by the financial needs of a growing family of nine children who in 1855 ranged from less than one year to seventeen years of age. In addition, the Utah War of 1857-58 and later disruption of immigration because of the Civil War may have dampened the enthusiasm to leave Scotland.

The letters from James Brady and John Thompson which arrived in the MacNeil home in the years 1852 to 1868 reflected both the real and ideal aspects of Mormon emigration. These letters were made up of glad and sad tidings out of Zion, and they undoubtedly helped shape and shake the MacNeil response to Mormonism and to its distinctive doctrine of the gathering.

James Brady to David and Ann MacNeil

Saint Louis, [Missouri]
21 May 1853

Dear Brother and Sister [MacNeil],

It is with pleasure that I now take up my pen to write you a few lines to inform you how I have Been since I left. . . . My health has Been very good all the time sinse I saw you — only too or three days that I was sea sick. . . . I would like very well to hear from you all. But there is no youse in talking about that at the present time.

Dear Brother my mind is uneasy and has been mostly all the time sinse I left you. I dont know the reason of it But one thing I know and it is this, that it is a pleasure to Be with the Saints of god. Although the people that I am with have the name of Saints, that's all that I hear about it and in deed Mormonism is all most Shocked out of me and if you saw the fixes that I have Been in sinse I left you would not wonder much at it, for if Saint Pete ware in there midst he could not put up with ther nonsonse. Belive me I would not put [up] with it, But I cannot help it at the present time. I dont want to Stop in this place and with the help of god I will go further. I have Seen the most of the Bretherin that is in this plase; that is three that left Airdrie Some time agoe. Some of them is gon to the valy this Spring and Some of them does not want to go. Your Archy has gon this season.[4] Old Brother Wilson told me he talked to him about you, But he said very little on the Subject. Brother Brown was here a few days Before i came to this plase. They tell me them that saw him that you would not know him. So that lets you see what a drunkin wife can doe. The

---

[4]Mention of "Archy" occurs frequently in these letters and appears to refer to a relative (uncle?) of David MacNeil, Archibald MacNeil. He was apparently the first member of the MacNeil family to emigrate. It has not been possible to identify Archibald's actual relationship to David. He was the son of David and Frances MacNeil and was born at Tranent, 16 July 1816; baptized at Airdrie, 20 December 1847; left for Utah 3 September 1849; and arrived in Salt Lake City 15 July 1853. His first wife, Agnes Brown, died in February 1849, and he married Helen Haswell in St. Louis, Missouri, on 5 April 1850. He was an active member of the Twenty-fifth Quorum of Seventy in Salt Lake City and died in St. George, Utah, 8 March 1891. See Airdrie Branch Record of Members; Twenty-fifth Quorum of Seventy Minute Book; Family Group Records.

story about her and your Archy did not rise out of nothing I Belive.

Dear Brother it is now the 26 of May & I comenced to rite this on the 10 But I thought that I would not Send it till we ware ready to start. We intend to go from this plaise to morrow for the Counsel Blufs. The moste of the emegrants is going to a plase not so far up the River. The name of the plase is [Keokuk, Iowa] it is only 2 hundred miles from this plase. The Saints is Counseled againste going up the River on acount of it Being Daingerous. It taiks 3 weeks to go from keoukuk to the Bluffs. We are going to go up the river to the Bluffs.[5] Howard wants to make up a little time going up the river. He has allwais Been in a hury sinse I Saw him and he is not any further yet than his neighbours and Im sure hees no ritcher than what I am Although he has got Some gold dust and some Bank nots in his posesion, I am a ritcher man than what he is for his heart and soul is in, But if he remains amounge [them for?] awhile I could profisy in my own name that it wont be so Plenty with him.

Dear Brother I have had my temper tried in a good many ways Sinse i saw you. You know it never was none of the Best and in deed it has mended nothing Sinse I left, But I guess it's all right. If I was getting every[thing] my own way I might forget my Self. We have got little or nothing prepaired for our Journey as yet. Howard opened a shop in Saint Louis when he Come and he has Been Seling off ever sinse, so that in fact he had rarely time to [?] ore any thing. But I dont Care much if he minds the main thing; that is to get plenty of tomy [bread] for our Journey. Perhaps you will wonder [at me] talking this way, But if you Saw the fixes that we ware in Comeing along, you would not wounder in the least at it. If you had saw me runing along with a lump of Beef under my arm and lying on [Brother] dobby to look smarter and get a knife, ill tell you would laugh. But thier is no [use] in talking. Little Said is easy mended.

---

[5] For a detailed analysis of the organization and movement of British Mormon converts to Utah see Taylor, *Expectations Westward*. For details on the Scots participation see Buchanan, "The Emigration of Scottish Mormons to Utah." A detailed contemporary account of the Mormon migration in the 1850s may be found in Piercy, *Route from Liverpool to the Great Salt Lake*.

I would Like well to Spend too or three hours with you all. I long to hear from you all and o, how I long to get a reed of the Star.[6] I have never heard or saw any thing that would Chear me up sinse [I] left. I may Say I don't know what i would give to get all the Stares that has Been Published sinse I left. You can read theis few lines to Both the Brother Adamsons and let Br. David know that if he gets the present volume of Stars for me I will not forget him.

I dont intend Bretheren and sisters to forget aney of you, Belive me, I Love the saints of Airdrie. It was with them that I heard the Principles of mormonism; it was with them that I learned some little of them; But I have learned little Sinse I left you. But I wont loes heart, I know theirs a good time Comeing.

I have rought [worked] Some little Sinse I left. I Belive I have maid about 20 dollars. Well, I had need of something. When I left Glasgow I had 5 Shillings and I gave 3 and sixpense in Liverpool for the harp of zion.[7] I had about 5 Shilings when I landed in this country. I got some little Coming across for some things that I did. I have got a pair of Boots & a pair of shoes. My shoes and my Boots went done when I came here. There is no youse in Bringing shoes or Boots with you to this Country, for the Leather gets so hard that you Cant wear them. They are as cheap hear as what they are at home. You will get a pair of Boots that will come up to your nees for 3 and a half dolers so that is about as cheap as you can get them at home. But I'll tell you what to doe; when donald goes your tenth you can ask him about the rait of the markets and I'm shure heel can tell you how much whiskey he gets.[8] [He] youst to get four cents.

Give my love to all the Saints. Remember me to Brother and sister Wilson and to Rab. You can tell Brother Baxter that I saw his sone and daughter going away. I dont know whether i will

---

[6] The *Millennial Star* was the Mormon periodical published in Great Britain from 1840 until 1970.

[7] *Harp of Zion*, a book of Mormon poems by John Lyon, was published in Liverpool in 1853 for the benefit of the Perpetual Emigrating Fund, organized by the Mormon Church in 1850 to provide loans to enable poorer converts to emigrate.

[8] Brady seems to be referring to some sort of barter system among the emigrants as they planned the financing of their journeys.

be along with them Crossing the plaines or not. Let them know that I send my kind love to them all. Latham and Wilsons folks landed here this day. I did not See Latham, But I saw the rest of them and they are all well. Give my love to all the Bretheren and sisters, the sisters in perticular. . . .

Remember me to Brother Lyon when you see him. I hope he will be comeing next year and a tun of young sisters with he.[9] I know he would get good sail for them; not that they are so scarse here, but they are so furry. I was going to Be introdused to one, But she had a baird on her upper lip the half lenth of your finger, so I looked at her and said nothing.

I need not say any more at present, But pray that the Blessing of the lord may rest upon you all. Brother [John] Dobbie sends his kind love to you all.

James Bready

[P.S.] Excuse my bad spelling and all theis Blots. Look over the top of them. I have a bad pen, Bad paper and Im sure its not good ink and you know I am not acostom to righing aney way. Dont forget to rite me.

I want you and Brother Adamson to rite me a letter and let me know all the news you can. Direct your letter to the care of Mr. William Thomson, Great Salt Lake City, Utah for me. This will find me and if you right when you get this it will be there as soon as me. I hope you will attend to this. I could not get this posted in saint louis. I saw William Smith yesterday. He cant get this season.

[James Brady]

---

[9]Attempts have been made to identify Scottish immigrants mentioned in these letters, but the absence of first names in many cases makes positive identification difficult. According to Essholm, *Pioneers and Prominent Men*, John Dobbie came to Utah in 1853, James Leatham arrived in Salt Lake City on 5 October 1853, and John Lyon on 26 September 1853. Some of the family names mentioned here appear among the names in the Airdrie Branch Record of Members, but early Mormon records are not as complete as one might expect. For example, the Airdrie records cease c. 1856.

James Brady to [David and Ann MacNeil]

[Salt Lake City, Utah]
[c. early 1854]

[The first four pages of this six-page letter are missing.]

. . . I was sory to hear you say that their is But 3 elders in airdrie Branch. Truly it is altered times But [by Heavens?] it is not much wonder.[10] John Baxter is gone to California along with John Weer. This is a free country. You can gou where you pleas and doo what you pleas. But the time is at hand when it will not bee so. Mary is living with William [Gates?] Wife. He is gone allso to cali[fornia]. This is dooing right in opision to the Counsil of the Presedent & that is at thing that I would not like to doo.

It is strange to think how some folks Belive that Mormonism is everything when they are in faverible sirconstances, But if the scail turns it is right the oposite. I had not seen Mary Baxter sense John went away. I dont now what she thinks about it. I intend to go and see her soon. I belive she is a good woman.

You say that you sent a letter along with [Irvin?] & a paper. But if you rite as son as you get this I will have word from you Before that he come to this place. I hope you will not wate to hear from me Before you rite But rite when ever you feel like it. When you rite let me now whereabouts Tom Lyon is. His folks never got a letter from him sinse they left.[11] They are very uneasy about him. I am in their house sometimes. Login is living with [lelsy?] at willow valy[12] Br Colvin very Bad. I was ther last sunday & his foot is no Better & he takes fits so that he cannot Be left alone anytime. I may also state to you that andrew Henderson is complaining of pains in his bones. The rest of the family is well.

---

[10] In 1849 there were ten elders in the Airdrie Branch. Brady is probably referring to the precipitous decline in Mormon numbers in Scotland after the peak of almost 3,300 in 1851, a decline caused in part by fewer baptisms, a high excommunication rate, and, of course, a high emigration rate. In 1853, for example, excommunications exceeded baptisms, and during the 1850s emigration siphoned off fifty-four percent of the growth created by new conversions.

[11] Thomas Lyon (b. 1826), son of John Lyon and Janet Thomson, eventually arrived in Utah c. 1859 and died in 1863. For details on the Lyon family in Utah, see Thomas E. Lyon, Jr., *John Lyon: Poet/Pioneer.*

[12] Willow Valley is near Tooele, Utah, about thirty miles west of Salt Lake City.

[Leatham?] is gon to Iron County along with Brigham an [Heber?] Kimbell and good many more is gon with them.[13] No doubt [Leatham?] will feel disaponted at Irvins folks not comeing. I dont now whether you will get a letter from Archy [MacNeil?] this male or not But I will doo what I can. Pleas to remember me to all the saints. As I have not room to name them you can doo it for me. When you adress your letter you need net Put upper California on it.

May god Bless you and your family.

James brady

[P.S.] Be sure and rite often and let me now all the news you can. You need not send the stars. I can by them cheaper here then the could Be sent. J.B.

James Brady to David and Ann MacNeil

Great Salt Lake City
28 May 1854

Dearly Beloved Brother and sister McNeil,

I received your kind and welcome Friday the 26 inst but the Paper you sent to me I did not get as yet. I supose that the mail was too heavy loaded & that they left the most of the Papers back on the road somewhere. Whether ever they will come this length or not I don't now. James Wilson sent me too papers from Saint Louis last month. I only got one of them. . . . I am glad that you ware all in good health & spirits at the time you rote to me. I may allso state that I am in good health & spirits & has Been, ever since I came to this Country. In fact I never was better [part of letter destroyed and words illegible].

---

[13] "Leatham" probably refers to James Leatham (1830–1921), a Scottish convert who came to Utah with his wife Margaret Irvine in October 1853. The "Iron Mission" was established at Cedar City in southern Utah in 1851 as part of Brigham Young's plan to make Utah's economy self-sufficient. Service in the "Iron Mission" was considered as important as a preaching mission, and American, English, Scottish, and Welsh converts who had worked in the iron industries were recruited to serve the church and Utah's economy in the manufacture of iron. However, after almost ten years of labor only a few viable castings had been made and the enterprise was abandoned. Arrington, *Great Basin Kingdom*, 122–27.

I am working at the quarry & living there. It is about 4 miles from the City.[14] The wages is very good. We have too & a half dollers per day but that is not enough for some folks. What I mean By that is that some folks go to California that had the above named wages everyday that they Could work. Their is great numbers of People working on the Publick works and their is plenty of employment for them all. Flower apears to be rather scarse this season But the Church is able enough to get as much as the folks on the Publick works will need. Last sunday [the President?] said to the Congregation in the tabernacle that he wanted them as a community to donate twenty eight hundred dolars by wheat for the Publick hand. This was on sunday & I am of the opinion that they got it and maybe for any thing I now, Before 10 oclock on mondy. So that lets you see a little of what a people can doo that is of one heart and of one mind.

I did not say that all the Inhabitants of this plase [are] of [one] heart and one mind But as general things they are People as far as my limited judgement extents that serves the Lord with thar whole heart and soul & my Belief is that they are all the time getting better. Notwithstanding all this, at times drones creeps into the hive & feeds on the honey in winter season as well as the good Bees. But Just wait a little—the warem weth[er] will come when the good Bees will need more room, then I am of the opinion that they will sting the drones to death so as they will not trouble them any more.[15]

Dear Brother I have many things on my mind that I could relate to you if we ware face to face But for the life of me I dont now how to Begin to rite them. You say in your letter that I am to let you now all the news I can. There is nothing strange or wonderful here but what is recordit in the [Deseret News].[16] This I have sent you regularly. . . .

---

[14] The quarry in Red Butte Canyon, east of Salt Lake City, was the source of the sandstone used for the foundation of the Salt Lake Temple and in the construction of a number of public buildings in Salt Lake City. The "public works" program was organized by Brigham Young to provide meaningful employment for immigrants. Arrington, *Great Basin Kingdom*, 154–55.

[15] Brady's language reflects the rhetoric used by Mormon leaders in denouncing "unproductive" members of the community. See, for example, Heber C. Kimball's comments in *Journal of Discourses* (hereinafter *JD*) 5:135.

[16] The *Deseret News* was the Mormon-owned newspaper established in June 1850 and still published by the LDS Church.

[lines indecipherable and parts missing, but Brady is criticizing those Mormons who turn from the truths they once accepted]

[I believe] . . . that it was Better [that?] they never heard the sound of the everlasting gosple then to stay in and then turn there Backs to it. It is just as Presedent [Heber C.] Kimble says that as sure as the lord liveth if an individul Comenses at the end of the row with the howe in their hand they have got to how that row & if they stop when they have howed a little & lets other people how past them, they are loosing time that they will not make up in a hury.[17] Another thing they will never attain to celestial glory unless they go Back and Begin & how their row like men & women. They have got to doo it sooner or later. The lords ways is strange to some & again it is quite familiar to others But its all [right?] that things should Bee as they are. Although their is a great many things rong, still it is right that they should Be sow. But the government that the lord has established on the earth is going to Put all things right just as quick as the nations of the earth are laid low which acording to report is on the straight road for it. But the saint of god has nothing to fear only to doo right and all will Bee right with him.[18]

You say in your letter that you were glad to hear that Archy [MacNeil] had got to the valey & that one of the Breed had gotien to the tops of the mountains. He is still working in the stone quarry. Whether he Intends to stay there this summer or not I dont now. He hardly ever said anything to me about you But I Believe that he would Be willing to assist in helping you out of the land of tyriny that you are in. Their is a great many People heare that talks of sending for their freends, but whether their will Be aneybody Brought to this plase or not I dont know—only thais that Can take themselves. At the last Conferenes they Sent men to

[17] Heber C. Kimball made a comment very similar to what Brady is reporting at Salt Lake City, 7 October 1853. His speech was reported in the *Millennial Star* 16 (1854), 177–80.

[18] The expectation that "the Lord's government" (i.e., that established through the Mormon Church) would soon take over is a persistent theme in the addresses of the Mormon leaders. See sermon of Jedediah M. Grant, 2 April 1854, in *JD* 2:145–54, and sermon of Heber C. Kimball, 5 July 1857, in *JD* 5:7–11.

diferent places in the states to gather the saints so their is to Be agathering Place in ohio & another in misouri.[19] The reason of this is I think that the authourities thinks that those that is not able to Bring themselves right through, By staying a year or too in the Staits they might furnish themselves with a more comfortable fit out than they Could other ways do by Coming with the Poor fund. For instance, when a man comes in hear that has got no team of his own, as handcarts doo, they have got to go right to suport their familys.[20] Well they have got no wood, no time to Bring any, no house to live in unless som person has a little spot to spare which is a rear thing to Be had during the season of the emegration.

I dont speak of theis things by the way of finding fault with [Utah]. No, not at all, for things in general are as well as they could Be expected & in fact many things are Better than I thought they would have Been. But the first year is the worst with the Poor that Comes here. That is thoes that have got no waggins or cattle. It takes a man too days with a ox team to get aload of wod. This is a good plase for to live in. It is a healthy country & it is a country that a man can live comfortable in after he is hear a year or to. I know some people hear that came hear too years ago just as Bear as I came, now they have plenty of Cous [cows] & oxin, and other things.

You say in your letter that I am to let you know if we have good meetings through the week. Well where I am at present we have first rate meetings. They are allmost all scotch & east country folks at that, that works at the quary.[21] When we quit our work at night some times we gather to gether and tak over matters just as we feel, But the Bishops if the several wards has meeting in their

---

[19]The conference referred to took place 6 April 1854. Brigham Young proposed that regional gathering places, where the immigrants could be prepared for the next phase of their journey, be established in California, Oregon, Ohio, and Missouri. See conference report in *Millennial Star* 16 (1854), 438–39.

[20]Brady's reference to "handcarts" is to individuals who used handcarts rather than to the organized handcart migration of 1856–60. See Hafen, *Handcarts to Zion*, 29.

[21]"East country" refers to the Clackmannan and Fife area of East Scotland, where many miners joined the Mormons and then emigrated in response to Brigham Young's request for specific tradesmen. Among such miners were the Sharps, Gibsons, and Condies.

ward every thoursday night.[22] It is generly held in the schoolhouse as every ward allmost has a school house in it and some wards has too. This meeting on the thusdy evening is a preys meeting. Again on sundy evening their is a preaching meting on in every ward and on satuerday night the quorim that I Belong to meets! So you see that we have lots of meetings. You will see an acount of the quorim that I Belong to in the paper that I will send you by letter. It is the 39 quorim.[23]

Now, about the lasies: you say that Bell Rolison sends her kind love to me & ec. Im sure that I feel to return my compliments to miss Rolison & alow me to say a word that when a young woman or a young man gets good Chans they ought to take it. This Brings to my mind the time that Dick Proposed But she thought that she was to young. Please to tell miss Rolison from me that she would doo well [to] Join the mormons again, that is if she feels like it. If not you need not mind. Allso Miss Christinia Brown, if you see here Pleas to give her my Best respect, allso her mother. Be sure and remember me to old sister Brown. Let me know when you rite how they are sitiated & how little sister Hill is. Let me know allso if Betty right is maried, allso if aney of the Miss Baxters is maried yet. Ill tell you I feel for the wee doos [doves]. But its one consolation that if they were all this length they could all get what they [want?].[24]

I dont know wat to think about Robert Pendelton & Miss Grant if it realy is the case I wish him health to his navel, marow to his Bones, long live and prosperity. You never told in [your letter] that John Crawford was married & little Lon, the tarter [rascal]. But I'll tell you, when I hear tell if sutch things it makes me laugh. I suppose that the young man thinks if they were to come here single that they coueld not get a girl for love or money. Well it may Bee the case But I know what I know; that their is aney amount of good girls here. Their is many of them that says they would rather wait for a year or to and get a young man than

---

[22] The LDS ward is the local congregation presided over by a bishop. It is the Mormon equivalent of the Catholic parish.

[23] Male members of the Mormon Church holding the priesthood were organized into quorums, which functioned as teaching and social institutions. The Thirty-ninth Quorum was presided over by Daniel Mackintosh, a native of Perthshire.

[24] That is to say, the lassies could get husbands.

to go in for second or third. They think that the first is to Be the greatest. For my own part I could get maried anytime I would just say the word But im not in a hurry. Their is a good time comeing. It is said here that their is 500 young ladies coming from one state in the union so if that is the case it is Bound to Be a good time.

You say that you saw a letter from James Wilson stating that he & young James was going to Canady, But Pair [Poor] man he did not get the length. I suppose By this time you [will?] have heard of him Been Murderd at saint Louis.

[James Brady]

Editor's note: On March 10 1854 James Brady and his Scottish friend, John Dobbie, received their "endowments" — the highest spiritual rites of the Mormon faith and he probably looked forward to the establishment of a family and a long life in Utah. However, the foregoing letter was the last he wrote to the MacNeils and the "good time" he spoke of never came, at least in this life. A black outlined entry in the Minutes of the Thirty-ninth Quorum of Seventy of 1854 August 19 tells of his fate.[25]

Moved by Bro. Mackintosh seconded by Bro. Jackson that we insert the following addition to our minutes.

That we the Officers and Members of the 39th Quorum deeply lament the loss of Bro. J. S. Brady who has been removed from our midst by receiving injuries from the falling of some rock upon him while laboring in Red Bute Kanyon on the 29th July 54 and died on the 31st July 54. During the short time Bro. Brady has been associated with the 39th Quorum we are happy to testify that he conducted himself with integrity and as became a Servant of the Lord, and possessed our entire love and confidence. May he rest with the righteous for a season and rise in the morning of

---

[25] Information on James S. Brady was gleaned from the Airdrie Branch Record of Members, Minutes of the Thirty-ninth Quorum of Seventy, and Endowment House Record Book. The Mormon temple endowment ceremony (consisting of "special washings and anointings, symbolic signs, instructions and sacred covenants [which] gave the Saints new insights into their relationship with God, their eternal destinies, and their earthly responsibilities") was begun in Nauvoo between 1842 and 1845. See Allen and Leonard, *The Story of the Latter-day Saints*, 169–70.

the 1st Resurrection to fill his place among the Saints in light is
our prayer in the name of Jesus.
Amen.

R. H. A[ttwood]

Ironically, when James S. Brady was buried in the Salt Lake City
Cemetery (the only burial of July 31), the sexton appears to have
recorded his name in the "Book of the Dead" as James S. Brock.
Without family he would not have been remembered in the Mormon community, and he disappeared from the records under a
mistaken name.

Two years after the death of their good friend James Brady,
Ann MacNeil's oldest son, John Thompson, left Scotland. For
the next twenty years his letters gave the MacNeils perceptions of
life in America, his views of Mormons and the Civil War, his
commitment to the Reorganized LDS Church in Illinois, and his
involvement in the coal miners' union.

John Thompson to David and Ann MacNeil

Belevue, [Nebraska]
Augest 1857

Dear father and mother,
I take up my pen to rite you a fue Lines to let you know
who i have bin gatin along Sinc last i rote you. I left iowa last fall
and Went over to ilinois and labered there all Winter at Cole
Digen. The name of the place is [Coal Town]. I rote you a leter
from that place, also another from Buflo to Which i have recived
no Answer.
In the Spring i Went to a place thre miles from that. I Was
Sick from Six or Siven Wicks With the Bulis fiver.[26] I Was then
Liven With James Miller and Wife Who atended to me verry Well.
But When i gote a litel bater i thought it Bast to leve this place as
it is Bad in the Summer With fiver and Ague. I left there in June
in Company With James Miller and Wife, also John Farel Who
came there thre Days before We left. We Started for Iowa City. I
Saw James Park there in the Camp. He Was gaten along vere Well

---

[26] An attack of sickness involving the bile—"bilious fever."

and thought of gaten With the time Company but Was told to Wate and go as pesident of the hand Carts Company.[27]

I lived in Iowa City five Wicks huntin Cole for a Scotish man by the Name of James Burns but he had not money to put it through. So We left For Councal Blufs Where We [arrived] Safe. I lived there too Days. I then Crosed the missouri River in the nebraska to Se and find Cole that i Can have Some Work into Winter, as nerlay all other Work is at a Stand Still. But We have not fund a vane that is Workabal yet but the prospicts is good and i believe i Will gat along hear. . . .

John Farel told me that you Stil Working in the qurry and that you had got your fout hurt but Was glad to hear that you Was bater again.

I Was Sorro to hear the Way that things had Went in Ardrie. Let Gaven know who i am gaten along.[28] I have no more at pres-ant but hope i Will have bater news in my nixt. Rite me and anser When you recive this. Give my respicts To all the famlay. Tel thm To do rite and gad Well bliss them. Also to [my aunt?] and all the Saints. . . . Your Son.

John Thompson

Derect Belevue, Sarpe Co.
Neberaskey Teritory
North America.

John Thompson to David and Ann MacNeil

Belvue, [Nebraska]
15 November 1857

Dear father and mother,

I received your kind and Welcom letar and Was glad to hear that you Was in good helth As this found me in joyen the Same Blissen. But [I] have not injoyed [health] all the time Since last i

---

[27] Most of the persons named in this letter appear to be Mormons whom John Thompson had known in Scotland.

[28] This "Gaven" may be the Gavin Findlay who apparently played a role in converting John to the Reorganized LDS Church in 1869. The Airdrie Branch appears in these years to have been in some disarray, hence John's expression of regret at how "things had went." This may also help explain the difficulty that David MacNeil had in keeping his family actively involved in the church.

Rote you. I thoute To escape the ague By Coming out hear But i find it is hear To. I have had the Shakers for nine Days in Suckcesin. I toke nothing for it thinking To Wure it of, But i found it Would Were me out first. So i tooke Some madson and Broke it and by Dranking Barks i have Capet it a Way. So i now injoy good helth thank the lord for it.[29]

I told you in My last leter We had Some prospacits of finding Cole. But it got Wate [wet] So i quite it. I then Went To Work hallin Wood for a feray Bote, at Which i Continued til i toke the fiver and Ague. Since that i have done no Work. Times hear Are dul. At presant there is no Work goning on hear. The onlay reson there Can Be founed for it is that the Banks have all Broke, So that there is no money in Curklasion. But i hear that it is the Same all over the Countary. But it is thought that things Will take a frash Start prity Sone and the Busness Will be Brisk Again. I hear that Some of the Banks in the este are Redemen there money Again.[30]

Winter Bagins To Set in hear. The River is ful of ice So the Bots Will have to Stope Runing for this Seson. I Belive i Will like this Countary and i think i Will Stay hear till I Can do Some good for you. I have not forgot you that are in Bablon, nether have i forgoten that Mormonism is true and of god and that it Will over Come, opose it Who may. But i have not had the privlag to atend miten much Since i Cane to this Countary and hear But litel About mormonism.

You Say you Will Send me a paper. It i have not Recived yet, but Will Be glad for you to Send me one as often as you Can. You Say in your leter that William thretans his mother to leve. It makes me Sorroy To hear that he [is] fulish. Tel him from me not To think himself a man To Sone but To Stay With mother til i Can Send [for] you. As for [Margaret] if She Will go She

---

[29] Thompson's illness was probably malaria, one of the most common diseases in the Middle West in the 1850s. Treatment included use of cinchona bark, the natural source of quinine. Dunlop, *Doctors of the American Frontier*, 90–91, 181.

[30] The financial panic of 1858 was caused by a rapid expansion of credit, too much speculation in railroads and western lands, and the lack of a central national bank to regulate the flow of currency, much of it counterfeit. The collapse of the Ohio Life Insurance and Trust Company in New York triggered a depression which began in August 1857 and lasted for several years. See Hammond, *Banks and Politics in America*, 707–17.

must[31]. . . . give my Respicts to gaven and Wife . . . Send me all the neu you Can. No more at presant but Remans your son.

John Thompson

John Thompson to David and Ann MacNeil

Nebraska [City, Iowa]
August [1858?]

Dear father and mother,

I take up my pen To let you know how I am getan along Since i rote to you last from Belvue but have received no answer To it. My helth is good thank the Lord and i hope this Will find you injoyin the Same Blisen. I left Belvue four months ago and came done the Missouri River about forty mils To nebraska City, hear I am liven yet but how Long i may Stay i do not know. Times are very bad hear at present. Wages are a doler and turtey five cents pur day but We dont get Study Work. I had a letur from St Louis last Wick. Times there are very bad, thay Can onley get about Too days a Wick, and i believe it [is] So all over the Country at present.

John Wilson is married and Jane hase had a Son. They are al Well. I Saw about one hundred from Salt Lake about To wicks ago.[32] Thay mate the tropus at fort Bridger going in To Salt Lake City and the Mormon Ware going done South. I have heard Some thing of Baxter and familey thay are going done South.[33] He Says mormonism ant the Same as it Was in the old Countrey. Magdalene and Jane is Married to George D Grant, So you Se my hopes is Blasted.[34]

---

[31] John's brother William was about nineteen years old when he threatened to leave home. His sister Margaret was twenty-one.

[32] There was a considerable "counter-gathering" at this time of people who did not want to remain in Utah.

[33] Reference is to the federal army's campaign to suppress the "Mormon rebellion" in 1857–58 and the subsequent Mormon plan to evacuate northern Utah and settle in the center of the territory in the spring of 1858. See Furniss, *The Mormon Conflict*, 180–84.

[34] George Davis Grant, a native of New York, was a Utah pioneer who lived in the vicinity of Woods Cross, Utah. He had a total of five wives; two of them, Margaret and Jennie Baxter, were undoubtedly the "hopes" Thompson refers to. Essholm, *Pioneers and Prominent Men*, 896.

I Cane get no tidens of your uncle [Archibald MacNeil] or aney of the rest that came out from Airdrie.

Dear father & mother you [may] think that i am Carles about you but i am not for i am doing my best to get you hear, but the way things is at present it will take me a good bit and i think it Will be best To get out To of my Sisters as thay can make more money hear than i can. [Letter is badly damaged at this point. Only ends of lines are readable.] [James] Miler and [?] is Liven hear. He is Boring for Cole if he finds it there Will be Some Chanch for making money. I forgot Caty [Miller] had Twins about To Weeks ago but thay are both Dead. . . .

> [your] affactnat[son]
> John Thompson

John Thompson to David and Ann MacNeil

> Neberaska City, [Iowa]
> 16 January 1859

Dear father and mother,

By this time you will think i have Left Neberaska and if so you will think rite. [most of the first page of this letter is illegible] [I] belive this place Wile be livelier in the Spring as We are only about Six hundred miles from the gold mins and this will be the main point for [outfitting].[35] I hard a spich delivered by one of the Companey that has the [Contract] from government for Carring the Suplies for the Army in Utah. He had Just Come from there. He Said he Saw Brigham [Young] and heber [C. Kimball], and thay told him that the United States tropes had no busnes there, that they Could rule the popel With out them. He gives them Credit for the improvements thay have made in Such a short Time. Brigham told him that he had not as Maney Wives as the pepel Said he had and that he had about thirty or forty children.[36]

---

[35] Thompson is referring to the gold strikes in Nebraska and Kansas early in 1859. Morrell, *The Gold Rushes*, 150–58.

[36] Polygamy was publicly proclaimed as a doctrine of the Mormon Church in 1853. Brigham Young had children by sixteen of his nineteen wives; between 1825 and 1858 he had fathered some forty-eight children. Of the fifty-seven children he had altogether, eleven died before reaching maturity. See Jessee, ed., *Letters of Brigham Young to His Sons*, xxiii, 357–59.

But i am glad that the Troopes has gone in as there is a good money has had the privelige To leive that Could not have got away anles Some Way like this.[37]

But i think i have done awfa [awful] for the Lord in the Way of Mormonism for i belive it is al a humbug, and in place of given money to a thing that Will never benifet me i belive i Will kipe it, and i Would advise you To do so to. Tel Willi to Kipe his money and Save it for a beter youse, but you may al do as you plece about it. As for me i have helped lofers long anife for i Will have to save my Self and so Will you. And i think David you ot To have known beter. So you Se my mind about things now.[38]

I am Sorry To hear the Way that Gaven is in but i Will help him as Sone as i Can . . . I am Bordin at the Same place that i was [when] i rote To you last. His name is Robert Carson and She has a Brother in glasgow . . . His name is Walter [Laird]. And if you are in glasgow Sone, Cale and let him know that thay are in good health. Give my best Respects To al inquiring Ferends . . . as ever your Son.

John Thompson

---

[37] There was a popular perception reflected in the anti-Mormon press and accepted by John Thompson, that Brigham Young's policy was to completely control movement out of Utah at this time and that the army's presence allowed dissidents to leave. However, during the "Utah War" Brigham Young commented to Orson Pratt that it looked as though Salt Lake City had "taken an emetic and vomited forth apostates, officials, and in fact all the filth which was weighing us down." En route to Utah by handcart in 1859, Thomas McIntyre reported an encounter with nine wagons of "Malcontents" and "Apostate Mormons from Salt Lake City — finding fault with everything and everybody. . . . There surely must be a stampede of Apostate Mormons from the valley." See Brigham Young to Orson Pratt, 30 June 1857, *Millennial Star* 19 (1856), 556; McIntyre, Journal 10, 19–23 July 1859.

[38] Thompson is apparently objecting to the practice of using tithing (10 percent of income) to assist the indigent members of the church. Those who had work were often expected to make extra contributions to assist the poorer members (interview with William Hartley, May 1987). See also Hartley's discussion of the development of tithing and its uses in "Edward Hunter: Pioneer Presiding Bishop," in Cannon and Whitaker, eds., *Supporting Saints*, 280–85.

John Thompson to David and Ann MacNeil

Nebraska City
2 May 1859

Dear father and mother,

I embrace the presant opurtunity of answern your leter Which I was so glad to recive. But i Was Sorrow To hear The Way that things Was With you but i hope that you have found good inployment before this and that you are in a place Where i Can rite to your Self. You Say that my Leter had hurt your filens. I am Sorro for it for i did not rite it With that intention. And you may Just rite What you think is Right and When you think i am doning Rong i Want that you Should tell me of it. Let ofence Come if it may but i am not very easy ofended therefore rite plane and do not trobel your Self to much about me. I ant fare gone out of the Way yet. But you do right and [teach] it to the famley and thay Will Blis you foreit. For i have always bin glad of the things you have told me.

You Say that I am to Loke at John Feral and Se What he had done. I am glad to hear that he is geting along Well. I mite have done beter to have Staid there but i did not think So therefor i Came hear, and i have not lost hopes but that i Can get along.[39] I know i am Slow, But i think it Will Come out Rite. You Say i Will never have any thing While i Sta With James Miller but you nide not trubel your Self any more a about that as i think We have [parted] for good. And i think i hav good Resons for thinking So. We oned a yoke of oxen to gither and Mr Miller Sold them and pocited the money and he and Wive is gone Some place and i dont know Where.

Times hear Loke a litel beter Since the Spring opened as there is So many Coming in hear that are goning To the Gold mins and it Will [Cause] money to Come in curklation hear, whither thay find gold or not. But the acounts from it is good and it is the generel [opinion] that there is plenty of gold there.

---

[39] John Feral or Ferrill was an emigrant who may have been living in Belleview, Illinois. There is also some mention of a Ferrill family in Utah with whom John MacNeil had some difficulties. See John MacNeil's letter of 27 May 1873.

And i hope So as it Will be a grate Benfite To this Countery if there is.[40]

I have hard but very litel of utah Since i rote To you Last only the tropes are Stil there. I hard that thay had Some Schourmishes With the indens. The goverment are prepusing trains for the plains. I gase one trane Will Start this Wick Loded With al kinds of goods for the tropes in utah. And i think thay Will pay good Wages for hands [but] i dont know Wither i Shal [go with them or] not. . . . . [41]

[Part of page is missing.]

Rite Sone and give me al the news you Can. May the Lord Blis you all I remain as ever, Your afacenitly.

John Thompson

John Thompson to David and Ann MacNeil

[Alton, Illinois]
14 Augest 1859

Dear father and mother,

. . . I left Nebraska about the later part of June and Came Back to the Stats. I Came done to St Louis Where i Saw the Wilsons. Thay are gutin along as Well as can be expected the Ways things is at present. Thay had a leter from James Mathes while I was there but no news of you. I tried to get Work there but it Was no good as the indain Says. The pits Was Working about three days a Wick for the Want of Sale for there Cole and farmers had all there hands hired thay Wanted and i Saw there Was no chanch. I Stade one Wick and then left.

Thay Were very kind and Wanted I Should Stay a While With them, but i left and i Came up the River to Alton in Ilinois

---

[40] Thompson reflects the optimistic mood of the Missouri outfitting center for the gold mines. A contemporary account predicted that by August 1859 fifty to a hundred thousand persons would be involved in the Nebraska-Kansas gold rush. See Byer and Kellom, *Hand Book to the Gold Fields of Nebraska and Kansas*, 13. According to Morrell, twenty-five thousand reached the mountains and only three thousand were engaged in serious mining. Morrell, *The Gold Rushes*, 154.

[41] By the spring of 1859, the United States troops sent to suppress the "Mormon rebellion" were located at Camp Floyd, forty miles south of Salt Lake City. With the outbreak of the Civil War the army left Utah. Neff, *History of Utah 1847 to 1869*, 512–16.

Where i [saw] your uncel and ants. Piter has got too pits. There Was one of them Working When i Came here but there Was no places empite [vacant], So he Started me to drive teme for him til Such time as trad Should get Brisk. He is doning a prity good bisnes. . . . He ons about twelve acers of Land hear. He rased a good Crop of ots this year. But thay have had there ups and dons as Will as other popel in this Countay, but thay are Well to live now and thay have had to Work for it. Your ant Works as hard as ever. There is four of us in the house besides there to Selvs. Lasly is gone Some Where about St Louis. You know about the way it usted to be With them and i think it about the Same yet. Your ant wants you to get Some news of your uncel David famley and Send hir all the news you can of them and the Rest of your Relitevs.[42]

The Smith, Burnets hasty and Mrs grame is all hear. William Smith has bin Sick but is now Well again. Burnet Wants you to Se if you can know Where William or his father is and Send him Word. I Rote you a Leter from Nebraska City about the fourth of may To the Care of Mr Master and i pad for it. But there is no answer Come to it So i Wont pay for this one.[43] I have but Litle more news to give you exceptin that Crops Look good this Season. We have had a firstrate Wheat and hay harvest and the Corn look good. There is plenty of frute this Season but it is very Smal.

I have hard but litle about Mormonism Since i Rote to you Last only What i hear from the aposteate Brothern that are hear from Salt Lake. Thay have all kinds of news and i know it ant all Lies thay Say about it but use your Judgment about it and i Will do the Same. Your uncel and ant Send their Best Respects to you. I have no more to Say, but may the lord Bliss and preserv you all til We mete again. Rite as Sone as you Recive this and give my all the news you can. your affictivatly,

John Thompson

Deract To the Care of William Watts, Marchant, Alton, illinois.

---

[42] Peter and Fanny Robertson and "Uncle David" are probably relatives of John's mother, Ann. She did have an uncle, David Boggie, who was born in 1788. Peter Robertson, a Scotsman, was one of the prominent citizens of Alton, Illinois, at this time. *History of Madison County, Illinois*, 109.

[43] It was possible during the nineteenth century to prepay for the delivery of a letter or to send it without a stamp and have the recipient pay for it.

John Thompson to David and Ann MacNeil

[Alton, Illinois]
15 February 1860

Dear father and mother,

I take the present opurtinity To Let you know how i am getin along Since i Recived your leter and was Sorrow To hear the way that thing was. When you rote to me i was then Liven with your uncel and ant. I had the bilus fever When i was liven with them, but when i got well i left and i have ben liven with Joseph graham wife Since that. I am working with a man by the name of Dunford; William Smith is Bossing for him. He has had a leter from [Graves?] this week which brings me news that my Brother William has got himself Badley hurt.

I am Sorrow To hear about it and To hear of the way he is placed but i hope you will give him all the atendincs you can. I will Send you Some money in about To Weeks and it will help a letel.

I expected To have Sent you Some money long ago but i have had my on troubls as well as you Since i came To this country. And them that thinks there is no trobels in the Countery are Sadlly mistaken. Things in this countrey are very flat at present and there is litel prospict of aney change befor the presidentel election and then we expect a change for the beter. I was down at [Graves?] at new year Time. I Seen Robert Pentlen. He was making it prety good at that time but this leter dont give aney news about him. Robert told me that Margrat was disipnted when you Received my leter but i Could not helpe it as things did not go as i expected, but i will have hir out as Sone as i can ras the money. This country is good for girls that is willent to Work. Thay have from 16 To 10 a month [and?] Bord.[44] . . . Give all inquiring Frends my best Respects. No more at present but remains as ever yours,

John Thompson

---

[44] Margaret, John's younger sister, was twenty-one at this time. There were high expectations on her part that her brother would be able to help her emigrate. This is the first of numerous references to the notion that America was a good place for immigrant women to prosper. That they get "bord" (board) probably refers to domestic servants getting part of their pay through food and accommodation.

John Thompson to David and Ann MacNeil

Coal Branch,
[Alton, Illinois]
15 April 1861

Dear father and mother,

I Have Had Word From Willim Wilson leter That you have Bine Wondern What had BeCome of me as you had not Recived aney from me for a Twelve months. It is Just about That Time now Since i Rote To you Last, But i have Recived no Answer To it yet and i have Bein Wondren Just as much What Was The mater With you That you have not Rote for The Last eighten or Tuntey months. If i Rote aney Thing afencef To you it Was more Then i entended To do, But i hope you Will Rite and Let me know all about how Things are With you now.

I have Bien working a Round and doing The Best i could At aney Thing i could find to do. It dont Sute for piopel To Stick To one Jobe hear So i have Bien Some Times Digging Coal and Some Times farming Just as it Would Sute. But for the Last Tue years There is But Little made at eather of Them. Your uncel and ant [Peter and Fanny Robertson] are hear Still and Doing Well. Thay have Boght [another?] Tuntey achers of Land at one hundred Dollers pur acer Which makes Too Thousent Dollers. He has Too pits, But only one of Them at Work for The Wont of Sale. He has got eight horse and Three or four Wagons and Cows and hogs a nufe of Them. But fanney Works a Round as if Thay had not a Doller in The World and Was not abel To pay for There Work doing. In Fact Thay Will not not Let There Daughter Stay at home. She has Bien [at] The Branch Twice Since i Came hear But She is not aloude about The house at all. I have Sein hir one of The Times But not Since She Came Back. I Belive She is Liven With one of hir Cousins in Alton.[45]

We are all in a uprore in This Country at The Present Time and War is unevitibel. I Rede a Dispatch To Day and from The acounts in it War has Comenced and no one Can Tell Where it Will end. The South Will not Come Back To The union With

---

[45] Thompson may be referring to a branch of the LDS Church in Alton, Illinois; if so, Peter's and Fanny's daughter, Lasly (or Lesley?) may have been a member of the LDS Church, but this could not be established.

Thout Some Traubel. From The Present aperence of Things Thay entend To Fieght Befor Thay Will give up To The North. But i Will Send you Too Papers With This Leter and you Can Judge for your Self how Things Will Be in This Countery Before a grate Time.[46]

We have had a long Wenter But not an extery Cold one. The Trees Begin To Blosem and Louk good again, the fall Wheat Crope Louks The Best it has Done for maney a year, and it is Thout By a good many That if The Wether is Faberl for The Weat, That We Will have good Times hear yet.

The miners have Started The union hear. It is Called The Illinois and Missouri association of miners Thay have Bien greatley Robed in There Water and misures in Some of the Places about hear. But our Coul has Bein haled With Teams and We have had Just Weght.[47] I was in William Smiths on Sunday and Thay are all Well. Mis Smith Wants Some of hir Boys To Rite to hir and Let Them know how Thay are gating along. . . . your affectanet Son,

John Thompson

John Thompson to David and Ann MacNeil

Cairo Ill.
12 May 1861

Dear Father and mother,

I take the Present opurtinity To Let you know my Where abouts I am a Present in Camp Defence, Cairo. You will Think it Strange To hear of me volinterin, But i am a Cissetion [citizen] of the united Staites of America and i am Willing To Stand By the Same. You know that Solgern is a thing that i never Was Fond of,

---

[46] This letter was written two days after the fall of Fort Sumter on 13 April 1861, generally seen as the beginning of military action in the Civil War.

[47] Thompson was working for James Mitchell, a Scottish entrepreneur who formed and operated coal mines in Madison County. See *History of Madison County, Illinois*, 518. His involvement in union activity is in line with a Lanarkshire tradition — Alexander McDonald, the most significant union leader in nineteenth-century Scotland, had his roots in Lanarkshire and became the first union leader elected to the House of Commons. See Gordon M. Wilson, *Alexander McDonald*.

But When Rabels Would Seak To Distroy the Best Goverment under the hivens then am i Willing To Sacrifice all i have on this earth Rather than Let Tierients and usurpers over Run the Freist Countery in the Woreld and in Slave and Daprive the Pipele of Free Spitch and Free Prees. The Pipoel of the North have Backad doun To Far with the South and thay thout the North Would let them have it all there on Way, But thay Will Fiend it Diferent before Long. For the North is up as one man for the union and Will niver Stand and let there Rights Be trampled on By Southern Tratiors That Would Like To Trampel under food the Freedion and Liberty Which there Patriotick Fathers Foght for and Wone at the expence of many a Life of as good men as ever live.[48]

We have about 5 or 6 Thousind Tropes hear under Arms and Ready for fight When Caled on and We expect more Troups hear every day. I understand there is To Be Fifteen Thousand men Statiend at this Point as it is the most importint Place in the State of Illinois. We had a Falce alarem last night and We Was all out in the field and ready in about fiftin minets. We Was There a Fue minets When the Word of Command Was given To the Captions To march there Compeneys To there Qurters. So We Went and Slept Sound Till morning at five oclock When We all had to Turn out for Role Call.

This is Sunday So We will have no Driel To day. Wick day We driel four Hours, one and a half in the fore noon and To Hours in the after noon and half an Hour for drus Pared [dress parade]. This is our days driel. Our Compney Was got up in Alton and is Called the Alton City gards. Caption Tucker in the 9th Ragement under the Comand of Cornel Pain. There has Bein grate Roumers of an acttack on this place, But We have had no fighting as yet. But When Thay Come We Will try and Be Ready and may the god of Batels Bliss and Stranthen the hands of those how are fighting for the freediam That Was wone To Them By There fathers. But i Will have To Come to a Close as the day is Werring By.

---

[48] Many Mormons interpreted the Civil War as divine retribution against the United States for its unjust treatment of the Mormons and as a necessary precursor to the Millennium. See Larson, "Utah and the Civil War," 55–77. Thompson's perspective on the Civil War as a "just" war may be one factor in his alienation from Utah Mormonism.

I left my things in the Care of Piter Robertson and Alexander Borthwick and thay Will Be all Right Should any thing hapen me. Pleas Rite To alton To the Care of James Mitchell Coal Branch and thay Will Be forwarded To me. I Will now Conclud Praying That god may Blis you all With helth and Stranth. . . .

Rite Sune and give me all the news you Can. I have no more at Present But Remens your efectioned Son,

John Thompson

Editor's note: The Civil War began on 12 April 1861, when the Confederates fired on Fort Sumter. Two weeks later John Thompson volunteered for the Union Army. He was wounded at Kennesaw Mountain, Georgia, in June 1864 and was mustered out in August 1864. Some of these letters describe in detail the military campaigns he was involved in, but because they are generally unrelated to the main theme of the collection, i.e., the response of the MacNeil-Thompson family to the Mormon gathering, they have not been included here. These campaign letters were written from Mound City, Illinois; Bridgeport, Alabama; Corinth, Mississippi; and Rossville, Georgia, in 1861, 1862, and 1863, and 1864. During his army period John Thompson is silent on the subject of Mormonism but he does not hesitate to express his almost chauvinistic patriotism and his belief that the United States had "the Best govermint on the face of gods Earth." Not until 1869 does he mention religion again—this time as a member of the Reorganized Church of Jesus Christ of Latter Day Saints. His letters continue with the beginning of one written from Bridgeport, Alabama, c. December 1863. It is included here because of the insight it gives into the developing relationship between John and his stepfather, David MacNeil. It also contained news of the death of his younger brother, William.

Bridgeport Alabima
[c. December 1863]

Dear father and Mother,

I Recived your Letter derected in Care of Peter Robertson and was glad to hear that you ware all well as it found Me the

Same. You Say in your Letter it is about a year Since i wrot to you and you Blame Me for Not writing to [you] oftener than i do. Well i with the Same Proriety Can Blame you as i have Not recived as answer to the Last tow Letters i wrote you. You Also Say in your Letter that you think i have forgot the old focks at home. In that you are Mistaken as i have all there that Belongs to Me and Some that i Never Can forget as Lang as i Live. David, i May have Acted a littel folish for there good and my own Since i Came to this Countrey But Still i have Never forgot them.

You Say that you think the Same Change has Come over Me that Comes over the most of Peopel that Come to this Country that thay forgets all But the Almighty Doller. Well David if you never get your heart no more ConCeintrated on the Almighty Doller then mine is i think it will never hurt you much. . . .

Well David i Cante Say that i Liek My occupation very well as you are Plesed to tarem it. I Never had a Lieken for Soldiern as i Gess you know that, But when Duty Calls Me, as a Citzen of what i Consider the Best govermint on the face of gods Earth, to give my aide to Sepress a Reblion that has Bein got up for the Pourpous of distroying that goverment and Estebishen a Dispat with Slavery as it foundation, then i [am] willen to give my aid in Supresen it. David i want you to give my your vues on this thing without Restrant. While i am writing this we Recived marchen orders.

Dear father and Mother, i have Just Recived your Letter with the Sorroful news of my Brothers Dath and i Can Sumpythise with my mother as i know what hir fellens must Be with Regard to his death.[49] But we must Submit to the will of God Altho it Looks hard in our famley. Daved do what you Can for his famly and Let me know in your nixt Letter how thay are Situated with to liven. If Gold wasent Such a discount to Pay for Paper i would Send you Some But we have [to] Pay about fourty Cents for Gold on the Doller. That is one thing the war has Caused to Rise in Vellue But it may Come all Right Befor long.

---

[49] William died as a result of injuries received when he was crushed in the pumping machinery of Board Loch Ironstone Pit, Kirkintilloch, Dumbartonshire, on 8 September 1863. He was twenty-three and left a widow and a son, Johnnie Thompson, who eventually came to Arizona in 1883.

We have marched about Sixty mills Since we Left Bridge Port and are now Camped at a Place Called Igons ferry in Teennessee, Eighten miles from Chattanago, where the most of our force of this depertment are Stationed at Present and gess will Be the most of this wenter. It is very Probebel that we may Stay hear for tow or three months as we have to gard allong the Tennessee River Betun Roscrans forces and Burnsides with our Devison So as to Cape Rebels from flanken us. We Can See them acrose the River and talk to there Pickets Every day. Our Devesion is Comanded By Jeff. C. Daves from Indana.[50]

Our Regment has Bein very fourtnet So far as we have Lost But very fue men in Battel. But we have never Bein in aney Generial Engagement Altho we have Bein in Places where the Balls flue thick and fast. But thank God i have Escaped So far with out Being hurt. We have Bein in the Service tow years and three months. Our time will Be out on the tunty fifth of July nixt and when our time is up i think i will Let Some one Else Soldier for a while.

Tell mother to Chere up and i will do all i Can for you when i get throu with this. . . . I will write again in a month. . . . your affectenet Son,

John Thompson

John Thompson to David and Ann MacNeil

Alton, Coalbranch
[Illinois]
19 November 1864

Dear father and Mother,

I received your letter of the Thurd of October . . . I hope [mother] Will Be all Right again soon. . . . I have Started To Work Since i Came Back for your uncel. The work is verry good at Present altho it is verry hard with a fello after Being of work for Three years and a half But i Gess i Will Get a Castomed to [it]

---

[50] In June and July of 1863 General Rosecrans defeated the Confederate forces under Bragg and advanced towards Chattanooga, extending the Union forces along the Tennessee River. During August they spent time repairing railroads and concentrating supplies and on 8 September 1863 they captured Chattanooga. William J. Draper, *History of the American Civil War* (New York, 1870), pp. 60–63, 97.

after a while. We are making verry Good Money at Present [even] if it is War times.

We have Just Got our Presidantel Election over and have Elected old abe again for another Teram of four years. So i think This Can be Set Down, as the voice of the American Peopel for War untill this Rebelion is Put Down which i think we Can Do throw Corse of time. But i Supose yours opinions and Mine differ widley on This SubJect as i Belive that it is Nothing But Right that This War Should be Carried on untill The Last Rebel in arms is Subdued and the Last Slave maid free. David, i belive if the Lord has Placed a Curse on the Peopel of This Country in the Shape of War it is Becase thay have Purmited The Existence of Slavery Amounst them for Such a Lenth of Time. But i Gess we would Differ in a Grait Maney things.

You Say in your Letter that i am To think Well Before i act and Let you know and you Will Give me advice how To Act. Well David, if it is aney Thing That you Can Give Me an advice on i Will Let you know and Be verry happy [to] have you Give Me all the advice you Can. David, i Might have Given you a Long Letter When i Wrot To you Concerning My Travels Throgh the Country But i think it would Be of Little Intrest to you.

You Say in your Letter that My Sister wants Me To Remain Singel untill She See me. Well if that will do her aney good and it ant to Lang [Long]. I asked you in My Letter To See My Sisters if thay Wanted To Come to this Country and who Much thay Could Rais for that Purpos. But i Gess you Will have Got The Letter Long Befor This if you Did not Let Me know.

Now David i want you To Do the Best you Can untill nixt Spring and i will do what i Can. Tell my mother to Chere up and all may yet Be Right. Tell aney that i Read hir Song on my native Country and i was Plesed with the Sentment But More So with the writing. George & Betsey Haig are Well and Send Their Best Respects To you also your uncle and anty. Give My Best Respects to Robert Haigs and all[51] . . . i remain your afficenat Son,

John Thompson

---

[51] The Haigs were apparently well known to the MacNeils and Thompsons in Scotland and it is probable that Betsy Haig, John's future wife, was a member of the LDS Church in Lanarkshire.

John Thompson to David and Ann MacNeil

Alton, Coalbranch
[Illinois]
5 February 1865

Dear father and Mother,

I Received yours of the 14th inst. and was happy to hear that you ware all well again as it found me in Joyin the Same Graet Blissing. Thank the Lord for it. David i am Sorrow to hear that Janet has had Such Bad work. But i will tell you what i will do for you. I will Send you one hundred Dollers to help you acrose the Sea & with what you Can Rais yourself that May be Suficent to bring you and famly to New york. And i will Send you tickets to Bring you from New York to hear. If you think with this help you and famley Can Come writ and Let Me know Soon.

You Say you had a Letter from La Salle with Mine from [an] ancquaintence of yours who you think will help [you] out to this Country. Well, you know him Best But i think if you Are Saving with what you and your Sons Can Maik and what i have offered you Can Come hear without aney further Asistence. The Distence from here to La Salle is About three hundred miles, a verrey good walk Befor Brakfast and one i Dont Expedt to take for a fue Days.[52] But if i Should happen to fall in with your friend Hamill i will treet him with Respect, But to open a Corespondence with a man that i never Saw in my Life nore knows nothing About would i think Be a Case that i Dont care about Pursuieng.

We have had Some trubell hear for the Last Too or Three [weeks?] with our Bosses. But i think the Dificelty is about Setteled or Soon will be, as we are Goning to have Waits on our Pit Head where all the Coal will be waid befor Leving the Platform in Place of Goning one or Too hundred Miles and there Being waid and the Returns Sent Back to us after Every one had helped himself To a Chunk or too as it want along the way.

David what do you think of Shermins Retreat now through Georgia? As your English and Scotch Papers had it, a verrey good

---

[52] LaSalle is located in northern Illinois, on the Illinois River, twelve miles west of Ottawa.

Retriit. I think [they] Captured Savannah with therty thousand Bails of Cooten, a Large amount of Rice, one hundrid and fifty Pices of Cannon, Eight thousend Prisaners and four or five Gun Boats and Transports with others velubels. And i Supose By this Time you will have Read an Acount of what Hood has Acomplished in his northern movemints. He has found out that Thomes is not the man to fuel with. He Drew him, as the Saing is, To where he wanted him; that was near Nashvele and acounts will Show what Hood Maid by it.[53] I think the Confedrecy Might as well give it up But it May be that the Lord wants a fue More thousend Slain Befor the Conflict is over. If So his will must be Doun. I Sopose you will have had the acount of the Fall of Fort fisher before this Time. There was a Grait Slaughter there.

David, i am verrey much Ablaged to you for your advice. Altho you need not be afred to writ aney thing in your Letter To me as all my Letters are Privet unles i wish them other wise. You ask me in your Letter how it is about houses hear. Well thay are verrey Scarce and as a Genirial thing Peopel Bild Houses for themselvs Except a fue that the Bosses have Bilt. But we will See about that when you Come hear as things Some time takes a Strange turen hear in Too or three months.

You Say in your Letter that you wish me to have nothing more to Do with the Conflict. Well i Dont Supose i will at Present.

George Haigs had a letter from home this week. He Says that things are Rather Slack with his focks. He and Sister is well. Give my Best Respects to the Haig Famley. William Smiths adress is Alton, Coalbranch, Madison County, Illinois. Your uncel and annty Send there best respects to you. Give my Respects to Dave Adamson [and] all Anquiring friends. I have but Littel More to Say at Present. Give My Love to Mother and all the Family when you See them and writ some. Your Affecinet Son,

John Thompson

---

[53] Thomas's victory over Hood at Nashville took place on 15 and 16 December 1864.

John Thompson to David and Ann MacNeil

Alton, Coalbranch
[Illinois]
19 April 1865

Dear father and Mother,

    I was Sorrow to hear that you Both had Bein Sick But hope By this Time you have Bein Restored to full helth and Strenth again. I have Bein Tolleribale Well Since i wrot you Last as far as My helth is Concerned But Work has Bein Rather Slack Since i wrot to you. But this is Nothing Strange hear at this Seson of the year, Altho i Beleve it is a Lettel Slaker this Session then it has Bein for Some years Past. The Reson Aperes to Be this: that the Capitalists of this Countery have Combined Together for the Purpos of Braking up the American Miners Association Which has Bein Established in this Countery for the Last four years and has Bein the Mains of Raisen the Miners Wagies in this Countery fifty Pur Cent higher then it Ever would have Bein had it Not Bein for the union that Exists amonng the Miners. The Blow Aperes to Be Amed at the Unions of all Labering Men Where ever Such a thing Exists in the Country. I Beleve the Laberiang Clases of this Countey Are Geten there Eyes opened to this fact which i think will Dow Away with Party feelling to a grait Extent in this Country and Laiboring Clases Will Begin to Look to there own Intrest and Elect Men that Will Legslate Justley for Labour as Well as Capitol.

    You Ask me in your Letter To give you Some advice As to what will be Best for you to Bring to this Country. Well, Bring a full Lout of Pit Clothing Apeace. You Might Bring Some Picks But if you have over fifty Pounds Apece you Will have To Pay for it on the Rail Road, So it might Come About as Cheap for you to Purches them hear. But i will find out the Rait of frait from hear to New york and Let you know. I would advise you To bring a fue Good Lamps with you as you Can Sell them for fifty Cents a pece hear and thay Wont be But Verrey Littel wait. Mens Clothing as a Generial thing is Pritey high hear.

    In Closed you Will find Tickets for Eight Persons Making Siven full Passiges. I Supose that Too of your famley Are under

Twelve years of Age and all Betwen that age and four Comes for half fare and under four free on the Rail Road.[54]

David, i think from the Present Apperence of things hear you Need Not Be in a grait hurrey Coming out if you Are Douing Aney thing well there at Present As i Dont think there will Be Much Work Douing hear befor fall. Besids this, the hot wether is goning To Be on Befor you Can Get hear. But if things is not goning well with you, [you] Cant Be Aney worse hear then you are there.

I have Just Got word that the Bosses Are goning to Stope there works untill we Come Down in our Price and Every thing Showes Aperence of trubell at Present. But then it is allways the Darkest hour Before Day. I will Send you a Paper this Week. I am goning to Town to Day and will get the Money Exchanged and will Send you the order in this Letter.

James Miller and kety Are hear. He is one of the Tools that our Bosses hear have Got for the Purpos of Braking up our Association. Him and Too or theree More thay Are working for three Cents Less a Bushell then what we have Being Working for. This is the kind of a Man Miller is.

David, i Gess By the Time this Reches you i will Be Married to Betsey Heaig. You need not think it Strange as Such things will happen. . . . yours Affectionety

John Thompson

Write Soon and let me know what you are Goning to Do. George Haig Sent of the Money for his focks Too Days ago.

PS the Rait of frait from New York to Alton is About $300s (Three Dollers) Pur hundred Wait. This Draft is Good on aney Bank in the united kingdom of Great Briaten.

---

[54] The persons John Thompson sent tickets for included David MacNeil (36), Ann MacNeil (54), and their children, Elizabeth Thompson (22), Janet Thompson (20), John MacNeil (18), David MacNeil (15), Annie MacNeil (12), and James MacNeil (10).

John Thompson to David and Ann MacNeil

> Alton, Coal branch
> [Illinois]
> 4 May 1865

Dear father and Mother,

I told you in My Last Letter that i was Goning To Get Married To Betsey Heig Which Came of on the 28th of Aprial. I would have Liked that you had all Being hear But i thought i had Being Singel Long Enuf and as i found a Girel i thought i Could Make a Wife of i Got Married. So you Need Not think it Strange as i think it is The Best thing i Could do.[55]

I forgot To Tell you in My Last Letter that your Rail Road Tickets is Good at aney Time you May Chanse to Come. I Also Told you that we had Some Dufficulty with our Bosses hear Which is Now Partley Settled and we Are goning To Resume Work Again at a Rudiction of one and Three Qurters of a Cent which our Bosses thinks will Anabell them To Sell Coal in Market with other Placies. The Great Trubel with us hear [is] that our vain of Coal is So Much Smaller then other Places and our Bosses have To Pay So Much More for Diggan there Coal that thay Cannot Compet with other Bosses.

I Would have Started To Work to Day But Abriham Lincoln the Lait Presedent of the United States is to Be Buried to Day and Mostley all Publick Works is Suspended for to Day in the State. He will Be Intered To Day at Twelve o Clock in Springfield, The Capitol of our State. Spaciel Trains have Bein Runing for the Last Too Days and i Expect there Will Be one of the Graitest Gatherings of Peopial that Ever was in the united States.

David, i think our Rebelion is about wound up in this Country, at Lest Aperiences Indacete So at Present. But i Think the Assassination of President Lincoln is one of the Severest Blows that the South Could have got at this Time as i Dont think Andy Johnstone Will Be Quit So Esey with them as Lincoln Would in Reconstruction of the union. From What President Johnstone

---

[55] John Thompson and Betsy Haig were married by the Rev. Melvin Jameson at Alton, Illinois. Elizabeth (Betsy) Haig was born in Scotland on 8 July 1842. These data concerning John Thompson and his wife were obtained from his military pensions file in the National Archives, Washington, D.C.

has Said To the Differient Delagiations that have Called to See him he Apears To Be Determint To Punnish the Heads of this Rebelion for the Tresion thay have Comited.

I have But Littel More To Say. Writ Soon and Let us know what you Are goning to Do, So that if you Are Coming Right away i Can have Some things Redy for you Such as a House and things that will be Indespencibell. . . . We Remain your Afficnet Son and Daughter.

John & Bettsey Thompson

Editor's note: The stage seemed set for the wholesale emigration to Illinois of the MacNeil-Thompson family c. 1865–66. John had magnanimously sent fully paid tickets for the transportation of his mother, stepfather, two sisters, two half brothers, and his half sister. At the same time the family was being encouraged to gather to Utah by their old friend John Marshall, who was preparing to leave for Utah with his second wife and family. Marshall didn't think much of John Thompson's marrying Betsy Haig and suggested that would be a deterrent to their emigration. Perhaps he was unaware that John had sent tickets. His letter suggests that David MacNeil had had another lapse in his faith commitment, another indication that David was not a particularly stable individual as far as Mormonism was concerned.

John and Elizabeth Marshall to David and Ann MacNeil

Moore St West Bromwich
Staffordshire. England
[c. late 1867]

Dear David & Ann,

You will Guess I have Delayed writing till I heard from my Son which I Did last week. . . . [56]

We have Been truly greaved to hear of John Thompson throwing himself away on one how from Charrecter Cannot make

---

[56] According to John Marshall, Sr.'s autobiographical sketch, John Marshall, Jr., arrived in Utah in September 1867.

him feel very Comfortable.[57] It may hinder you from getting away as soon as you might have Done had he Remained single, as the Lord helps them that helps themselves. We will have to Continue Dilligent in our labour, Be Economical in our liveing and our Chance to immagrate will Be the Mare Sure.

I have Been Managing a Small work and Selling the Iron Since my Son went of. Trade has Been very Bad here a long time. From My own means I Dont Expect to Be able to go next year. You See what my Son Says about trying to help Me out. I Dont Expect he will Be able to Do anything like what I would require. I have to pigs worth [£]5''0''0. Should I Be able to keep them till april they will Be worth [£]12''0''0. But it is uncertain that I Shall Be able to Bring them up. My house goods May Bring Me eight or ten pounds. With a [pice?] pound lottery I think of geting up, would go a lump of the way toward taking us out. The Rail way will Be laid 500 Miles Be yond the frontiers which will Expeediate the Journey very much.[58] I will write you again ere long and let you know My prospects.

Please write Me Soon and let us Know how you get on. Let Me kn[ow] if you have yet Returned to the Sheepfold of Christ. If you have not, think of your familey loss. I have put this question to you Before. You never repplyed to Me on this point. Please Excuse Me for Meddling thus. I shall Be glad to hear from you and to learn that your Doing well and Enjoying good health as we are at present. May God grant that My wish is correct and in Conclusion we hope to meet [Soon] where the honise in heart all go.[59] We Remain yours as ever.

John & E. Marshall

---

[57] Despite Marshall's assessment of John's choice of a marriage partner, the Thompsons seem to have been very happy together. See Elizabeth Haig Thompson to Elizabeth Thompson, 9 April 1876.

[58] Until the late 1860s, St. Joseph, Missouri, was the western terminus of the railroad. Taylor, *Expectations Westward*, 119.

[59] John and Elizabeth Marshall arrived in Utah in the Captain Roylance Company, 20 August 1868.

John Thompson to David and Ann MacNeil

Caseyville.
[Illinois]
25 August 1867

Mr. David McNeil:

Sir, i hear from a Letter that Robert Winning has Recived from the old Country that you have Started a Clothan Store in the Whifflat and i Expect you & my mother & famley have Given up the Nothin of Coming out To This Country Soon.[60] So i have Made Inqurey in St. Louis About the Rail Road Tickets i Sent you and found out that thay Will Not Be Good Much Longer. So if there is None of you Coming out To This Countery Soon, Please Too Send the Tickets Back as i C[an] Get Part of the money B[ack] i Payed for them.

I Was up at Alton and Stayed Too Weeks at Robert Winnings. I Seen your uncll & Anty. Thay Are Getten Along Prety Well in this Country. Thay have Built a large Brick House on there Land and i Gess thay Are Worth a Good Maney Thousand Dollers and Graben for More. I have had verrey Poor helth this Summer But am feeling a litel Better again. My Wife and Child is Well. Peter Brownlees Wife had a Daughter one Week ago.

I have But Little More To Say. Labour hear has Bein at a verrey Low Eabbe for Some Time. The Men hear have About four Cents, Pur Bushell for Diggan.

There Was a young Man Lost his life hear Last Week. Thay Ware [putting?] Back the Powder in the [hole?] When it Exploded and Blawe the Coals in his face and Smashed his head verrey Bad. He Died that Night. His name is Philip Carnes. His father & Mother Live at Carnbrow [Lanarkshire]. There Was Three Brothers of them in This Countery . . . your Afficetnet,

John Thompson

Editor's note: No letters from the period between August 1867 and July 1870 have survived. After the MacNeils rejected

---

[60] Whifflet is a mining village in the vicinity of Coatbridge, Lanarkshire. In the 1871 Census David MacNeil is listed as a draper, a dealer in clothing and dry goods.

John Thompson's generous offer to transport the family to the United States, it is possible that none were written. In previous letters, John had referred to his stepfather as "father" and even "David," but in this letter the use of "Sir" may indicate some alienation between the two oldest men in the MacNeil-Thompson family — it should be remembered that David was only nine years older than his stepson. When the letters from John resume in 1872 they are all addressed to his sister, probably Elizabeth. In the meantime, the focus of immigration possibilities shifted from Illinois to Utah as a new set of letters arrived at the MacNeil home, this time from David and Ann's oldest son, John MacNeil, who began reporting on conditions in Utah in the summer of 1870.

3

"Rough Country & Rough People"

Letters from John MacNeil, John Thompson,
and John Marshall
1870–72

The last letter that John Thompson wrote to his stepfather appears to signal the end of John's efforts to help his family emigrate. By going into business in 1867 as a draper in Wishaw, Lanarkshire, David MacNeil in essence rebuffed his stepson's efforts to bring the family to the United States. However, the urge to emigrate persisted, and in 1870 John MacNeil, aged twenty-one, became the second member of the family to leave Scotland for the Mountain West.

John was the first child born to nineteen-year-old David MacNeil and his thirty-seven-year-old wife, Ann Boggie Thompson, the widow of John Thompson. He was born at Carnbroe, Parish of Bothwell, Lanarkshire, on 5 December 1847, and four months after his parents joined the Mormon Church, he was "blessed" in the Airdrie Branch of the church on 26 June 1848. In March of the same year his half sisters, Janet and Elizabeth Thompson, were also blessed. As other children were born to David and Ann they too were blessed in the church, David in 1850 and Ann in 1852.[1]

During the next twenty years the MacNeils seem to have had some sort of relationship to the Mormon Church in Scotland. However, none of the children became adult members of the church until John MacNeil was baptized on 9 July 1870, by Brigham Young's business manager, Hamilton G. Park, who was serving a

[1] Airdrie Branch Record of Members.

mission in Scotland.[2] Three days after his baptism, John left Glasgow for Liverpool where he joined a group of some 200 Mormon emigrants on the *Manhattan*, bound for New York.

It is possible that John had been baptized earlier at age eight, the usual baptismal age for Mormon children. Records may have been lost, and Hamilton Park may have been making sure that John would have at least a recorded connection to the church as he set out for Utah. It is also possible that the lateness of the baptism may indicate that the family was not particularly close to the church during the 1860s.

Whatever his precise rationale for joining the church, John's early letters suggest he came to Utah to improve his economic lot: "Laying Mormonism aside," he says, "this is a better country for A poor man than the Old Country ten times over." While his letters display some sense of ambivalence toward the Mormon Church, he also condemns the "d — d Mean Scoundrels that are here under the pretence of Mormons." In spite of his efforts to believe in Mormonism while rejecting Mormons, there is little of the religious idealism of the "Spirit of Gathering" in the letters he wrote to his parents.

John's account of his first few months at the home of the William Douglass family in Smithfield, Cache Valley, reveals a tendency to expect too much of other people. These early letters are a portent of John's future difficulties with people, institutions, and employments. By constantly looking to the future and expecting too much — of strangers, kinfolk, work opportunities, religious institutions, or the economic and political system — John MacNeil was setting himself up to be constantly disappointed.

John MacNeil's letters were not all negative evaluations of life in Utah, however. He persistently encouraged his family to follow him, and within two years he had sent money to bring either his brother David or James to Utah. John naturally missed his family, and even singing the "auld Scotch sangs" did not ease

---

[2] About the time that John MacNeil was baptized there was a significant decline in the number of baptisms in Scotland. The few baptisms that occurred were treated as major events in the *Millennial Star*. One of the main functions of the mission of Hamilton Park appears to have been to revitalize the inactive Saints, and he may have contacted the MacNeil family in the early 1870s in that context.

his homesickness. He wanted his family to share in the benefits of the new land. In spite of his desire, he would bring them only if he could pay cash. Some might borrow with no intent of paying back, but John MacNeil, with traditional Scots pride in his independence, would have none of that. When his brother David offered to send him money during a period when he was unemployed, John responded that he would rather die than accept assistance. John hoped to buy land and settle down as a farmer with cows and crops. However, he was attracted to mining as a way to raise capital to buy land. John's early years in Utah foreshadow his later attempts to gain an economic edge by mining for coal in Almy and Rock Springs, Wyoming, and for silver at Alta near Salt Lake City and at Silver Reef in southern Utah. There is no evidence that after John MacNeil arrived in Utah in the fall of 1870 he ever communicated with his half brother John Thompson in Illinois. Indeed, if the letters that survive are representative, there appears to have been little correspondence between John Thompson and his kin in Scotland after David MacNeil went into business as a draper in 1867. At times there were gaps of eighteen months or more between letters.

The one letter written by John Thompson between 1870 and 1872 was addressed to his sister Elizabeth Thompson, who was a milliner in the vicinity of Wishaw. This letter gave the family still another perspective on America and especially on Mormonism. In contrast to John MacNeil's letters, it had decidedly religious overtones. At one time he held Mormonism to be all a "humbug"; John Thompson now encouraged his family to investigate the claims of the Reorganized Church of Jesus Christ of Latter Day Saints, which he had joined in 1869. Both he and his Scottish wife, Betsy Haig, were apparently rearing their children in that faith.

In addition to the divergent views of John MacNeil and John Thompson, another John wrote to the MacNeil household to enthusiastically endorse Mormonism and life in Utah, even though he admitted mistakes and errors on the part of individual members there. John Marshall's sometimes earthy but always positive letters are a microcosm of the Utah scene. The conflict between the Mormons and "gentiles," the efforts of the "Josephites" (the Mormon term for members of the Reorganized Church) to convince the Mormons that Brigham Young was a usurper, the challenge of the "Godbeites"[3] from within the fold, and the difficulties that new settlers faced are all grist for John Marshall's mill. His was the voice of a committed Mormon who tried to get his old friends to come "to where the honise in heart all go."

John Marshall was born in Glasgow 10 December 1821, the son of John Marshall and Janet Wright. The family name was originally Minto, but John Marshall's grandfather, James Minto, changed his name to John Marshall c. 1795 to avoid detection as a deserter from the British army and probably also detection as a bigamist. He had at least four "wives" living at the same time in Scotland and the North of England! In 1846 his grandson, John Marshall, married Margaret Wood at Glasgow, and by 1854 they had had six children—although only John, the eldest, survived to maturity.

Like many converts, John Marshall had a dramatic personal experience which set him on the road to being receptive to the message of the Mormon Church. On 1850, January 16 he was seriously injured in the explosion of a boiler at the Mossend Iron Works in Lanarkshire. Fifty-two years later he recalled that this accident led him to reflect on his life and to promise that if his life were spared, he would commit himself to serving God (see Appendix B). He was then an active member of the United Presbyterian Church, but had begun to question the scriptural basis of its teachings. On 1850, June 6 on his way to a weekday meeting of the UP Church he claimed that a voice told him to go in the opposite direction—eastward instead of westward. He made several attempts to continue his journey to the church, but kept getting promptings to continue eastward. After visiting a friend at the Calder Iron Works, he made his way to Whifflet railway station, one mile east of Coatbridge, intending to take the next train to his home. Stopping at a house in the village to inquire about the next train, he was invited to stay until the train came. He mentioned that he had known the Mrs. [John] Thompson who had lived in that very house some years before and was told that that she had returned to the village after having married a Mr. McNeil. He went directly

---

[3] William S. Godbe, an English immigrant, led the "New Movement" in an attempt to reform Mormonism, c. 1869–70. Godbe was excommunicated, but the movement eventually became the nucleus of the anti-Mormon Liberal Party. See Ronald W. Walker, "Commencement of the Godbeite Protest," 217–44.

to her home and found that she and her husband (David MacNeil) were Latter-day Saints. "Here the New and everlasting gospel Door was thrown open to me," and when the train came he "had No use for it that day." He engaged the MacNeils in a long religious conversation ending in some sort of "Revelation" at midnight on the bridge near where the Luggie Brook emptied into the River Calder.

The MacNeils, then, were the means of converting John Marshall to Mormonism. He believed that he had been led to their home by inspiration, because although he had lived only a mile from where the Latter-day Saints in Holytown worshiped, he had never heard of Joseph Smith or Mormonism until he visited the MacNeil home in the village of Whifflet on that fateful Thursday afternoon of 1850 June 6.

In spite of the dramatic nature of his conversion, John Marshall was not actually baptized into the Mormon faith until 17 April 1851. He was then almost immediately excommunicated for "Neglecting meeting and the performance of My religious Duties" but was rebaptized in May 1851. Shortly after the still-birth of their fourth child in October 1851, the Marshalls moved to Shatlybridge, County Durham, England. His wife requested baptism in 1853, but, according to John Marshall, the missionary who promised to baptize her was so busy courting two sisters that he neglected his potential convert and never came to perform the ordinance. She felt slighted, "kicked hard against the truth," and consequently never joined the LDS Church. In the following year Margaret died in childbirth at the age of 32.

In May 1855 John Marshall married twenty-one-year-old Elizabeth Joyce Robson at Barley Maw, County Durham. That same year, he was once again "cut-off" from the Mormon Church after which he apparently returned to Scotland for a time, and in May 1857 was rebaptized for the third time at Holytown, Lanarkshire, near where he had first heard the Mormon message. Shortly after this, his second wife was also baptized at Holytown. Thereafter the family returned to West Bromwich, in the English Midlands, from which they moved to Utah in 1868, settling in Bountiful. Marshall followed his trade as an iron worker and helped establish and operate a furnace in Salt Lake County. He and his wife Elizabeth had five children born to them in England and five in Utah.

While living in Bountiful he was contacted by John MacNeil, who had arrived in Utah in 1870. Marshall's letters to David and Ann MacNeil reveal a rare ability to distinguish between the human and divine aspects of religion, and this ability no doubt played a role in keeping him within the Mormon Church. The inability to make that distinction seemed just as surely to hasten John MacNeil's departure from Mormonism. Unlike John MacNeil's honesty, which propelled him further and further from his Mormon associates, John Marshall's honesty seemed to give him a balanced perspective. He laid no claim on special "piety Nor santity," but was simply a "plain fellow, ever has been, ever will be." He had a solid commitment to Mormonism and he wanted from the very start to build the kingdom in spite of the imperfections that he saw in it.

Around 1875 the Marshalls moved to Pleasant View in Weber County where John established an iron works in Ogden, engaged in farming, and was active as a High Priest in the Mormon Church. He died 3 January 1905 and was eulogized for his "useful, well spent life" and for his many "acts of kindness and benevolence."[4] In a very real sense, John Marshall was the epitome of the successful Mormon pioneer. Before he died he actually experienced the "good times coming," which never seemed to arrive for his friends the MacNeils.

When these emigrants were reporting their varied impressions of Utah and the Mormons, the territory was just beginning to feel the impact of the newly completed railroad. The Mormons accounted for almost 98 percent of the total population in 1870, but in the next decade or so that commanding majority was reduced to around 62 percent. Mining, which in 1870 employed 3 percent of the labor force, more than doubled during the 1870s. There was increasing pressure on the Mormons to accommodate the larger non-Mormon population by making changes in the way schools were organized. In addition, federal efforts aimed at eradicating

---

[4] Data on John Marshall from genealogical records of Cleone Marshall Wayment, North Ogden, Utah, who also provided a copy of an autobiographical sketch which John Marshall wrote in 1882. Dean L. Marshall, Modesto, California, made available a copy of the original Life History of John Marshall, written in 1902, which appears in Appendix B and contains Marshall's account of his conversion. Tributes paid to John Marshall on his death are in the "Journal History of the Church," 3 and 6 January 1905, citing the *Salt Lake Herald* and the *Deseret News*. See also Essholm, *Pioneers and Prominent Men*, 1024.

polygamy increased tensions between Mormons and non-Mormons and stimulated the emergence of active political competition between the Liberal Party and a countervailing church group, the People's Party.

John MacNeil to David and Ann MacNeil

Queenstown,
[Ireland]
16 July 1870

Dear father and Mother,

I take up my pen to let you know how i got along. I had a very good passage [from Glasgow] to liverpool. There was a good deal of sickness on board & pitching up. We got to liverpool about four oclock on tuesday 15th. Brother Park[5] introduced me to the people you seen at the boat, but when it was all counted i would have got along a considerable deal better without them. For this reason: the only man capable of doing any thing was a dumfarlain [a dolt?] and he was as stupid and thick wited as a goat. The fact is i was the smartest man in the lot but your not to be laughing at me.

When we landed in Liverpool there was no one there from the office to direct us how to get along, so we thought of getting a cart and sending the luggage along to the boat. There was [sharks?] any amount but [we decided to] carry our selves if need be. The very respectable Gentleman we Spoke to said he would only take 6 shillings to take our luggage to Sandon Dock, two miles distance. We would not give it, so me and a sister went to look for the office. We found it and got our tickets all right. The rest of the people were Sitting attending the landing. Me and the sister came back to them and took them to the office. Then i came back and employed a cub and took my traps to the ship & left the rest of them sitting all night.[6]

I got on withoght bed or tins & didt get of[f] again. I bought what did me from a brother and i made my bed with what i had.

---

[5] Hamilton G. Park had just baptized John MacNeil on 9 July 1870.
[6] John MacNeil sailed on the *Manhattan* 13 July 1870 from Liverpool and paid sixteen pounds in cash for his passage. Liverpool Emigration Records.

I got a very good passage yet. I have no more to say at present but remains yours for ever,

John McNeil

Give my respects to all inquiring friends.

John MacNeil to David and Ann MacNeil

New York
26 July 1870

Dear father & Mother,

I take up my pen to let you know how i got across the ocean. We had a very rough voyage from [when] we left Liverpool. I have been Sick & pitched up. Nearely all on board were sick. You must excuse my Queenstown letter, wrong dated, wrong every thing. I never knew anything about Queenstown till we were within sight. We had morning & evening Meetings on board. The weather was so very rough that it was miserable up on deck. I got wet to the Skin several times attempting to stay on board deck. There was such a sickning smell below, i could not stay below. We had plenty of music on board.

I have eaten very little since i left. The food you get steerage fare a pig would not look at. We had cofie & bread to breakfast (sour bread). We had dirty water soup & boiled beef & potatoes for dinner. We had coffie & sea biscuits for Supper. You could not eat the meat we got. If ever your spared to come, do not come with the intintion that you will have every thing you require on board. You will have nothing, unless you treat the steward & you would have to always be droping Money into them. Some of them had every thing that they riquired with them, pickles, preserves, hern, ham Stake, & every thing nice while i was Starving of hunger. Be sure to take oranges or lemons to taste your mouth after sickness. Be sure & fetch ham & cheese.

We got to the banks of knew foundland on thursday 21. I found brother Richardson on the vessel & soon made his acquaintance. He says he had a note from brother Douglas regarding me.[7] He says he will see me all right.

---

[7] Thomas Richardson's family joined the LDS Church in England, settled in Nauvoo in 1841, and came to Utah in 1847. William Douglas had joined

There was about two hundred & fifty Saints on board, the most part of them Swis saints. There was one child died (Swis) & was buried in the see. There was two Births amongst us. The Swis are very dirty & lousy.[8]

Be sure & fetch every thing tasty for you will get nothing on the vessel. Warm clothing is very necessary till your within two days sailing of newyork. When we were within two days sailing of new york it turned very warm & we could get up on deck & had games both with the Sailors & with our selves. Be sure and fetch bread.

We seen lots of fish on our trip, porpoises and whales. I do not know that i have got any more to say at present. You need not expect any more word from me till i am landed and looks around a little. . . . Give my kind love to brothers and sisters and all inquiring friends. No more at present but remains yours forever,

John McNeil

John MacNeil to David and Ann MacNeil

Smithfield[9]
[Utah]
Teusdy 27 September 1870

Dear father and mother,

When last i wrote you we were in castlegardens.[10] We stayed a day and a night there and then got into the cars. I liked the cars better than the vessel. We were only two days traveling on the rail when two men coming along the line placed a raailway sleeper

---

the church in Glasgow in 1851 at the age of fifteen, immigrated to Utah, and eventually settled in Smithfield, Cache County, in 1861. They formed a partnership in Smithfield in 1864 and had a prosperous mercantile business until 1869, when they were called to serve missions in Great Britain as a means of getting them out of competition with the cooperative stores owned by the Mormon Church. By 1871, however, both Richardson and Douglas had returned to Smithfield and once again began to compete successfully with the "Co-op." Holmes, ed., Journal of James Sherlock Cantwell.

[8] The manifest of the *Manhattan* records 139 adults, 44 children, and 17 "returning missionaries" among the passengers. Liverpool Emigration Records.

[9] Smithfield is located forty miles north of Ogden in northern Utah's Cache County.

[10] Castle Gardens, New York, was the port of entry for immigrants.

[railroad tie] acros the line and when we came up against it the Cylander of the Engine burst into shivers. But the engineman struck it of an Shunted us back to the next Station with 1 cylander. The block had to be cut out with an axe before we could get it out. There were three trains come meeting us at the time but they seen us in time to haul up. When we got back to the Station they telegrafted to the next station and the two men were caught.[11]

We were ten days on the rail. We landed in Ogden on the 6th of augst. When we arrived there the Small pocks were raging there so they thought it advisable to take us all luggage an all down to [Salt Lake] City. When we were about half way to the City we had to shunt to let a train past that came from the City. When they were passing they Stoped and let out Brigham Young, George A Smith & Daniel H Wells.[12] They Stepped into our train and went right through Shakeing hands with every one as they went along through the cars.

When we went to the City we had to Stay there all night. They took the people that had no where to go to the tything yard.[13] Stayed there all night. But i struck up an acquaintance with a family from Ayrshire & one of the sons had to come to the City for his luggage also. . . . He was acquainted with a party of the name of Boyle that lived in the City so he took me with him there. They were old focks & hadnt not very much to offer us but they gave us what they had & gave us a bed to sleep in.

That is the only bed ever i Slept in since. The young men dont lie in dours in the summer time. They lie out at the Stack fit [foot]. I was lying down one night at the hay Stack & when i laid down my head there was a snake began a hitching up [its] head so i had to pick myself & skidadle to another place. I have killed

---

[11] According to Professor Maury Klein of the University of Rhode Island, a historian of the Union Pacific Railroad, this incident appears to be an example of personal vandalism rather than part of a labor dispute. It probably occurred between New York and Chicago. Telephone interview with Professor Klein, 5 May 1987.

[12] Smith and Wells were Brigham Young's two councillors in the First Presidency of the LDS Church.

[13] The tithing yard was located in the center of Salt Lake City and had an "immigrant house" where new arrivals could stay until they found work and living quarters. The Ayrshireman that John mentioned is probably Andrew Livingston, who traveled on the *Manhattan* with John MacNeil.

several of those snakes. The boys here take them by the tail & crack them as you would do a whip.

I have Stayed with Sister [Cynthiann] Douglas 3 weeks and could not get any work. Thomas Richardson come no further than Chicago & he told me to go on to Douglases & he would be along in two days but it was 3 weeks before he came along.[14] Sinc then i have been working 3 weeks making a road in Logan canyon. My pay is a bushel & a peck of wheat a day. But that is finished so i am out of work again but i am getting a little acquainted know & i hope soon to get work. Money is not to be had here for work nor nothing else. It is an awfule rough country & rough people to.

My reasons for not writin sooner was waiting on Thomas Richardson & when he came home i was called on by the bishop to go along with some more men to work on the canyon road.[15] When i get work i will give you my address. It was rather a new thing to me to rise of the ground in the morning with my shirt frose to ma back. My reasons for not given you my adress is i am not sure whither i may stay in this place or not. I will go where ever i can get work. Sister Douglas has been more than kind to me. . . . Your for ever,

John McNeil

John MacNeil to David and Ann MacNeil

Smithfield [Utah]
Monday 3 October 1870

Dear father and mother,

. . . As i told you in my last letter i could not find work before i went to work in the canyon [letter torn] When i came back [letter torn] i engaged to work to Sister D[ouglas] for my board, but i do not [know] how i will get along. My trousers are

---

[14] Arrangements had apparently been made by Elder William Douglas in Scotland for John to stay at his home in Smithfield, Utah. Richardson probably stopped off in Chicago to arrange purchases for the business that he and William Douglas planned to open on their return from their missions. Douglas made a similar trip to Chicago c. 1869. Douglas, Biography, 5.

[15] The bishop who called John MacNeil to work on the roads was probably Samuel Rosskelly, bishop of Smithfield.

getting all worn out in the seat and i do not see where i am to get any thing to mend them seeing that i am engaged to work for my board. But i will stay here till my last pair of pants is on me and that will not be very long for i have got two pairs through already. My top boots were done when i got here. My pit shoes[16] got worn out in the canyon. I have nothing but the strong boots bought before i left but when they are done i will have to go some place else to get more, should it be back to the States for run naked i will not. I believe there is places in America where i can get a patch to put on my [pants? letter torn]

Let [Brother] Douglas know how i am. [letter torn] . . . tell him his wife and little one are all well and tell him i have his wife fightable abought him fetching home another woman.[17]

It is just the same here as it is at home. You can find lying deceit and any amount of swearing & cursing but no seduction.

I have tried my hand at everything nearly since i have been here. I have pitched Bundles for 3 days. I have worked on the thrashing maschene 3 days and i have ploughed a little & milked.

Tell David[18] this is the place for the gun. I went out one evening & bought home nine large Ducks, what they call green heads here, in about half an hours shooting. There is plenty of prairy chickens, pheasants and all kinds of ducks but i never seen a hare or rabbit. We have got a few Bairs though & wolves.

I am very lonely here. I have nothing to read at nights to amuse me. I wish you would send me a Sheet or two of Songs and a paper or two. At present i am well with the exception of a bile [boil] on the bridge of my nose which has nearly closed one of my eyes.

I want you to write soon and let me know how David & old Lindsay gets along in regard to the work. Whither he is in the level yet or not. Let me know about James Sharp and whither you

---

[16] The term "pit shoes" refers to the heavy shoes worn by miners in Scotland.

[17] John's attempt at humor turned to reality on 15 January 1872 when William Douglas took as a plural wife Annie Capeland, whom he had met during his mission to England and who later bore him five children. On the same day, his business and missionary associate, Thomas Richardson, married as his plural wife Sarah Capeland, Annie's sister. Douglas, Biography, 3; Endowment House Record Book.

[18] John's brother David MacNeil, Jr.

have gotten any word from Matthew Wright, or John Marshal. I heard when i was in the City that the Lindsays were in ogden and that Walter was married and the wife wears the britches and he has not the life of a dog with her. I had not time to go and Search them out when i was there[19]. . . . Give my respect to John Hendry and family. . . . Yours truely,

> John McNeil
> Smithfield, Utah Territory
> North America

[PS] I received the paper all when i went to the Store this morning with my letter. I had myself weighed & i was 154 = 11 St.[20] There is thousands of Geece here at present in the fields and 2 is enough for a man to carry. This is the place for the gun.

John MacNeil to David and Ann MacNeil

> Smithfield [Utah]
> friday 18 November 1870

Dear father and Mother,

   . . . I received your welcome letter & i was very glad to see it for i have been looking for a letter for a long time. It rather downed me a little to hear of Davids accident & the loss of his work but i hope he will keep up his heart & allow me a little time. He will find that supposing he was here that it will be a good few years before he will be as comfortable as he is now if ever. Tell David not to get over anxious about me or about coming here. Rather tell him to content himself till such time as i can make you a home to come to.

   I can tell you the stangers home is no better than it is caled. I get plenty of good food but i have to stand as much for it. Brother Douglases wife & family make a regular wash the dishes of me if i do not obey the littlest of the family. She orders me to do what i am told & above all the unmannerly uncivilized children that ever i seen, they beat them. I presime you wold not like to be

---

[19] John Marshall arrived in Utah on 20 August 1868. Walter Lindsay was a member of Airdrie Branch and came to Utah in 1862. He married Elizabeth Burt c. 1859. Essholm, *Pioneers*, 641, 1000.

[20] He weighed eleven stone; one stone equals fourteen pounds.

sitting [at] a table and one of the children take a chunk of Bread & hit you a smash on the face with it & the Mother sitting there & only smile. She has got four children, the oldest a little older than Mary Hendry & she takes the liberty to spit in my face before her Mother.[21]

The wemin hear whistle [and] swear & any time they get a bill to leave them. It is quite a trade hear for wemin to leave there men. They get half of all the property that belongs to the man.[22]

I heard old Martin Haris Witnes to the book of Mormon Speek. He is an old man 88 years of age & quite childish. He takes all the p[rai]s to himself. He says Joseph Smith could not print a almanac in his day but he did it all.[23]

You talked about me not giving you a better description of the City but I could not because i did not see that much of it. You asked me about the Lindseys, Mashels, & McNeils. Well i cant get out of this plase to find out any one.

I got a lend of a few sacks the other day to go & beg some of my pay for my work on logan canyon road but i could not get a curnel of wheat. I hear that Brother Douglas is gone to England to labour. Lot Smith gets the name of a wife beater & the wemin dont like him.[24]

---

[21] When John MacNeil was living with Cynthiann Douglas, she had four children — Margaret, b. 1863; Eleanor, b. 1865; William, b. 1868; and Martha, b. 1870. By 1886 William and Cynthiann had had a total of eleven children, one of whom died in infancy.

[22] There were well over two thousand divorces in Utah between 1847 and 1890, a rate considerably higher than the national average of one divorce per one thousand existing marriages per year. According to the Campbells, "Many Mormon marriages during this period were unstable, and official attitudes towards divorce were quite lenient." There were few official guidelines as to what was and was not permissible in the plural marriage, which left it up to individuals to devise their personal solutions to difficulties, including divorce. Eugene E. and Bruce L. Campbell, "Divorce among Mormon Polygamists," 4–23.

[23] Harris was an early associate of the Mormon prophet Joseph Smith. He mortgaged his farm so that Joseph Smith could print the Book of Mormon, but later he separated from the church, c. 1834. He came to Utah in 1870, rejoined the Mormon Church by being rebaptized, and lived in Cache Valley until his death in 1875. Jenson, *Latter-day Saint Biographical Encyclopedia*, 1:271–76.

[24] Between his service as a leader of the Mormon guerrillas during the Utah War in 1857 and his role in laying a foundation for the Mormon settlements in Arizona, Lot Smith served in the British mission. Some of his time was spent in Scotland, where he became familiar with the MacNeils. As of 1870 he had five wives. According to Peterson he was a bundle of personality contradic-

Sister Synthian Douglas is about as good a Mormon as old mary Sharp.[25] I do not have to work hard nor no other person work so hard as they do in the old country. I feed the cows & do the chores. No body works in the winter here unles about the house. I spend a good deal of my time in shooting. I have killed 47 Geece 19 ducks & Several prairy chickens . . . i want some of your likenesses & some papers & songs to amuse me. Write soon & let me know all the news you can . . . [last page of letter is missing].

                                        [John MacNeil]

John MacNeil to David and Ann MacNeil

                                        Smithfield [Utah]
                                        Sunday 7 December 1870

Dear father and Mother,
      Your welcome letter came duely to hand on the 29th Novr and i was very glad to see it. I am very glad to hear that David is able to work again although i do not like the idea of the spirit of Saving leaving the house. I see you sent my letter to Brother Douglas. Well if [it] done you any good, it done me no harm.
      You may tell my Brothers & Sisters they need not be uneasy about My safty because i am as safe here as at home no matter what i say, unless i kill some one or Steel horse or cattle as some daring Divels has done before.
      You wonder at me not having mentioned being to a meeting. Well i have attended the Meetings but they are not like the old country Meetings. All they preach about hear is water ditches,

---

tions and was "sometimes rough and callous in his dealings with his family, but not without warmth and love." John is apparently reporting the rough side of his nature. Peterson, "A Mighty Man Was Brother Lot," 394; Jenson, *Latter-day Saint Biographical Encyclopedia*, 1:803-6. Later John and his brother would experience the other side of Smith's personality as he tried to help them get settled. See James B. MacNeil to David and Ann MacNeil, 12 October 1876.
      [25] There are a number of unflattering references to "old Mary Sharp" in these letters, and it appears that she was one of the local Lanarkshire "characters." Later he refers to "Mary Clark," who is likely the same person.

field fences, canyon roads, cooperative Stores & Such like things.[26]

You talked about Me trying some of our acquaintences. Well it is easyer said than done for this reason: i cant get out of the place i am in. There is no conveyance of no kind to go by hear. I am looking out for a chance of a teem going to Ogden So i may get a hurl [a ride]. It is 40 miles to ogden from Smithfield. That is where the Lindsy family is but i know nothing about any of the rest of the folks.

There is not much religion troubles the people here although there is exeptions. There was a woman had a visit here the other day from an old Ancient Nephite. She dreamt the night before that there was an old man come to her house & sure enough next day the same man came to the house and took dinner with her & told her Several things worth knowing. One was that the time was nigh at hand for the ten lost tribes to come from the north and live amongst us & also for some of the saints to go back to Jackson County & that many of them would die by the road and some would be changed in the twinkle of an eye. He said he was one of the oldest nepites & asked for Several of the people in the place & She went to the doar to see if She Could See any person to call in but could not see any one. He went out & disapeared. He said he had to have three witnesses in each place. That is all that i learned about it.[27]

---

[26] John is objecting to the practical, community-building emphasis in Mormon sermons and is contrasting it to the theological emphasis that he probably heard frequently in Scotland. Hill argues that this social, practical emphasis is an integral aspect of the Mormon religious experience. Hill, "Mormon Religion in Nauvoo," 172–74. In this sense John was seeing the very essence of the Mormon religion. Like many others, he did not recognize ditch digging and road building as being in the same league with praying and formal worship — but all of these were part and parcel of the redemptive community Mormons were attempting to build in nineteenth-century Utah. The fact that John found fault with this emphasis on building up the kingdom as a physical community may be a reason why he never became truly integrated into Mormon society. The "cooperative" movement was promoted by Brigham Young beginning in 1869 and was a frequent topic of sermons preached by Young and other leaders. It was viewed as a means of making the Mormons in Utah self-sufficient and was a step toward the "more perfect union" Joseph Smith had envisioned in the 1830s. See Arrington, Fox, and May, *Building the City of God*, 110.

[27] According to the Book of Mormon, three of Christ's disciples in America were given the promise of remaining on earth until the second coming. Appearances of one or all of these "Three Nephites" have become part of Mormon

There is a great exitement here about Silver. They have found several seams but they have yet to learn whether it will pay or not. They propose takeing me into one of the companys if it turns out well as Share holder & blaster of the rock.

I received the paper all right but the songster was gone out of it. You must be careful in Sending a song that it dose not be seen. You must stamp it as for two papers. I want you to try it again and send me some of your likenesses. David promised to get him & tomy took and Send.

I am very lonely hear & i have gotten to stand a heap of insult & abuse but i am thriving under it all. Patience Will perhaps turn the table for me. I weighed My Self the other day & i was 160 [lbs] 11 Stone 6 lb and i never had better health in my life. Shooting 68 gece, 19 ducks, several prairy chickens, 3 hairs &c &c . . . your dear son. . . .

John McNeil

John MacNeil to David and Ann MacNeil

Smithfield [Utah]
30 December 1870

6 weeks since i got a letter

Dear father and mother,

. . . I wish you all happy New Year. It is not going to be a very happy one for me i fear, but i will have to put up with it i Suppose till i can Shift for the better. My position here is miserable. A Mean Curse of a woman to deal with is worse than dealing with the Divel. I have seen many a Mean Woman but Sister Douglas beats them all & her Young ones is worse than herself.

As regards Mormonism here i do not think much of it. It is not the thing here that the elders represent. [I] can testify the principles as taught are the Same but they are not practized by no one. There is as much Selfishness, deceit, lying and all other bad practices are just as prevelant as they are in the Old Country. And as regards the word of Wisdom, Drinking liquors Such as tea,

---

folklore. See Fife, "Legend of the Three Nephites," 1–49. According to Mormon belief, Jackson County, Missouri, will be the site of the second coming.

coffie whiskey & tobacco Smoking they all drink as much & Smock as mush as they can get.[28] For good association the boys here is about the worst of company.

I am heartily Sick of this place if i could get away, but patience will Work it out. People here that know brother Douglas Say he is as Mean as his wife. If that be so i am long enough here but the worst of it is i cannot get away.

We have had Snow & frost here this month enough to freeze the old divel, and i am getting the full benefit of it. I lie on the flore in the kitchen on a matress of the childs about two feet long & my legs lays on the bare floor & in the Morning when i waken i do not know whither it is Me or not. With cold i am froze nearly stiff. The question may suggest to you, why dont she give you a larger matress to lie on. She Says i must just be like the indians[and] pull my knees up to my chin. She is any thing but a good woman. She is a thorough bred Yankie as Meen as hell. She tried pretty hard to get my blankets & Shawl of me but i could not see it. I was not a week here till i happened to go into a Scotch womans house living near by when She told Me that Sister Douglas wold like to trade Me out of My blankets and Shawl. So one night as true as the woman said She asked Me to Swap them for a california blanket about 20 inches broad. I said i thought not. She is a pealer [aggressive; always ready to fight] so when i would not swap She took the Shawl and put it on the little girl to School and they burned it up at the Stove.

Since Douglas went away She has had five or six men doing her chores: that is runing for water, feeding Stock, choping wood

---

[28] The Word of Wisdom is the term for the Mormon dietary rules against the use of tea, coffee, liquor, and tobacco. These restrictions were not strictly enforced as a test of faithfulness until the twentieth century. However, Brigham Young admonished the members of the church to observe them, if not for health reasons, then for economic reasons. Arrington, *Great Basin Kingdom*, 250. See also Alexander, "The Word of Wisdom," 77–88. Although John appears to be reporting inconsistencies between Mormon practice in Utah and in Scotland, he may be reacting to the disjunction between rhetoric and reality within any group that sets up a particular standard of behavior as an ideal. Indeed, in a letter to Brigham Young, Hamilton G. Park reported that one of the big problems in Scotland at this time was the *failure* of members to observe the Word of Wisdom. He and Lot Smith had tried to convince the Scottish Mormons that they should abandon "the prevailing evil" — whiskey and tobacco — for financial, intellectual, and spiritual reasons. See Hamilton G. Park to Brigham Young, 15 October 1869, Brigham Young Letterpress Book.

& so forth & none of them would stay with her but they had all homes to go to but me.

I see by your last letter that David is able to work again & is back in the level in Kirkwood.[29] The reason that my letter is so bloted is all the time i am writing i have to shut my letter every few minutes from the girls ho come behind Me and read it and go and tell ther Mother what i write. I will finish up by wishing you a happy new year . . . your affectionate Son,

John McNeil

John MacNeil to David and Ann MacNeil

Smithfield [Utah]
Sunday 29 January 1871

Dear father and Mother,

I take up my pen to let you know I Received Your welcome Letter. It found Me enjoying good health and Comparitively good Spirits and I Sincerely hope this will find You all enjoying the Same Great Blessing. I have been wearying very much for A letter From You. I had Concluded that you had Furgotten all about me. This is only the third letter which I have received Since I Come to the Country. I have wrote Over 12 letters I am Sure.

I was well pleased to see the Likeness But it is Just as Like Me as a horse. Now, if You Seen Me Now You would Not Call Me Seldom Fed and Scarce of Bread. I am as fat as I would wish to be Now, I weigh 161 [lbs] [Part of the letter seems to be missing here]

The Snow which was up to My Neck Nearly, but I got back alive thank goodness. I could been Earning 3 dollers per day had I took My Chance with the rest of the Emigrants. Two days after I left the City, John Lindsy was there and fell in with two Scotch boys that I parted with in the City and took them up to Bingham Kanyon and got them work at two dollers and a helf a day. But it is My Luck you know. I am going back the first chance I Get though.

I expect to have News for you before Long. As regards David Sending Me Money I Say No he will Not. If I cannot Get

---

[29] Kirkwood, a mining village two miles south of Coatbridge, Lanarkshire.

Along without that I will die first. I know to well how it is Earned, but I hope before Long to have better prospects. John Marshal is in the City Some where and I hope I will run Acros him to before Long.

You say Brother [Hamilton G.] Park is Coming home in the Spring. If you [can] send Me 2 pairs of good worsted drawers and do Not Make them to large, and a good Shot Bag,[30] for I lost the One I brought with Me, and the incect glass or Cloth Glass.[31] I would Like very well if I had a Violin and a Violin tuter Book or My Instrument. Now I am certain I could Learn Some thing. I have got the time Now. I am not hard wrought [worked]. The people here do Not Believe in hard work.

Mother Lindsay wants you to Send her all the information you can About Matthew Bishop and wife. I am Sorrow that John McLean[32] is Badly yet. It was all a hox of Brother Douglas to write and tell you that he had No particular Use for Me. He had Not, but his wife Needs A Man all the time, and he knew that. But the reason I was Sent here was No Man would Stay with her, Not even her Brother and Douglas knew all that, for I found One of his Letters one day and took the priviledge to read it.

They are Not all angels that preach the gospel, but it is a little Lesson which May be profitable to Me. Douglases Connections are all without exeption the very people which I was Counceled to avoid.[33] I think I have Said about Enough at present So I will finish up by wishing you health and happiness. Give My Love to Brothers and Sister Also My respects to John Hendry and Family Robert paterson and Family and all Inquiring Friends. Your Afectionate Son,

John McNeil

---

[30] A "shot bag" is the bag in which miners carry the explosive charges used in mining operations.

[31] An "insect glass," or magnifying glass, might be used for examining ore samples. Apparently John was planning to enter the mining profession again.

[32] His sister Janet's husband.

[33] This might mean that John MacNeil had heard about the conflict that Richardson and Douglas had with some of the local church authorities over the operation of their mercantile business prior to their call to the British mission in 1869. Douglas returned in August 1871 (after John MacNeil had left for Evanston, Wyoming) and within a few months Bishop Rosskelly was sending letters to Mormons in Smithfield prohibiting "members from purchasing any merchandise from Richardson and Douglas." Holmes, ed., Journal of James Sherlock Cantwell, 27 November 1871.

John and Elizabeth Marshall to David and Ann MacNeil

> Session Settlement,[34] Davis
> Coy.
> utah Territory u.s.a.
> 26 February 1871

Dear Davie & Ann,

You could see By my note to Lambert, he was Not punctual in Calling on You, or we should heard from you much Sooner.

Beleive me we were glad to hear from you & more astonished to learn your son John was in utah. I posted to him today & invited him to Come to me. A New line of Railway is going South. In Spring work will Be plenty.

Whatever took him to Cach[e County] It is the Best wheat Country in utah. The valley is 90 miles long & well filled with Settlements. I have Been up past the mouth of the valley on my way to Idaho Territory. This is a bueatyfull Country to some Minds. I like it. It is one Continued Range of Mountains & valleys. My house is on the main Road of travel to the Northern Settlements from the City. As Soon as I got your letter my wife said she would like to See you here. I wrote you 9 Days Before I Sailed stateaing that I was going, so I thought when not geting an answear you was offended about the gun [and that I had] Been geting a liveing by Dishonesty. I alwas had more Respect for you & yours to take any advantage of you. I got into it with my pistol. The Riffleing of it was Not to my Mind yet it was a good pistol. I sent it to have it Reriffled. They New when I sailed. It was Returned on Saturday evening & I had to leave at 5 oclock on Monday morning. They Sent me another one & Not my own. I had not time then to look after it But had to take what I got. You Can get on among the Brums if they Dont know your leaveing. Enough of this.[35]

---

[34] Sessions Settlement, ten miles north of Salt Lake City, was founded by Peregrine Sessions in 1847. The name was changed to Bountiful (a place-name derived from the Book of Mormon) in 1871.

[35] David MacNeil's relationship to this vague account of a mix-up over having a pistol re-rifled before Marshall emigrated is unclear. However, Marshall didn't want the MacNeils to think he had taken advantage of them in the transaction. "Brums" are citizens of Bromwich in the English Midlands.

David we should Be truly glad to See you here & Settled. Just Now is a rather trying time oweing to having our land to pay for By the first of June. The Clerks in the united states land office are trying all they Can to Baffle the Mormons to Do them out of there lands.[36] They are gentiles. They try to find out whether we have complyed with all the rules of the government. By making Certain improvement I Could had mine all right provideing I had work this winter at the furnacace. The winter has Stop us. Anyhow I am starting of twomorrow from home to See about another Job. You See I have to Do So as the [grass]hooppers Cleaned me out last year. We will Be able to raise our Crops this year as No hooppers have laid there eggs here this time. If you think of Coming out this year the Sooner you Start after the Middle of March the Better as you will have all the Summer Before you to provide in for the winter. With your two Sons or three you would Soon get along. Write By Return & let me know if you think of Coming out at all.

If you Did, let your luggage Be light. All that you Can Buy in the old Country Can Be Bought here & most of things Nearly as Cheap as they are with you. For yourself & Boys light balanced tweeds. Black is good anywhere But in Spring & Summer this is Such a Country for Dust, light or lilac prints. A feather Bed if you have one, good Scotch Blankets. Dont lumber yourselves with extra Shoes, glass Nor Crockery. Bring Some good Brandy, a little whiskey & Composition powder and aparateas made of tin to hold 3 Candles underneath & a Small tin Kettle above it is one of the most usefull things on the Railway that I No of. You Can light your Candles any time & Boil your kettle when you have a mine to. Whatever water Cans or water Bottles you have on the water keep them to the end of your Journey. I Bought six Cups & 6 plates enemeled Iron they were. Cups 1½ d each, plates 2d each, Called Damaged ware. Wallow Blue Coloured. I used the plates aboard Ship & quart tin Jugs Cups & plates I have yet.

---

[36] Strictly speaking, title to land in Utah was not legal until after 1869. Until then, Mormons held their land as "squatters." With the influx of non-Mormons after 1869, a General Land Office was established by the federal government and was a "potential source of antagonism." The Mormons had to exert themselves to preserve their claims. Arrington, *Great Basin Kingdom*, 249-50.

I Did not See [Gavin] Findlay Nor [David] Adamson when here. Findlay Could Done well here. I heard of him Sometimes. He Could Joined the Josephites here if he had wanted without any truble to anyone.[37] We Can go or Stay or Be of whatever faith we may Choose No one interfears. There is 7 Different isms here at present.

Let me know if Lambert sent my letter to Willie. That queens head is No use here.[38]

We are all in good health at present except my wife She is not so well at present . . . we Remain, yours affectionately,

John & Elizabeth Marshall

John MacNeil to David and Ann MacNeil

Evenston [Wyoming]
27 March 1871

Dear Father and Mother,

. . . I received your letter of the 23rd all wright and I was verry Sorrow to hear how things are Looking with You. I want You to tell David to keep up his heart and have patience. Theres A good time coming. And all the rest of You Also.

Just as I got your letter with John Marshels Address I was ready to start for Ogden bidding Farewell to Smithfield. Me and Douglases wife quarreled Before I Left and I was Left her Severel days before I Started. The party I Stayed with took Me down to John Marshels at Session Settlement. I Left My trunk in Ogden till I Come Back. I found [John Marshall] all wright. I stayed with him over night and Started Back for Ogden Next day having made Up my mind to Start for Evenstone Coal Mines in Wyoming territory 80th Miles east from Ogden. That is where I am at present and I think this is the place I ought to have went to at first

---

[37] Gavin Findlay (b. 1824) was baptized originally in 1849 at Airdrie. In 1851 he was baptized a second time and then was "cut off" in 1852 (Airdrie Branch Record of Members). In September 1869 he was baptized and ordained an elder in the Reorganized LDS Church at Salt Lake City by David Hyrum Smith, son of Mormon founder Joseph Smith (Record Book A, RLDS Archives).

[38] Perhaps a reference to British postage stamps not being of use in the United States.

if I had knowed they are Mostly all Mormons that are working here.[39]

I expect to have better News for You in My Next. I have only gotten Started to work when I received your Letter. I can Make four dollers per day and Not work very hard either. Come up the Mine every day and take dinner. I suffered with My hands very bad. They pay every Month and I have Not wrought A Month Yet.

I had fever and ague before I left Douglases but got over it all wright.

As regards Mormonism being the Cause of My Suffering you may tell them all it isnt so. It is the d — d Mean Scoundrels that are here under the pretence of Mormons. Those are the kind of Folks that Makes Me and Such as Me Suffer when we Come to the Country but that do Not Mak any difference to Mormonism. Brigham Young or Any other Man in the Church Cannot prevent a Man from being A Scoundrel if he Chooses to Make himself one. Enough for that. Mormonism is Just the Same in My estimation as ever it was.

Laying Mormonism aside this is a better Country for A poor Man than the Old Country ten times over. But Coming as I come Not knowing any one it is pretty [hard] I Can tell You.

I have Not Seen Lindsays folks Since I wrote Last. John Marshals are all well and doing well. They have a team of oxen, A cow a good Log house and gathering things around them fast. [He beged?] me to tell you to come Along Next Season. He has got A house with two ends And he Says You Can have one of them to live in till we Can get one of our own.

If there is no possibily of You all Coming this Next Season it would Be advisable to Send David here. Me And him Could Make as Much As by us A good place farm in a year. I want you to never Mind Sending My Organ [accordion] till Some of you Come your Selves. I See you Are determined to Stick to the Cloth Business till it either Sends You to Your Grave or the [poorhouse?].

[conclusion of letter is missing]

[John MacNeil]

---

[39] Although John was critical of Mormons in Smithfield, here some ambivalence creeps in with his admission that he did not go to Evanston because he thought the miners were *not* Mormons.

John and Elizabeth Marshall to David and Ann MacNeil

Bountyfull
Davis Coy
Utah Territory U.S.A.
20 April 1871

Dear David & Ann,

We feel so pleased to hear from you & with cheerfullness I repply. Yours of 25th March got to hand safe this morning. My wife is stumping around again for which I feel truly thankfull. I am at home very sick haveing got poisoned at the lead ore smelting. I am recovering By useing proper remadys. Other wise all are well. My son John is a tall smart fellow at home with me, unmarried. [He] is 24 year in aug. He was with misses, proud & glad to see your son John who had your letter at Cache with my address the same time as I had your first. He set of to see me next Day. Got here Sunday march the 5th wet & weary.

I had By previous agreement to go of next Day. Ere I left he wished he could fall in with a waggon going to Ogden so as to start from there to evenston Coal mine.

While I was on the way to the City, Blankets on Back, I met a team going to ogden. I told fellow to call at my house & See if John wished to go then. The fellowes waggon was empty. It is Seldom anything But loaded waggon go or Come on long Journey. Misses advised him to stay, the fellow advised him to go. He went.

I met my Boss in town as I had to work for he would Not Be ready to the end of the week. I got Back that night with a heavey heart. There Came on a Storm of hail Snow & Rain & wind such as I had never been in. I got home worn out with carreying a Bundle of wet Bedding.

I wished the Devil had had me many a time that night for leaveing home that morning. But the greatest truble of my wife & me was about where your John was on such a pityless night, as I New the road he had to go & it Being an uncovered waggon that they would stop somewhere on the way unless the Storm Caught them in the Sand ridge which is 17 miles & No house. I wrote next Day to the place he said he was going to. To which letter last Sabath we felt Joyfull at geting a repply. He had such a night in the above storm just as I feared he would have. After writing to Evenston Coal Mine I sent By the Burts to the Lindsays to know if they had seen him. I got No repply yet.

But John has turned up all right with 5 Dollars a Day at evenston where, for your Sake, I wish your other two Boys were at work also, then you Could get out this year. Were you & wife, your Daughter & Boys & Lizay Thompson all here in two years, with such a familey you would not need to wish to Be a kin to any monarch at hay cutting time.

I shall go 50 miles East of the City to where I shall Build me a New house [and] settle there with familey. It is a prettey valley. This is a pritty vallay But feed for Stock is Scarce here & abundant there. I am taking Steps to Secure for you 40 or 50 acres of land for you & familey along side of mine. Land that president Young made purpose Journey to go & See and Said it will grow anything. I Sent word to John about it. I would wrote you Sooner But Delayed to hear from John.

G[avin] Findlay Could Done well here as any man. Smiths geting from 4 to 5 Dollars per Day. Many Come here [and] loaf about town for weeks or months (already there are more men than there is work for) instead of turning out to the Country Settlements where persevering men that take up land (that Can Be had easey) get rich & independent & able to Do Something to Build up the New Kingdom.

There was a Josephite Branch at Birmingham 5 miles from Bramwich Composed of Excommunacated Curses. I often Confronted them. I heard sum of them preach the Best Sermons advocateing pollygamy to Be of god & Brigham the right man to lead the people, turn round & publicly Declare the opposite. What would you think of Such Curses. 3 of them met me one Sunday afternoon at Bromwich station. They [were] Coming to hold an out door meeting. One offered me his hand. Get out of my sight or I shall kick you to hell [I said]. They turned pale. I told them to go on. I was Coming to open there meeting. They were out of Bramwich By way of the toll road in 15 minutes & I Never went Near. I was going by next train to visit Dudley Castle & went. Two of them have Beged they way Back to the Church.

There is about 100 of them in the City. That is there own Statement. I Know Some of them well. I have it hot with them at times. One tells the other I [am] a good honnest man they would like if I Could See my way Clear. I have Done so till Now. David I Cannot Discribe in this note what I know to Be true respecting the Deceit of Emma the wife of Joseph who was on his way to these valley when Emma By an act of Deceit Caused him to return. Two Days after he was life less.[40] The men are here that were through his last trubles with him as well as his first trubles. The wives [Joseph Smith] had are here. Brigham keeps them Comfortable & that is all.[41]

David I Dont Carry much piety or santitey about with me. About the same old Card I used to Be. Utah haint agoing to Be for [giving?] up. The folks are Busy sowing & planting. Dont intend going to South america. Nothing of the Sort. There is Now 5 or 6000 gentele here at present.[42] They have Not Come to make a row Nor it wont pay them to make one if they wished it. They have come to hunt after us and invest Capital in mines. . . .

Them fellow has Done the Saints much good. The have Brought there money among us & it has Done us good. I was up in Cottonwood kanyon Sunday 16th inst. The snow then was 18 & 20 feet Deep. Then on Sunday night, monday & monday night & tuesday it Snowed all the time. I traveled 18 miles on foot with Snow Drifting in my face, sick & faint Carrying my Blankets & Changeing things. There is No Snow in this valley. I & the familey are Busy planting as every one else that has land. We Dont mean to Bid good night to utah yet.

Every thing is on the improve Except genral padday o Connor. I seen him yesterday & the same Coat he wore 7 months ago more seedy than ever mine was after 12 months. Look out, he is a Damned Curse to the mormons. He will go to hell & soon to. He is wasteing away like as governor Shaffer Did. I seen that Curse in

---

[40] The notion that Emma Smith contributed directly to Joseph Smith's death by requesting him to return to Nauvoo was popular in Utah. Newell and Avery, *Mormon Enigma*, 189.

[41] One of the plural wives of Joseph Smith was Eliza Snow, who was also a wife of Brigham Young in the sense that he supported her, but there was apparently no connubial relationship between them. This may be what Marshall is referring to.

[42] Gentiles — the Mormon term for non-Mormons. Marshall is probably overstating the number of non-Mormons in Utah at this time. The census of 1870 lists only 730 persons as *not* being members of the Mormon Church. Poll, et al., eds., *Utah's History*, 692.

his Coffin. He was about to Do something But got stopt. Pat Connor has stopt the mormons from Drilling.[43]

Samuel & willie Kirk are here from ardrie side.[44] They know you David. I forgot to state I read the Josephite tracts in England. They have given me them here also the godby or New move tracts. There is Nothing in it. They talk of the times and Seasons.[45] Some things may be true, But all there smack wont Blind my eyes. Both these god forgoten lots predicted During the absence of Brigham Young on his last trips South that he had gone to Seek out a place of retreat for the Saints & he would not Come Back. They took Bets on it. He Come Back. I seen the Company arrive. Next week at the Oct Conference I hard him say Before a 11000 people he Did not mean to Be Driven from his home any more, Nor wood Not. He went South last Dec. He had gone for good that time. He opened Conference the 6th of this month & Stated to the Satisfaction of many if Not all that he is going to make a Railroad to Cotton wood 16 miles to Bring in Rock for the temple. It will also Suit the gentles for the freighthing of ore & other Smelting materials & another line to Spanish fork 60 miles South of the City. The gentles are proud of this move yet the Josephites has him away. But from observeations of my own, I know they are every Day trying to make mountains out of every midges[46] toe the Can treade on.

It is true in Some instances what Findlay says about giveing up there homes & improvements to New in Comers. Well, the most of the City Bugs are like that unless you know Some one. It is not like that in the Country Settlements. If it was So, Such has Nothing to Do with the truth.

---

[43] Patrick Edward Connor was commander of U.S. troops at Fort Douglas, an implacable foe of the Mormons and a leader in the Utah mining industry. J. Wilson Schaffer was Territorial Governor for a brief term but died (October 1870) in the midst of his anti-Mormon campaign. Both men were opposed to the Nauvoo Legion and succeeded in having its "drilling" stopped.

[44] Samuel Kirk from Scotland was living at Brighton, Utah in 1870. Kearl, et al., comp., *Index to the 1850, 1860, 1870 Censuses of Utah*, 231.

[45] The *Times and Seasons* was a Mormon paper published in Nauvoo and was often used by critics to point out changes that had been made in Mormon belief and practice since the 1840s.

[46] A "midge" is a very small gnat-like insect, common during summer near Scottish marshlands.

I might have [Capsized?] my wife to after we Came here. The Day I landed my son got the Best & only place to Be found. It was a large New unfinished Dobie house. One end partly ruffed, the other not. The window Built up with Brick, No floor, in the ground two feet Deep under the Joycts, No Door. I got lumber, made a Door, a table, 3 Benches, a mantle peice. Put a floor in & with out Stove or grate & the familey wet through in Bed many a night & at Day time, with half a roff & an early winter & this for 11 weeks made us think it was hard. I Could not Deniy the truth Because of this. And this was Not the worse of it.

An Englishman going to work at the Railroad rented us his house for the winter or till I got my house finished, his wife going to her mothers the while her people was rerefoofing a stable. To Do this they, unknown to me, put these logs on the Saw mill frame over the top of mine. Keept mine Behind in this way for 3 week, till I found it out. The mans house was a warm house. We had left an open Cold one in Nov. When two Days in it, the woman gave us Notice to quit Next Day. She would come to live in it herself. I lived in it 9 Days & left. Went into my New house, half roofed after they keeping me Behind for lumber. Said there Cattle had more Need of a roof then me. There winters provisions was in the house while they feared we were going to winter on them. I went to my New house the last of Nov. My Children all in the croup through the warmth of the one & Cold of the other. This arose from ignorance. The gospel truth had Nothing to Do with it.

Findlay, poor man, Came along way to Shit on mormonism. What a pity it was he Did not get the medicine Sooner. Pollygamy is as right as our other prineple.[47] My wife told me to take another wife long ago if I wanted to, But she would like if we were Better of in first place. I have thought So to. Also when the Lord wishes me to take another wife he will also place the means at my Disposal to keep them Comfortable, otherwise I wont have them. All that are liveing in it has not taken this Course. Polligamy

---

[47] In the nineteenth century many Mormons believed that polygamy was an essential principle of exaltation. In 1876, in answer to an attack on polygamy in the Edinburgh *Scotsman*, David McKenzie asserted in an editorial that plural marriage "is an essential article of our faith." *Millennial Star* 38:136–38. John Marshall, however, did not practice plural marriage.

& many woman through it, has Been grossly taken advantage of By Damned mean Curses. The Lord our god is Not to Blame for the actions of ill Designing men. You No the gospel is like a Net. It had to Catch all sorts. It has Done so.

This is a very healthy Contry. I Beleve you would have Better health here. Your likeness is a true one. My Son will Send his. When it sutes you Send another or two.

I know where overton is and the whole Country around it from lanark to glasgow & Muirkirk to Coltness yea to the Shotts.[48]

I gave a familey house room gratis for four months in my house the first winter. I Did not Do as I was Done By. How much more I would I do for you if you Needed it . . gess at it. Come on. We Can get the stuff in the mountains to Build with for Bringing, & each Build a house in 2 weeks or 3 at most. Plenty of timber at hand where I am going to. Is not So here. Write me Back soon. I got 4 or 5 papers. Space run out so I conclud. Remember us to the old ones. Tell Findley from me, any Damned mean get up will Suit him or Josephiteism would not Satisfy him. Yours as ever,

J & E Marshall

[PS] We would be glad to see you here.
Your Johns address is care of Alexander liveingston,

Evenston Coal Mines,

wyoming Territory,

u.s.a.

John MacNeil to David and Ann MacNeil

Evenstone [Wyoming]
Friday 28 April 1871

Dear Father and Mother,

. . . I Am Digging Coal Again You See And I think I Am doing pretty well. I think I Am Making 5 Dollers per day. I am Living With a Family of the Name of Livingstone who Crossed

---

[48] He names areas adjacent to Airdrie and Coatbridge.

the Sea with Me. They Are AyrShire people And very kind people. It was them that got Me work here. They wrote to Me in Cash Valley and told Me to Come here.[49]

I had a letter from John Marshall on the 23ed And he has been sick A few days but he is Getting better. Me And John [Marshall] has Bought 160 Acres of Land in Rodgers Valley And he intends Moving there in the fall And Build him A house on it and Make improvements on it till we Come to it.[50] He tells Me You have been Sick. Well I Am very Sorrow to hear that You have Such poor health But keep up your Spirits All of you For there is A good time Coming.

I Am paying 5 dollers A week for Board But we get plenty of Good Grub. We do Not work So hard as we did in the Old Country. We Come home every day at 12 oclock And take Dinner. The Coal is 27 Feet in hight. They Only work Abought ten or eleven feet of it at first. It resembles kirkwood Main Coal very Much.[51] If David was here Now, Me And him Could [make enough] in One fall As Sett Us All up. If David would Like to Come here And You Can get Along without him For A Little while, I would Like You to Let Me know And if You have Not Money to Send him I will be Able to furnish it in A very Short time. John Marshall is very Anxious that you Could Come here.

I had the fever & Ague before I Left Smithfield But Got over it All wright. I stayed Over Night with Tom Grant Brother to Walter Grant on My way from Cash. He Lives in Wellsville.[52] . . . Your Loving Son,

John McNeil

---

[49] The Livington family on the *Manhattan* consisted of Elizabeth Livingston (45) and her children Andrew (20), Elizabeth (18), Agnes (7), and Alexander (4). Liverpool Emigration Records.

[50] Rhodes, not Rodgers, Valley is in Summit and Wasatch counties, Utah. There is no evidence that John MacNeil or John Marshall made a purchase of land at this time in Rhodes Valley.

[51] Kirkwood Main is a coal mine near Coatbridge.

[52] Wellsville in Cache County had many Scottish settlers and was known as the "Scotch Town of the North."

John and Elizabeth Marshall to David and Ann MacNeil

> Session Settlement, Davis
> Coy
> utah Territory u.s.a.
> 27 September 1871

Now Dear freinds,

I must Confess I have Delayed writing you. Yet we Expected you writing ere this. At all eventes we hope your all well & harty. Do not let Dispondency take hold of you. Your John is all right. My familey is well, Except the wife & She is much Better. Her Sickness has Cost us much. Also our loss By hoppers last year & this, haveing Been the hottest Summer for 17 years, which has also Been injurous to the Crops, has all tended to keep us Down. I find Somthing to Do Be times that makes ends meet & a little Beer & whisky at times lifts the old fellow to the old pinnacle. The wife has Nearly quit takeing Medicine. I Buy her a Bottle of wine weekly. With a few Crackers & Cheese, Seems to Be Bringing her around.[53]

Dear Davie & Ann, fear not to Come here on account of tales. It is all right. We aprehend No Danger from any. John got here from Evanston all well July 23rd. I was working in town till aug 10th. When he got to town on his way to look for work at the lead mines I was Engaged that morning to go to a lead [ore] smelter at the head of american fork kanyon 54 miles South East of the City. My passage & Board found. I took John with Me. He was found also. I took him to help me at the furnace. It was Nearly Burned out when I left on the 20th aug for home & this mostly to get a Change of Cloths. John had his things with him. I was hurried of without a Shirt to Change. John Stayed Still till I go Back. The Boss at My advice Stopt the old furnace. Is Building a New one & altering the machinery.

---

[53] The twentieth-century interpretation of the Word of Wisdom as enjoining the use of beer and wine was not observed among nineteenth-century Mormons. Such beverages were not generally considered to be the "strong drink" mentioned in the original revelation in Section 89 of the Doctrine and Covenants.

[John] read me your letter he got Before leaveing Evenston. He Never got the Song Book. Send No More till I tell you what to send. John thought you rather low of Spirits. You wondered if Rhodes Valley was in Utah. Yes, 45 miles East of the City & the most healthfull valley in Utah, 12 miles long & from 5 to 8 wide. Has the largest quanty also the Best timber of all the Valleys in Utah & there is many valleys. Salt Lake Valley Extends 95 miles North of the City. I have Been Beyond that up into Idaho & also 74 miles South of the City. Cache valley runs East North East from the North end of Salt Lake valley. Cache is 90 miles long. Rush valley 900 [?] miles. I have Been to the head of it. Utah Territory Extends East to the green River, 160 miles from the City (it is a mighty River) & over 300 miles West where it Joins Nevada & Wyoming in the East. It is 95 miles North where it Joins Idaho Territory & 400 miles South where it Joins Colorado Territory. The range of mountains runing every where through the Territory is Called the wasatch range. The Different valley that I Could Name is very Numerous. Besides them I Dont know & others I have forgoten. Rush valley runs through Nevada Territory to Calafornia[?].

The land in Rhodes valley is all hay land. A familey with a house & 40 acres of land in such a place Can in a Short time Boast of independence. Splended Crops of wheat potatoes & other things are raised there this year. You Can Build a good log house in a week. John would like if you were all here espaceily Bro David, which would Be the means of helping you all out. This is his view of it & right to. Every thing gets Cheap here. Work is plenty, wages pretty good in most Cases. John has $4-0-0 per Day at present. Boards himself, time & hours per Day. Since Commencing this I am manageing a Smelter [one] mile South of City $6-0-0 per Day. Smelters Dont run Steady. Engine tenters 5 Dollars per Day.

My house is 4 to 5 miles from the great Salt Lake on the east Side, in full view of it & the islands that intersect it for many miles. They are progressing rapaidly with the temple. My wife & me went through the endowment house. Had our washing & anointings & were married & sealed for time & eternety on the 11th Sept 1871. She will Be Baptized shortly for my first wife when I will have her sealed to me allso and a host of others. David everything is of the most sublieme grandure Connected with these ordinences here. Two of the Sons of Hyrum Smith officates & Eliza Snow.[54] Your John was Baptized Before leaveing evenston. All are Baptized here anew Before they are recognised as members of the Church.[55] Our enemys Sometimes try to get up a fuss which always works to there own Disgrace.

Let me know if you got the papers 3 in a parcel. I Send two By this post. Remember us to all your familey with John Hendry. My wife with me has the will to help you out if we had the power & John Hendry. Time & industrey alone will Bring this about.

Cotton print hankerceifs are high here & long white or Blue Cotton Stocking are not to Be got here. When any of you Should Come Bring My wife & me each a few pairs of white & Brown Cotton Stocking, a few Cotton hankerceifs. I will pay for them on Delivery with a few Scotish Songs the following Named ones amongst them with a 3d Comic reciter. . . .

I am in Recept of a note [from John] to Day Sept. 25th. He says he is geting on first Class. A Dry Comfortable place to work in. He is very annious for me to go & work in the Mine with him. Your not aware that I am a miner. A fellow has to play Jack of all trades & play the Devil to Some times. Trade is Brisk, money is plenty & like to Be so for along time.

Davie & Ann we Should like to See you here with all your familey. I would Not live in the old Country Nor wife would not,

---

[54] The "House" refers to the Endowment House on Temple Square, which Latter-day Saints used for endowment ceremonies before the completion of the St. George Temple in 1877. Latter-day Saints believe that the endowment is necessary for exaltation in the Celestial Kingdom — the highest degree of glory in Mormon theology (see Chapter 2, note 25). "Sealing" is the part of the marriage ceremony in which a man and woman are joined "for time and all eternity." Given the Mormon belief (at least until the turn of the century) in the validity of plural marriage, it was, and still is, possible for a man to be sealed to more than one woman (but not, of course, the reverse). John Marshall is contemplating here the prospect of having his first wife, Margaret Routledge or Wood, baptized and then sealed to him, with his second wife Elizabeth acting as proxy for his first. However, according to the records in the LDS Family History Library, his first wife was not sealed to him until 1959. Perhaps the second Mrs. Marshall did not particularly like the idea!

[55] Rebaptism has been practiced in the LDS Church since 1832. In addition to the original intent of signaling admission to the church and remission of sins, it was performed for forgiveness of transgression, when records had been destroyed, for health reasons, and in connection with endowments and plural marriage. See Quinn, "Practices of Rebaptism at Nauvoo," 226–32, and "Echoes and Foreshadowings," 12–17.

yet I have the Notion to pay it a visit. In Case I am intruding on your time I will Conclud. You have Been silent a long time. Write soon to your old friends,

John & Elizabeth Marshall

John MacNeil to David and Ann MacNeil

Bountyfull [Utah]
Fridy 22 December 1871

Dear Father and Mother,

I received Your Welcome Letter bearing date Octr 26th And it found Me enjoying Good health And Spirits. I have been Detained From writing Longer than I Might have been Marshall having Sent Your Letter to Cottonwood Kanyon And I was on My way Home At the time having been Forced to Leave there through the Great Snow Storms that have been in the Mountains.

I had A Very Good Job there working in the Mines, (Silver Mines) At 3 Dollers per day And Board but the Snow has fallen So heavy this Last two or three weeks that Several of the Mines has Stoped working, having been Scared Out through Snow Slides.

This is Something You Dont know Much About in the Old Country. I will try to Give You Some Idea of it: the Snow fell 12 to 14 feet on A Level So that on the Mountain Side it Cannot Stick. It Breaks Away when it is 3 or 4 feet deep And runs Down the Mountain Takeing every thing before it trees, & rocks tons weight. And if A Man happens to be in its way there is very Little Show for him. There was Several Men killed with it Already here So I thought I would Skin Out in Time. So I Am At home Living with Marshall At present And have Not decided where I May Go Yet to work.

Marshall And family Are All well At present Although he has Been very poorly for Several weeks Back through having been Leaded[56] At the Smelting furnaces.

---

[56] "Leaded" refers to a sickness caused by miners inhaling noxious fumes at the furnaces and mines. It is also referred to as "lead colic."

I expect there is Great talk in the Old Country About the Downfall of the Mormons but I Can tell them A Secret: the Mormons have No fear. They Are happy And Contented, there is Not the Least Excitement or fear whatever.[57] On the Contrary they Are happy And rejoicing. You will See by the papers that they Are Afraid that Brigham has Gone South for the purpose of enlisting the Indians in his Cause but thats been done Long Ago. There on hand.[58]

John Marshall Junr And Me went to A dance the Other Night And there I Seen A Brawney Son of the Mountain (Indian) raised Amongst the Mormons with A pair of Sholders On him that Any Man would Envy. With Mussell Enough to take A Common Man in each hand And Squeeze the Live Out of him. And he was Dancing with the Mormon Girls And enjoying himself Like A red fellow. Those Are the kind of fellows that will be of use in the right time.

I was in the City the Other day when I run Acros Tuncan Kelly for the first time. He was very Glad to See Me And would have Me Come to there house to See his father. So I went down to the house And Seen And had A Chat with Old Chon.[59] He was in very Good Spirits, well pleased with every thing.

Me And Marshall fell in with A Scotch Woman in the City One day who knowed Archie McNeil And All About him. She would Not tell Me All She knowed but I Learned As Much As that he was A poor Miserable Good for Nothing Curse to Low to be Owned by Any Body. She told Something About A Child being Blamed on him in the States Just After he Come to the Country. Him And Several Others that Come Along with him Conducted

---

[57] By 1869 opposition to Mormon domination of Utah politics and economics was beginning to coalesce and unsuccessful efforts were made in 1870 to unseat the Mormon delegate to Congress, W. H. Hooper. William McGroarty received only 105 votes in 1870, but in the next election the candidate of the non-Mormon Liberal Party received 1,500 votes. Lyman, *Political Deliverance*, 14–15.

[58] On practical as well as humanitarian grounds, Brigham Young believed it was good policy to maintain friendly relations with Utah's native tribes, although the notion that there was never any conflict with Indians has been overstressed. Indians saw the Mormons as intruding on their homelands and were not inclined to fight for them. See S. Lyman Tyler, "Indians in Utah Territory," in Poll, et al., eds., *Utah's History*, 357–69.

[59] MacNeil may be trying to create a humorous effect in imitating a Highland accent by writing "Tuncan" for Duncan and "Chon" for John.

themselves Disgracefully, Drink And Women being there whole hobby.[60]

I Am Glad to hear that David has plucked up Courage Again And Started in the pit. Although I hate the idea of either of them having to do it but I hope the time will be Short that they will Need to do it.[61] I thought I would had Money to Send for David by this time but My Castle in the Air tumbled down for their was A Man Cheated Me Out of 40 dollers. It is that And the Like of that has kept Me Back but I Still Live in hope of Seeing You All here.

I have Nothing More of Importance So I will Draw to A Close By wishing You All A happy Cristhmus And A Good New Year. Give My Kind Love to Brothers and Sisters And All Inquiring Friends. Also Tomy Rogers And Jerry. Let Tomy Eat My health in Sweeties on New Years.[62]

You Need Not Mind Sending Me Any Clothing Unles You have A Mind for I have All I want Now. It Aint Such hard times with Me Now As it was when I Left Cash Valley.

I will Send You the Names of Some Songs to Get for Me: the Lord Bateman Song or I am fond of A Lark with the Girls in the Dark, Whool be An Old Mans Darling, Jolly Old Sam the farming Man or 40 Years Ago, Rolling home in the Morning boys, And Ten Thousand Miles Away, And the I am A Jolly Dog And I dont Care A fig, Can Any One tell Me where Nancys Gone, At Midnight on the Sea, And farewell Mother Adew, Adew or the boy in blue, We were A Couple of Gay fellows Coming home from Brighton, And My Name is peler Simple. Send Me A Sheet or two. I had All I Got Stolen but I will take Care of the Next Ones.[63]

---

[60] It is difficult to put too much credence in John MacNeil's report about Archibald MacNeil. John seems to have had a tendency to take gossip and unsubstantiated charges at face value. "Uncle Archie" is mentioned in a number of the letters and it appears he is a relative of David's, but research at the LDS Family History Library has not been able to establish what the relationship actually was. The title "Uncle" may be honorific, but given the fact that he was also born in Tranent, Archie may have been a "Scotch cousin," a very distant relative.

[61] John MacNeil's two younger brothers, David (21) and James (17).

[62] "Tomy Rogers and Jerry" may be family pets, perhaps a dog and a cat.

[63] These songs are a mixture of traditional Scottish ballads ("Lord Bateman") and popular nineteenth-century songs such as "We Were a Couple of Gay Fellows Comin Home from Brighton." For a sample of two of the songs the MacNeils used to entertain themselves and others, see the Appendix.

Give My respects to Lizy, Janet And husband, Marget And Robert Paterson,[64] John Hendry And Wife, Also James Sharp and All Inquiring Friends. Tell David to Keep up his heart. Theres A Good time Coming. I remain as ever, Your Affectionate Son,

John McNeil

Editor's Note: While John MacNeil was trying to settle in Utah, his half brother John Thompson was establishing a family in Illinois. The lack of letters from Thompson may indicate that they were destroyed or that there had been a breakdown in communication between Illinois and Scotland, or perhaps both. When the contact was renewed, John Thompson indicates that he has been attracted to the Reorganized LDS Church and suggests that his sister watch for the Scottish RLDS missionary, Gavin Findlay, whom John Marshall castigated in his letters to David MacNeil. John Thompson's quiet, religious tone is in sharp contrast to John MacNeil's strident and contentious perspective.

John Thompson to Elizabeth Thompson

Bunker hill
St. Clair County. Ills.
5 February 1872

Dear Sister,

I Recived Your kind and welcom letter and also the Parcil which you Sent to us. We was Glad to hear from you that you was in Good helth and it found us InJoyin the Same Grait Blissing. Thank the lord for his Goodness.

Dear Sister we thank you for the Presents which you Sent to us untill you Are Better Payed. You will See from the Abouve Heading that we have Moved Since i wrot to you last. Work was verrey Dull in Caseyville for a long time. My Wife and Children did not have verrey Good helth for about a year, So i thought that a change of air would do them Some Good. We Moved from Caseyville in the later Part of Least July to a Place Called Belleville, the County Seit of Saint Clair County. Since then we have Moved to the abouve Named Place and thank the Lord the helth of my

---

[64] He refers to his half sisters and their husbands.

Wife and Children has Improved a Grait deal with the Change and are all well at Present Except a littel Cold that Some of the Children has caut.

But the work is Not Much Better hear then it was at Caseyville. Work has Being verrey dull in this Section of Country for the Last Tow years and has Every apprence of contuning So for the Nixt Sumer althoug we have always had anuf to Get along toleribell well and have always had a Comfortibell living During all the Bad times. Thank the Lord the Giver of all Good to Mankind upon the Earth.

Dear Sister, a Grait Maney changes have taken Place Since i last wrot to you and amoungst those Changes Mr. Robert Haig sen has Deperted from this Earth. He Died on the 4th of July 1871 at Caseyville.[65] The old man Suffered a Grait Deil for the want of Breath in the latter years of his life But his famley was verry Good to him, Espishley his oldest Son George, in Providing for his wants while he was not abell to Do aneything for himself. The old woman feels a littel lonley Since his Daeth. We have also had an addition to our famley Since i last wrot Which Makes three Children that we have now. The last one is a Boy and is Naime is Robert Haig Thompson. He is one year and four Months old on the 16th of Jannery 1872.

We have had a verrey long weinter this Sesion. It Commenced about one month erleyer this Session then usuell and has lasted Pritey Studey Since its commencment. We have had a Grait Deal of Snow this winter and it has Being Sleeting Nerley all day to Day.

Dear Sister, i was Glad to hear that mother had Got over hir Sickness and was well again and i hope that hir Days May Be Maney and usfell upon the Earth. You Say that you would like to come out to this Country to See me but you Would not lick to leve Mother. I hope you will try and Give hir all the Comfort and Can in hir old age as we never can Do to much to hir for the Suffering and [anxiety?] that thay have for there Children.[66]

---

[65] Robert Haig was John Thompson's father-in-law. He was a Scottish immigrant, but it is not known whether he was a Mormon.

[66] It is perhaps significant that John does not mention his stepfather, David MacNeil, in his letters. There appears to have been some estrangement between the two — exacerbated by differences over the politics of the Civil War, by David's failure to emigrate in 1867, and also now by religious differences.

I was Sorrow to hear about John Bening chited out of his twenty five Pounds.[67] But if he has no Graider loss then that he will Be Luckey for there is a Grait Maney Men in this Country that try to Chiett all thay Can and think that thay are Smart when thay do it. The facte is that it is hard to know Who to trust. I was Sorrow to hear about Jenets Husband Bening Sick for So Long a time But i hope that he will Soon Get well.

Dear Sister i would like to know if there is aney of the Elders of the Reorganization under the Ledarship of Young Joseph Smith Priching about Glasgow. We had Gavin Findley hear with us a year ago Least December But he Left hear and went East to Pinnsylana. He wrot to us in the Spring that he was Goning home to Scotland and he Promised to writ when he Got home But we have never hard aney thing from him Since. Please to let us know if you have hard aney thing of his Since he Got Back there. He was a Member of the Reorganization and was ordained to the office of Elder and i Expected to hear of him Doning Some Priching amoungst the Pepol.[68] We have a Branch of the Church hear although we are fue in Number. There is a Good Maney Branches around in this vecinety of Countrys and thay ceep adding a fue to there numbers and i Expect that the work of God will Start with More viger then it has for Some time Past as there is a grait work to Be acomplished in the latter days.

When You writ let us know what the miners is Erning Pur Days waig. Lizebth Says that i am to let you know that She is Six years Past and is Goning to School and that She Got a Card from the School Teacher for Beining a Good Girel . . . your Brother and Sister,

John and Elizabeth
Thompson

---

[67] The reference is apparently to John Thompson's half brother, John MacNeil, who reported being cheated out of forty dollars in a letter of 22 December 1871.

[68] John Thompson was baptized into the Reorganized Church at Caseyville, Illinois, on 19 February 1869 and ordained an elder on 27 March of the same year. Record Book B, RLDS Archives. L. Madelon Brunson to author, 27 June 1983. It is not known whether Gavin Findlay ever went to Scotland as a missionary for the RLDS Church.

[PS] Joney says tell my antey that he can Say his Prayrs and go to Sabeth School with his father and Gets tickets. Robert Send a kiss.

John and Elizabeth Marshall to David and Ann MacNeil

Marshallville, Sessions
Settlement
Davis County
utah Territory u.s.a.
2 March 1872

Dear Davie & Ann,

Yours of the 8th inst. Came to hand this morning. Your John & me perused it with much intrest when home from meeting. I have not felt more healthy & lively for years than Now all the Bad effects of Leading haveing Disappeared. We have Been at home Now for 14 weeks & liveing the right way while many who have Been less fortuneate & Compelled to work through the winter in the Mountains have lost there lives in the Snow slides which have Been many this winter.

John is in Splended health and my Children But my wife, god Bliss her, has Been very ailing savral weeks But is Something Better at present. Our ploughing & sowing has Begun.

Me & your John will go to Rhodes Valley in a few more weeks & each Build a house. I feel vexed that your David is not inclined to Join his Bro in utah. John would not return Back to Scotia. We would like to See every Soul of McNeil & Thomsons here in Marshallville Just Now.

Do not Stay from utah Because our very Sincere freinds have Been laying in waiteing making Sure of Bringing a mamoth Drag of Superior fish to land. But oh Dear Me, some have pulled to strong at the Drag ropes, they have overturned the might fedral net. The Consequence is the fish is sliping out and settleing Back to there useal element. United states attorny Genral at washington sent a Message to the god Damned Curse McKean telling him to accept Bail for the men in prison & to Be moderate in the same. McKean & his Brimstone Scented Curses is Now ordered to washington, No Doubt to give an acount of his Career in utah which has Been anything But prophetable. But listen, he would Not take Bail for our Boys. The reason I suppose is he is ashamed to Do it Now at the Dictation of others while he so long has tryed to have presiDent Young locked up But Could not reach the key. President Young is not locked up. He is in his own house, has the previledge to walk half a mile from his house or ride in any Direction he may Chosse. The others are Confined in the City. They have all they want to eat Drink and wear with a Bagtell and Billard table to amuse themselves at and all else they want.[69]

If there had Been 12000 troops at Camp Douglas instead of 1200, Brigham would Been locked up or they would tryed it. But with the Bigest Number at hand it would not paid them. We Can enlist thousands of indians when they Could not get one. You know how the Devil likes yon peculiar kind of water. 20,000 of them would made a Bad Job of it to let the Smell of there powder Been felt.[70] The long Blockade on the Railway would make them look small. Davie what I am goin to tell you Now is what I seen. The Natural formation of the Kanyons through which the u.p. line runs offers the Best fecillitys for Destroying trains of any lentgh of any thing to Be found on this Continent. They have tryed to Shit on us. Now we expect to Do so to them and rub it in after. The Lord is not always going to strive with the wicked. He has said whom so ever you Bliss I will Bliss & whomsoever you Curse I will Curse. So think it not wicked of me

---

[69] Judge James B. McKean was appointed Chief Justice of the Territorial Supreme Court by President U. S. Grant as part of the Grant administration's efforts to suppress polygamy. Eventually McKean succeeded in having the "Lion of the Lord"—Brigham Young—indicted for adultery, later changed to murder. Before Young could be tried, however, the U.S. Supreme Court quashed all indictments. In 1875 McKean again presided over legal actions against Brigham Young, this time in a divorce suit. McKean's extreme actions in this case led to his removal from office in March 1875. See Larson, *Outline History of Territorial Utah*, 229–31.

[70] Marshall's claim that the Mormons would be able to call on the services of twenty thousand Indians are grossly inflated. Although it was not uncommon for Mormons to threaten an Indian uprising in order to exert pressure on U.S. government or even to provide Indians with whiskey, Indians in nineteenth-century Utah did not number in the thousands, nor were they one homogenous group that would be inclined to obey a Mormon call to arms. Interviews with Floyd O'Neil and Gregory Thompson, University of Utah, 12 and 15 June 1987.

[or] any of the persecuted of the annonited of god to Curse Such Damned wreches.[71]

Capt hooper our Dellagate to Congress has Employed the most Eminent attorney at washington & Sent him hear to act with the honr T. Fitch & other attorneys on the Defence. The Mormon Murderer will Be tried March the 4th. We Dont Doubt at all that anything will Be the matter Beyond a little Excitement at the time of trial.[72]

John has seen Lot Smith here & H. G. Park he has seen twice. But I think he is a tinker, like many more in good situations.

Yours of Jany 26th Came Safe to hand with 4 papers & two Sheets of Songs. John is with me Still. Has Done Nothing Since Now 25th. He started twice to Cottonwood But work is Slack oweing to the Snow which has fell in larger quantiteys this winter than any previous one. I advised him to stay out of it to spring opens & all Danger of slides over. He is uneasey about loseing so much time. I am loseing time as well as him & has a Numerious gang around me. Then I Cannot get much else to Do But go to the furnaces where two weeks work will make me ill for a month or two.

If I had my property Sold here it would Enable me to Settle Down in Rhodes valley in Such a way that I wont Need to truble about furnaces after. Johns run out of money savral weeks ago. He is vexed as David wont stay at the pit till he makes what would Bring him out & also that he has not got the money to Send for him which he will Do when he gets it. It would lift Johns heart up if one of them or all of you were here. He is Cheerfull enough with all. It is Being idle thats whats the matter. He makes me & the wife talk to him Sometimes when in his Disatisfyd moods he has a mind to go here & there. It wont Do. We keep Showing him the way to make us independent of haveing to work for [others] & settling and makeing a farm in Rhodes valley with two cows & you have it. The grass is two to 3 feet high through summer & fall & all the hay you Can Desire for winter. If one of your Boys was here early in this year they Could make pretty well of it up to Now.

---

[71] There is no evidence that confrontation between government and the Mormons in 1872 ever reached the stage described by Marshall.

[72] As explained above, the trial of Brigham Young for murder never occurred.

I am going to Rhodes valley this summer to Build me a home. Your John & me would Been over there while we have Been at home here But was wateing for the order to go & help to make the Ditch to Bring the water from the provo river on to the land for iragating with. But they wont Begin to get it out till the snow is gone. The provo river is Second to none for trout of the largest Size. Boys, Mere 8 to 10 years old, go into the water & throw them out with there hands & plenty of Shooting. The water there is Soft & like the valley is Counted on Being the most healthy Locality in utah. The land we have Bought is a mile from the settlement or City in which I have agreed for two City lots of an acre & ¼ each to Build our Dwellings on with Stables, orchards & etc.

John is Short of 90 Dollars that he Should have had. He got a watch worth 50 Dollars. He has 40 Dollars out & little prospect of geting it. It was provedential of him geting the watch or the 90 would all flickered.

John would feel much more Comfortable if one or all of you were here. Excuse me in atemping [to] advice you that you Be on the look out that as Dull time Do not overtake you Being prepared to flee to Zion as the present good time Departs. For go it will, as many good times has gone Before. I Stayed over long my Self. I was Strong & healthy when I Came here as I am to Day But I am not So heavey By 50 lbs as at that time. Nor Dont want to Be. I am 165 lbs at present. I was over two hundred then. Unless geting Sick at Lead smelting, I have had No sickness here and I have worked like hell & Thomas at one thing or another ever Since I Been here. I would not take 1000 Dollars in gold to Day for my property & stock & has had a young & growing [family] to support.

Many of the yanks look about as pleasent at you as the Calfs at father when they see an old Country pitching & working all the while. I will answear for the Sin of heard work. The most of them in this Settlement are Satisfyed how little I Care about look[s]. It is little they middle [meddle] with anything as smart as themselves. The yanks are mighty talkers of what they have Done But you Never See them Do anything.

I must Close this epistle hopeing you will Remember me & wife to Besy & Janet & all who know us as you may meet them. You Did not tell me if old Neilson of Mossend was liveing. Let me know if you ever travel about [Dalserf] Kirk Near Motherwell.

Write oftener & Send the papers as regular as you Can and let us Be hearing of you and all the lot Coming out Soon. Dont Be staying to lay your Bodys Down on overton Braes. I have Been on top of Malsley Castle. The vale of Clyde is Bueatyfull But it is not the appointed place for those that have learned of the revelations of god to man in this age.[73] Come out of her o my people. Fear not what the world say about us. There is as good men & weman here as ever lived on the earth Since the father of Abraham apostitised. But all are Not So. This is the thrashing floor. All have got to Come that the wheat may Be Sorted out from the Smot & the Sorting has Begun in Deed. Of a truth the Josephite & them other Damned fools, the [Godbeites], has Done a good stroke By Rolling out of it. They make But poor progress I assure you. Write me soon. Beleive us as ever your sincere freinds,

John & Elizabeth Marshall

John MacNeil to David and Ann MacNeil

Bountyfull [Utah]
Wedensday 6 [March]
1872.

Dear Father and Mother,

I received Your Welcome Letter Bearing Date Jany 26th And I wearied Very Much To hear from You. Your Letter Come to hand Feby 30th. I was Glad to hear you Were All in the Land of the Living Although I was very Sorrow to hear that the Cobbler was Still Bothering You father.[74]

I was Sorrow to hear Also that David had Not Stuck to the Pit for A Little, As My Luck has been so Bad Since I have been here that I have Not had the Opportunity to Send Nothing to help You. It Made Me feel very Bad to think You was the first to Ask

---

[73] Marshall mentions places near the MacNeil home with which he is familiar — Dalserf Kirk and Mauldslie Castle are near Overton, Lanarkshire. He seems to be saying that the MacNeils should emigrate rather than die in Scotland.

[74] Some tradesmen may have been demanding money from David MacNeil — he was apparently having a difficult time keeping his business afloat.

Me for Money, And Me Not to be in A position to Send None. It Made Me feell Like Clearing Out.[75]

I have Worked 3 Months And A half Since I Came to the Country, And one Month I worked in the Mines. I Got Nothing for it. If it had Not been John Marshalls Advice And his Unboundless Kindness And Hospitality As Well, I would have Cleared out the first opportunity. I have Been Living with him 15 weeks Now, Doing Nothing And No prospect Until Spring. You Need Not trouble YourSelf by Mentioning Money to Me Any More. I Am As Anxious to Send it As You would be to receive it. I Am Only Sorrow it is Not in My power, for this reason: I Never Shall have A home here Until Youre All here.

It is Expected this will be A Good Season for work here. As Speculators have Been holding back And Business has been At A Stand Still for Sometime Owing to the Expected trouble And Trials but As Usual its About to end in Smoke. The Mac Kean Cleak is All Burst And they think Shame of themselves. I Expect by the time this reaches You things will be Sufficiently Opened up So there will be plenty of work for every Body And if God Spares Me Perhaps I May have A Little better Luck this Season. Suffise it to Say i Am Going to hope for the Best.

I have Seen Lot Smith twice of Late in Salt Lake City And had Quite A talk with him. He invited Me to Come to his house And Visit him And Seemed Awful Good. He Said he thought if You Would Make An effort You Could Come here without My Assistance Whatever. I told him I thought Not. He told Me to Give You his respects.

I have Stayed Over Night With John Kelly Several times. He is Getting Along Very Good. This place is Zion for Any person who has Never had enough to eat in the Old Country. If I would do As Doncan has done, I Could Send for My focks to As well, but I Wont borrow Money Where ever I Can Get it With No prospect of ever paying it. But She Dont Care So She Gets it. Those Are the kind of people to Get Along here. There is too Many of his kind here Already. She is too holy to be holesome.

---

[75] David, Jr., apparently left the coal pits as a miner early in 1872, but when he married in July 1872 he gave his occupation as a journeyman engine smith — an occupation still associated with mining.

She is Deceitful and She Lies besides. She is No Good. She All Sends her respects to You.

I dont Know As I have Any thing More of importance to tell You. I Am Enjoying The Best of health At present thank God. Brother John And Elizabeth Marshall Sends there kind Love to You All. The Lindsays Adress is Eden City, Ogden Vally, Weber Coy. . . . Your Affectione Son,

John McNeil

John MacNeil to David and Ann MacNeil

Evanston [Wyoming]
13 May 1872

Dear Father and Mother,

It is With Pleasure I take up My pen Once More to Let You know how the World is Using Me At present. I received Your Welcome Letter Bearing date (April 4th) And Was Sorrow to here of Mothers poor health. It Also Makes Me Feel Bad to hear how foolish David Acts. If he knowed how hard I have tryed to Get You hear I think he Would Act With A Little More Judgement And have A little patience. I Am Just As Anxious to See him And All of You here As You Are to See Me for Without You here theres No home in Utah for Me.

I Am Afraid the people here is too Much on the Gouge, So Much So, that A Single Man has No Chance to Make Any thing. When he pays board And keeps himself in Clothes And perhaps Goes idle half the Year it dont Amount to Nothing. A Married Man has All the Chance in the World. Young Men that Wants to Stay in this Country Marry the first Girl that Will have them, for the Very Good reason that A Man Can keep Himself And A Wife easier, And pay rent by half, [then] he Can keep himself. You May think this Strange but it is to true.

I Stayed A Week With Lot Smith And he treated Me Like A Gentleman. He Was Sorrow that he did Not find Me Sooner. He Says he Could have found Something for Me to do Around his place All Winter. At Any rate he Said I Could have had My Board All Winter free of Coast. He Also Offered Me A Yoke of

Oxen to Go And put up A house on My Land And flour to keep Me While I Was doing it, but I was On My Way to the Coal Mines At the Time So I Could Not except his offer.[76]

I Am Working At the Coal At present. At the Same place that I Was Last Winter but I am Not Making So Much As I did Last Winter. There is hundreds of Chinese Working here, digging Coal for One doller per day Which Makes White Mens Labour Very Little thought of. Still, I Am in that I Will Make A raise Yet.[77]

I Started on the first of April here to drive A Sump. Me & An English Man. It is very Wet. We have to Change Our Clothing twice A day. I have been of Work 3 days With rhumatics pains but I Am better And Working Again.[78] I Am Living With A Scotch family the Name of Kennedy from AyrShire, Acquaintances of David Irvin.

I expect You Will have heard the News of Brighams release. Judge Mc Keans Court has been found Illegally formed And All his procedance Null & Void. They held A two Weeks Conferance And the president Was there the Second Week in good health And Spirit.

The reason there is No papers Coming to You it is run out, And I had No Money to renew it. But I expect to be Able to Send them You Soon. . . . I remain as ever Your Affectionate Son,

John McNeil

Adress As before to Marshall.

---

[76] Given the generous offer that Lot Smith made to John, it is obvious that he had a warm spot in his heart for the MacNeils. One has to wonder what might have been John's future if he had accepted Lot Smith's offer and had become more fully integrated into Mormon community life.

[77] According to Leonard J. Arrington, almost all Chinese living in the western states in 1870 were involved in mining. See Arrington, *Changing Economic Structure of the Mountain West*, 8.

[78] John later describes his joints as being very stiff, and he may have had arthritis. This is another factor which must be considered as we attempt to get the measure of this emigrant — at the age of twenty-four he exhibits signs of painful and crippling arthritis. No wonder he seems to be discouraged with his misfortunes.

John MacNeil to David and Ann MacNeil

Alta City,
Little Cottenwood Kanyon
[Utah]
18 August 1872

Dear Father and Mother,

It is With pleasure I take up My pen once More to Let You Know how I am Succeding At present And to Answer Yours Bearing Date June 20th.

Since I Wrote You Last I had to Leave of Digging Coal for it Was Killing Me. I Am at present Working in the Silver Mines, Little Cottonwood Kanyon And If I Could Get Steady Work I Could Make Lots of Money if I had David here. We Could Make a Stake (Yankie for Money) in One Season Which Would Make him Stare, by Contracting, but I Know No One Who I Can trust. Besides Yankies Wont Work hard Consequently I do Not Like to go in with One of them.

I Am Very Sorrow to hear that David is Thinking of Marrying in the old Country for I know that I Can Get An Easier Living in This Country than I Can Get in the Old Country for killing My Self Working.[79] And Not Work half time either. Although I have had poor Luck As Yet in this Country I Know that I will be Better of here in A few years than he is Likely Ever to be in the Old Country. This is A Curious Country. One Man Will Come to this Country And Make his fortune in A Year; Another Man May be here A Livetime And Not. But I have Good faith My turn Will Come And that Before Long.

As regards Coming Back to the Old Country to Dig Coal for My Living rest Satisfied that is A thing that Will Never happen. I Might Come Back on A Visit to the Old Country Providing I have Enough of Means but I Would Make Sure before I Started that I Had Enough to fetch Me here Again.

David May do As he Chooses About things but My Advice to him is to Come to this Country. If he dont Care One fig for Mormonism this is the Country for him to be. If he has fallen in with A Good Girl who Sutes Him, I dont Say dont Marry, but

---

[79] David MacNeil married Mary Murray on 16 July 1872 at Glasgow.

Come to this Country And Send for her. You Will do Well here take My word for it, but he Can Please himself About it.

I have Gained More Experience by Coming to this Country than I would have Learned in A Lifetime there. Suppose I Never done Any Good in this Country I dont Grudge the Money Ive Spent in Coming here. I Can Get A better Living And Work 3 Months in the Year than I Could Get in the Old Country Working the Whole Year round. Besides if i dont Get rich in Money I Will in Stock [livestock] Which is As Good As Money, but I expect to have Money to After A little.

I Am Getting 3 dollers per day And Board but in this Country A person has Got to Look Ahead for Winter, Which has through Me Back Considerable. I have been Unfortunate enough Not to have Work in Winter And had to pay Away What I earned in the Summer. As regards Coming Home I Can fetch Myself Any time I Want to. A person has Got to keep A Little Money for Winter Not Knowing Whither You Can find Work then or Not but theres A Good time Coming And I know it.

I had A Letter Along with [yours] from [John] Marshall And he tells Me that his wife is Suffering Very Much through Sickness And he is Afraid that She will Slip Away Suddenly Some day. All the rest of his family Are well . . . I Remain as ever Your Son,

John McNeil

Write Oftener And I Will Answer

John MacNeil to David and Ann MacNeil

Alta City
Little Cottonwood Canyon
[Utah]
17 September 1872

Dear Father and Mother,

It is with pleasure I take up my Pen Once More to let You Know how I am Succeding At Present. Since I wrote You Last I have had A Little More Success, then Usualy falls to My Lot. I was Working At four Dollers per day when Last I wrote You. But this Last two weeks I have Been Working For Myself on A Contract, which I took, And have done well. Clearing 65$ per week,

And Expect to have three weeks work at it Yet. And Another party waiting on Me finishing that, to Get Me to run A tunnel for him.

I have Good prospects here if I Only had My Brother here, to help Me to take Advantage of them. I Am Beginning to Be Better Known, And My Ability in Mining is taken Notice of. I have Been forced to take A Mormon boy in with Me, And Learn him to Mine, for want of A person I Could put Confidence in. So that You See Yourself how it is with Me, And how it would be if My Brothers were here. Im Bound to Say that if I had them here one Sumer, Now that I Am Acquainted, we Could have horses to ride of our Own in A few Months. I had to Learn that boy And Give him half of the proceeds of My Contract, Namely 65$ per week. And Get My hands And head Belted with the hammer to the Bargain. I Am Enjoying the Best of health At present.

I have Been to the Bank, Namely Wells Fargo & Coy., And have Bought An Order or Check on the Bank of Scotland. (or Any other Bank will Cash it). It demands twenty pounds, for which I payed 116 dollers in Green Backs, they Being worth Only 85 Cents to the doller in Gold. Which is 15 Cents I Loss on each doller. But I Am More than pleased to be Able to Send even that Small Amount with the hope Soon to be Able to Send you More. That is Only My Last two weeks wages.

I want this Money to be Apropriated to the Sendind of My Brothers here, which ever of them will Come.[80] I would Like David would take My Advice And Defer Marrying Until he Comes here. And if he will Come, I wish You to Give him the Chance. And if there is A Girl there, which he would Like to Make A Wife of, I Shall Lend him My Assistance to fetch her here. And I Give him My word he will find An Easier Living here than he is Able to find in the Old Country. And A better One to. I will Enclose the Check in this Letter And if Any of My Brothers will Come, I will be happy to receive them. If they Conclude to Come Let Me know.

As regards Crossing the Sea, beware of Sharks in Liverpool. I had to threaten to kick Ones backside for trying to hoot it on Slick. It is Not so bad in Newyork, but You require to be Careful both places. Send them, As I Come, with the Saints. And Above

---

[80] Cost of passage from Liverpool to New York in 1872 was approximately sixteen pounds.

All Give them or him Something to eat Crossing the Sea, for I
was Nearly Starved. The Grub was So badly Cooked, And so
Little of it, if it had Not been for the Piece of Cheese You gave
Me, I think I would have died of Starvation. The Grub was Not
fit for A Sow to eat. A piece of Cheese, A Lemon or A few
Oranges, or A piece of boiled ham, or Something that is tasty, is
Good to have on the Ship. For when You take Sea Sick, Your
Stomack requires Something to Sharpen it. And wear Your worst
Close on the Vessel for they will be No Good to You when You
Come here, the Salt water rotes every thing You wear on the Ship.

I would Like You to fetch My instrument Along.[81] And A
Jacket Something Like what I brought with Me only A Little
Larger. They Are Not worn so Short here. And Velvet Collar on
it. Do Not by Any fire Arms there Unles A Shot Gun which is
Costly here And Very Useful here. Rifels And Pistols Are Cheeper
here than in the Old Country And better. If the Musical Albums
Are Not to Costly, I would like One of them. Fetch My Music
Book to. I think I Can Learn Something here Not having to work
So hard. I have Got Some Life And Energy in Me here, which
Seemed to be Dead in Me there After A days work.

The Kellys have Got their Mother hear, but they do Business different from Me. They Borrow Never thinking how to pay.
This Money which I Send is My own Earnings, Not Borrowed.

You Need Not be So much Afraid About the weight As
You was with Me, for it was Never checked till it Come to Salt
Lake City. And then I was Under My weight of baggage. If Any
of them Come Let Me know, And Give them Marshals Adress in
Case I Aint Aware of their Arrival So that they know where to Go
to find Me. But I will try And be there in waiting.

I would Like to have A pair of Black Molskin Britches.
Stout (this is an Awful Country on Clothes) Made to Butten up
the front. I want Lizy to Send Me A Nice Neck tie, And Ann to
Send Me A Scotch Balmoral Bonnet. My white Shirts Are All
Gone. Only One. And they are All the rage here. If I would Not
be Asking too Much I would Like two of them, fancy ones ruf-

---

[81] John had studied the violin under a Mr. Watson in Scotland and also
played the accordion. According to his granddaughter, Mrs. Gladys Thorne, he
was also much sought after as one of the best square-dance callers in the Bountiful area.

feled in the Breast. I Aint Very Conceited Just Now, but I Am Going to be when I Commence to Spark, Which Must Not be very Long, or else I shall be An Old Maid Soon.

If You want Any English Coin Chainged do it in Castle Gardens Newyork which is the proper place. Marshall And Family Are well, with the Exception of his wife, who is Constantly Ailing. They Send their kind Love to You All. Marshall Suggested Something About Me telling You to Send A few plated rings, finger rings. I want You to keep Tomy Rodger, till You Come Yourself. And then Emigrate him Also if it is possible. I have Nothing More of Importance to tell You. I have Not Seen Lot Smith for Some time, being Out in the Mines. . . . Your Affectionate Son,

John McNeil

John and Elizabeth Marshall to David and Ann MacNeil

Session Settlement, Davis Coy
utah Territory u.s.a.
10 October 1872

Dear David & Ann,

. . . I hope my last note to you Did not affend Sister Ann. The fact is am a plain fellow, ever has Been, ever will Be. I have Nether piety Nor santity about me. Never had much of it. My opinion is that god loves the hounest in heart therefore they Dont Require Coverings of Santity to give there actions a glace.

There are many here have a Name in the Church worth thousands who for five Cents would again put Jesus to Death. Brigham Come out on them at times. Such are ocasionsonly Droping of. They Came to make themselves up at the expence of others. They had No intrest in the Building up of gods kingdom & about all who Come here with a Different intension must undoubtedly mis the mark they aimed for. Down gos Mormonism and to whitewash themeselves, Blackball somebody, something or every thing. The end of Such hypocrites will Be awfall.

Every man or woman is free to go just where they please, when they please. People are, as your John knows, fliting & moveing to & fro Daily the year round, to the East west North & South. It is But a 21 Day Journey from Liverpool to this place & there is room for all to Dwell & Do right who want to. We have Never had another opinion of any of you than that you wanted to Know & Do right.

The lands of utah are Being taken hold of on a Scale that makes people look on & wonder. During the last few month every unocupied lot in & around the City has Been Bought & much enquiry is Keept up about City lots. Many have sold out as I am going to Do. Buy horn Stock, go out to the out laying Settlements, taking up or Buying farms. This last I have Secured for you & me with City lots right in the Settlement for Both of us. If your familes would take no Notice of the accounts of partys who return But Come out here with you Set to work & Build up a home reliying on the help of god combinsded with your own energy, in a short time you Could have a happy home & the most independent one you [ever?] will possis. There is in no land lords Nor poor house Clerks Buming around here.[82]

And as to your Daughter ann, my Son is an industrious young farmer. He is Just waiting till you Bring her with you. I Dont Say it Because he is my Son But the truth. There is few to pass him in Smartness & he is geting well of. He has 40 acres of land here & 40 in Rhodes valley. He has two good Brood mares, two colts waggon &c. This is the Country where home Can Be truly made happy. There is None of those inducements here to Draw men from the familey Circle making home miseryable and ultimately Breaking it up, parting man & wife, all ending in murder, suicide &c as is So often the case in the old Country. It is the truth. Beleve me or not. And Such Doings is unheard of.[83]

---

[82] John Marshall is trying to convince the MacNeils to discount the stories they hear about Utah from returning emigrants. According to Bancroft (c. 1884) there were few signs of "abject poverty" in Utah, the "idle and dissolute being discountenanced by the community." Bancroft, *History of Utah*, 698. However, this does not mean that there was plenty for everyone or that Utah had an egalitarian society. The struggle of the MacNeils to make a living is testimony to the difficult task of keeping one's head above water. In spite of efforts of the Mormon leaders to promote equality, by the 1870s Utah was rapidly being integrated into the national norm of an "unequal pattern of wealth holding." See Allen and Alexander, *Mormons and Gentiles*, 105–6.

[83] However, murder, suicide, and family disintegration were not unknown in nineteenth-century Utah, although compared to more urban areas Utah had fewer crimes, less debt, and fewer paupers. Bancroft, *History of Utah*, 692.

There is as good a publishing medium in Utah as most parts of the States. We have a handsome Theater. We have our Dances in our settlements and other amusements and Besides people is not Compelled to Be Mormons. There is an english Church, a methodist Chapel & Catholic Chapel Built in the City & altogather there is Six Diffrent Sects here Besides the Church of the true and liveing god.[84] They have Done much good puting up Such Buildings, has found work for many of our people and the gentile brand has the previlidge of worshiping among there own or go to our meetings as hundreds Do. In our old & New tabernacle there is set apart [a place] for outsiders who always Behave themselves well. Anything else would not do.

I have found out where Maxwells live at. The Name of the place is peoa Not peas. It is in Summit County. Arthur Died a year ago. John & Ralph is Still there doing well.[85] It is about 6 miles of the settlement in Rhodes Valley.

I Begun written This letter Before I got your last. Pleas to forgive me not writing Sooner. Your John is Doing well. Has a Contract of a mine in Little Cotton Wood. I have Been out there at the Smelter. I would Done well my health Being good & prevention is Better than Cure. I was useing an preventive which keept me hale & harty. But my wife has Been so very Near going home. She Sent for me twice to Come home. Twice I Came home in two weeks. Now I am at home waiting on her. She is Some what Better to Day Sunday Oct 6th.

What I have Said here [about] your Ann & my Son you will Excuse. I showed him your letter where in you Speak of the Disobedence of your famiely. I had a test of it with my first wife. [If] it is your lot I hope you will Be able to overcome. Coolness on your part is the Best.

Sister Laird & famiely come in last week. Rob is Dead. He has gone to Goshen[86] to Paul Gourley that is 10 miles South of

---

[84] An Episcopal church was established in 1867, a Catholic in 1871, and a Methodist in 1869. See Lyon and Leonard, "The Churches in the Territory," in Poll, et al., eds., *Utah's History*, 317–36.

[85] Several large Maxwell families from Scotland lived in Peoa during this period. Arthur and Ralph Maxwell's sons, Arthur, Jr., and James A., served as bishops of the Peoa ward. Kearl, et al., comp., *Index to the 1850, 1860, 1870 Censuses of Utah*; Jenson, *Latter-day Saint Biographical Encyclopedia*, 4:632.

[86] Goshen is located seventy miles south of Salt Lake City in Utah County.

the City. Walter & miron Lindsay Called here two weeks ago. They live in Eden City, ogden valley, Weber County, utah Territory. Walter has a good farm.

I went to Rhodes valley July 5th I Built a house on the homestead. I agreed with an aquantance for two City lots. We would Be glad to see you all here. If that ever Comes, I shall Be glad to wellcome you. It was No want respect to you that Caused me Delaying writing. I had a Busy time at home this last Summer. I had not time to write By Day & So Sleepy at night. I could not keep my eyes open.

We are having a great Conference This time. All has Been peace here for sometime. That Damnation Stinking filthy rag the Tribune printed By Godby & Co has a peice every Day in there paper sluring and sneering the Saints.[87] As our publishers Dont Seem to take any Notice of it exasperates them.[88] At our election for Delegate to Congress, you take my word for it there, he Did not get more than one in 50 of the gentle vote. Thomas Hakins is at liberty that was Tried for poll going. Dear friends, we are yours as ever,

[James & Elizabeth
Marshall]

[PS] My Son Dont Seem to feel any Disapointmen at your Statement respecting your ann & him. Girls here soon get Saucy. He would Sooner have a girl for wife from the old Country as I would were I in the Market.

---

[87] The *Salt Lake Tribune* was originally founded in January 1870 as the *Mormon Tribune*, but by July 1870 the name had changed and it became the major mouthpiece of anti-Mormon sentiment in Utah. See McLaws, *Spokesman for the Kingdom*, 177.

[88] Marshall is referring to the *Deseret News*, the church-controlled newspaper. Although both newspapers would often trade barbs, the general policy of the *News* was to try to ignore the *Tribune*. Ibid., 141–66, 178–79.

4

"Working Hard and Making Nothing"

Letters of John MacNeil, James Brady MacNeil,
John Thompson, and Elizabeth Haig Thompson
1872–75

Building the "city of God" in North America was part of the Mormon plan. Consequently, thousands of Mormon immigrants flocked to Utah to help fulfill Isaiah's prophecy about "the house of the Lord" being established "in the top of the mountains." However, precious little of this religious sentiment appears in the MacNeil letters written from Utah between 1872 and 1875. Instead they stress how difficult it was to sustain a living in Utah by mining.

About the time John and James MacNeil were moving to Alta and its silver mines, Brigham Young was reminding Mormons that they should not expect silver mining to solve all their economic problems. Too often miners in search of wealth were the most likely to plead poverty:

> Whenever I see a man going along with an old mule that can hardly stand up, and a frying pan and an old quilt, I say "There goes a millionaire in prospect." These millionaires are all over the county; they are in the mountains, on our highways and in the streets. And they haven't got sixpence.[1]

Church leaders believed mining did not promote the kind of personal, institutional, and community stability that they thought was necessary for the establishment of Zion. Moreover, the mines were owned and operated by non-Mormon capital (much of it from British investors) and church leaders felt they had no direct role in "building the kingdom." However, as has so often happened

---

[1] Sermon of Brigham Young, 7 April 1873, cited in Arrington, *Great Basin Kingdom*, 242.

in Mormon history, the church had to adopt a more pragmatic stance. Mining was in Utah to stay and it would probably attract large numbers of non-Mormons as laborers. To keep some semblance of control over the enterprise, the church therefore gave approval to Mormons who wished to work in mines, but it asked them to consult with their bishops first. The bishops in turn were asked to determine if the man's departure for the mines would create a problem for the community, and the miners were cautioned not to become involved in the "vices of the Gentiles with whom they associated." Mining was viewed as a means to an end rather than a lifelong occupation: money earned should not be invested in more mining claims but in land, livestock and agricultural machinery. In this way an occupation which might disrupt the development of stable Mormon communities could be used to further more desirable religious and social ends.[2]

This church policy toward mining was followed by both John and James as they tried to find their niche in Zion. But mining never brought what they most wanted—the security of land, family, and community. The letters of John and James MacNeil are replete with accounts of the dislocation caused by shifting markets, the hard, grueling physical labor involved in mining and the long absences from home. On a number of occasions their old missionary friends from the Glasgow Conference, Lot Smith and Hamilton G. Park, offered them other work, but they ran away and headed for the mines. Their experience and enculturation in the mines of Lanarkshire and the possibility of becoming "millionaires in prospect" was too strong. However, the hope persisted that mining was but a temporary expedient and that soon they would leave underground labor and enjoy the "good times coming" as farmers in Utah's valleys.

The letters from 1872 to 1875 not only reflect the extent to which the lives of the MacNeils were shaped by mining, they also reveal how they personally responded to the religious environment. John was quick to pick up on the contradictions he witnessed between Mormon rhetoric and Mormon reality. He saw these as signs of duplicity and hypocrisy rather than as evidence that ideals are never fully realized.

---

[2] Ibid., 241–43.

After John married the widow Annie Cooper Warrilow in the Endowment House in February 1874, the tone of his letters shifts from ambiguity to a firm conviction that Mormonism was filled with "hokey-pokey," and there was a rapid decline from a troubled believer to a thoroughgoing religious skeptic. To those who, like his father, had difficulty accepting his rejection of Mormonism and his refusal to write only "Cheery News" from Utah, he said in effect: "Don't take my word for it — come to Utah and see for yourself."

In 1873 his younger brother, James Brady MacNeil, came to see for himself. What James saw, or, more precisely, how he interpreted what he saw, differed so much from John's interpretation that one wonders if they were indeed in Utah at the same time! James Brady MacNeil was born in 1855 at Cairnhill, Lanarkshire. He was named for the Irish friend of the MacNeils, James Brady, who had died in Salt Lake City six months before James MacNeil was born. As far as can be determined, James Brady MacNeil was not a member of the LDS Church in Scotland, although his father appears to have taught him the basic beliefs and he was no doubt familiar with Mormon missionaries such as Lot Smith and Hamilton G. Park. Like his father and his brothers before him, James probably worked in the mines of Lanarkshire — the Census of 1871 lists him as a "labourer." In June 1873, at the age of eighteen, he joined a group of Mormon emigrants on their way to Utah. Just as John's letters reflect the skepticism and criticism which eventually led him to completely reject Mormonism, James's letters reflect a tendency to "see the hand of the Lord in Utah," which culminated in his baptism and eventually his participation in the Mormon settlement of Arizona.

James was not blind to the contradictions that troubled his brother, but he did not interpret Mormon errors as a sign that the Mormon principles were flawed. His belief, he said, was not based on what certain people did but on the "word." He was not baptized in order to get along with the Mormons, but because he believed that Mormonism was true. Like John, James also went to the Endowment House and received his endowments.[3] Unlike

---

[3] See chapter 2, note 25.

John, James saw nothing but good in the endowment and expressed hope that his family would also have the opportunity to receive their endowments soon.

The relationship between these two brothers had its share of rivalry and there are suggestions that James felt John was too heavy-handed in his efforts to control him. This rivalry, and their apparently deep-seated personality conflict, undoubtedly exacerbated the religious tensions which were emerging. From the accounts sent to Scotland, we also learn that mother Ann MacNeil and her daughters had sided with John; father David, however, seemed to align himself with James's point of view.

The family dispute that seems to have been present in the MacNeil home for many years surfaces — should the family emigrate to North America? Ann and her daughters apparently did not want to leave Scotland and David, Sr., vacillated considerably. In 1867, when John Thompson sent tickets for the whole family to emigrate, David attempted to establish a drapery business and the tickets were canceled. Around 1873 he tried to open another store which once again delayed his emigration. He apparently preferred to struggle as a small-time entrepreneur in Scotland rather than face the uncertainty of life in Utah.

Only two letters from the Thompsons in Illinois have survived. They contrast sharply with the striving and conflict that characterized the letters from John and James MacNeil. John Thompson was also a miner and attempted farming without any measurable success. Notwithstanding this, he writes that he is gaining good experience which will serve him well in the future, and he acknowledges he has developed some spiritual values which will outlast material successes. How he might have fared in his quest for a balance between material prosperity and spiritual contentment remains unknown because in August 1875, John Thompson died in a coal-mine accident in Caseyville, Illinois.

News of struggle, aspirations, conflict, doubt, faith, and death came to the MacNeil home through the letters of 1872 to 1875. Whatever the precise response was to the letters in Scotland, the plaints of "John the Skeptic" and the psalms of "James the Faithful" demonstrate the diversity that characterized the life of Mormon immigrants in nineteenth-century Utah.

John MacNeil to David and Ann MacNeil

Alta City
Little Cottonwood Canyon
[Utah]
13 October 1872

Dear Father & Mother,

I received Your welcome Letter bearing date Sept 11th And was Sorrow to hear of Mothers Declining health, Also Sister Anns. But My prayers is that God May Spare them both to See Me And this Country Yet. I Am Still Mining Yet And Doing well. I Sent You A Check for 20 pounds in My Last Letter And Am Anxious to know if You Got it All right.

Father. I do Not want You to feel Uneasy About David Marrying. That will be All right if he has Got the Girl of his Choice. As My Mother Used to Say, As they Make their bed So let them Lay. She is A Mighty poor Affair if She isnt better than he Can pick up in this Country.

Women has the easiest, Lazyest, Life in this Country that ever Anyone thought of. They Are All Ladies here. This is the Country for wimen. I would Advise All wemin to Come to this Country, where they Are treated best. As regards polygamy they Need have No fear, for No woman Need Go into it Unles She Chooses. There is Lots of work for wemin that they Can Sustain themselves At Comfortably withought Going into polygamy. Besides, there is More that do Not believe in it than ther is of the other.[4]

You Complain of My Not describing the Silver Mines. *Well* I Shall try: first the Men or prospecters, take A pick, And Shovel

---

[4] There has been a tendency for Mormons and others to underestimate the numbers involved in polygamous relationships in Utah during the nineteenth century—a figure of 3 to 5 percent is often cited. If only men are counted, of course the figure is much lower than if women and families are included. According to Lowell C. Bennion, "a significant minority of Saints" in 1880 were actually involved in plural marriage. He estimates that in the larger towns of the St. George Stake, 40 percent or more of the Mormons were involved in polygamy. In Davis Stake (where John MacNeil lived) the incidence was lower than in southern Utah; it ranged from 32 percent in Centerville to 5 percent in South Weber. Overall, approximately 20 to 22 percent of the Mormon population was probably involved in the practice. See Bennion, "Incidence of Mormon Polygamy in 1880," 27–42.

And Clime All Over the Mountains hunting for A crevice, or hitch, which we would call it, running Out on the Surface. When they find that, they Sink right down on the end of it, which is Likely to Lead to A body of Ore. It is Mostly driving Stone Mines And Sinking Shafts in Solid rock or Going down on One of those Hitches. I Am At present working on One of that kind by Contract And Making on An Averidge About 8 dollers per day. And As I told You in My Last, paying the Same Amount to A boy whom I had to Learn And who Understands Nothing About Mining, for want of Some of My Brothers being here.

I will Send You A paper And will try to put A Little ore inside of it. There Are three kinds of Ore: Oxid & Carbonite Ore & Cloride, which Generally Contains Carbonite Also. And the Oxid Generally contains Galena which is Like A bar of Lead when Cut & Containing A Great portion of Lead. The Ore Just Lays in round bodys or Masses in the hart of the Mountain, no regular bed or Seam Like Coal. Those Spurs or crevices which we would Call A Hitch, Generally runs to the body or Mass of Ore.

Marshall And family are All well with the Exception of his wife, who is still Aling. I had A Letter from him Along with Yours And he Said I had Seen her for the Last time in Life he thought, but I hope Not for She is A Good woman.

I do Not know of Any thing More worth describing, but I will tell You One thing: that is, this is Going to be the Greatest Country [in] the world. Its riches in Mineral Are Boundless. It is Going to far Outstrip California Or Any Other place.[5]

I want You to buy Me A peddle for My Instrument And Send it with the Boys. I Am Going to Send A $50 dollar bill (Fifty Dollers) which Must be Used thus: pay Your Passage till New York with English Money then You Can pay the railway fare with this bill. And if it takes A Little More than this All right.

Robert Laird of Bellshill And family Are All here Living in Salt Lake City and working in Cottonwood Canyon.

If the boys Come tell them they Must [bring] warm heavy Clothing. A Good Overcoat heavy As possible [is] All the better in this Country, which is cold in winter here, And Just As Extremely

---

[5] By country MacNeil means Utah. Mining for silver at Alta began in 1869. Between 1870 and 1880 some 3,500 claims had been staked out in an area only 2.5 miles square. See Arrington, "Abundance from the Earth," 192–219.

warm in Sumer. Old Country Boots or Shoes do Not Last Long in this Country but boots & Shoes Are Very Costly here from 8 to 10 dollers per pair. Clothing from 20 till [?]0 dollars for A very Ordinary Suit. As regards Squandering My Means Since I Come to this Country I have Not done it, which Marshall Can Testify to.

I Shall Send you one copy [of] the Best paper in America for general News of every kind. Every thing is Quiet And prosperous Around Salt Lake City. They have had A plentyful Season All Around. No Grashoppers. They have had A Good time At Conference And every[thing] Going plesent here.[6] . . . I remain as Ever Your Affectionate Son,

John McNeil

John MacNeil to David and Ann MacNeil

Bountyfull [Utah]
5 December 1872

Dear Father and Mother,

. . . I received Your welcome Letter in Answer to the receipt of the Money And was Glad to hear that it was All right. I have Just read A Letter from You to Marshall to night Decr 4th I have delayed writing on Account of Sister Marshals Low State of health. We have Not Known whither She would Live or die but She Seems to have Got Over it And is on the recovery Although Slowly.

I Got through with my Job in Cottonwood Conyon And have been At home over three weeks. When I was About Finished I Got A Stroke on the Eye, the bad one, which weakened it So Much that I have been forced to Lay Over on Account of it. I was Sorrow to hear of Davids poor health. Also Mothers. I want You to Let Me Know in Good time when the boys Are Coming So As to Look out for them. Brother Marshale told Me to tell You, You Need Not Send No rings to him. Send 2 good ones to me Any-

---

[6] "Conference" refers to the semiannual, church-wide meeting of the LDS Church held in Salt Lake City, usually during October and April. This is the occasion for the leaders to exhort the members to continued faithfulness. That John could report that a "good time" was had at conference indicates that he is not yet as alienated as he later became.

how. I would Like You to Send A pocket Dictionary too Me. Also I would Advise James to fetch A Fiddle And Music Book for he will find Plenty of time to Learn them hear.

The Last time I wrote to You I Enclosed A $50 doller bill. You Seem to Say As Much As that Mother And Ann wont Come here. All right dont force None of them, or trouble Your Brain so Much About people who will Not Listen to You. If they want to Stay there Let them Stay. They will find Out who was there friends Perhaps when it is to Late. Let every One please themselves A Little More than You do And it will be better for You in the Long run. Any One who is Urged to Come here wont Stay Long, believe Me, So that it is only Lost Money. But perhaps You Picture it A Little too black. I hope So. I Should Like to See All of them All here Yet.[7]

I Am About to Go to Cottonwood Again to work Again until the boys Comes if I Am Spared. I Seen Lot Smith the Other day And he told Me to Give You his kind Love. I have Not Seen None of the Kelly family for long Enough And I dont Care Much. They Aint No friends of Mine.

Remember My Instrument And the Peddle And book. I received the Likenesses of Mr & Mrs Watson And was very happy to know they were well. Give them My Respects And tell him I would [like] to have the Opportunity of Learning Music now. I think I could Make A better Job of it.[8]

Remember to Give the boys Some Oranges, Lemons, Cheese And Something of that kind to revive their Appetite if they happen to be Sick on the Sea. I have Nothing More of Importance So I will draw to A Close. Fetch Some Songs. Dont be so Scared of the boys having over weight As You was with Me. I had under weight. . . . Your Affectionate Son,

John McNeil

---

[7] Here is the first direct evidence that there was opposition to emigrating from Ann Boggie MacNeil and her daughter Ann, Jr. John seems to be suggesting that his father should leave them and come by himself. Factors that may explain why Ann would not come to Utah must include her age — she was sixty-three and did not enjoy good health — and her desire to remain near her relatives. Her stepmother, Mary Waite Boggie, was still alive, as was her sister Janet Boggie. Not to be discounted is the fact that Ann, Jr., seemed to be doing well as a milliner. Lacking the religious impulse that motivated many emigrants, Ann and her daughter simply did not see any need to pull up their roots and move.

[8] Mr. Watson was John's violin teacher.

John MacNeil to David and Ann MacNeil

Alma Station [Wyoming]
Sunday 16 February 1873

Dear Father & Mother,

. . . I receive Your welcome Letter baring date Jany 6th And was Sorrow to hear of Your Accident through the Shutter falling on it.

I Am working At present in the Coal Mines Evanston. When I wrote to you Last I was Suffering from A Sore Eye that Got better And I have had Another Stroke on it with A Coal but it is Getting better Again. I Am doing well At present but do Not know how Long it May Continue. I had A Letter from Marshall Along with Yours And he tells Me his wife is recovering Steadyly. He tells Me he had Seen John Hendrys Sister in Salt Lake City. She Arrived After I left for the Coal Mines And I did Not See her Yet.

If David Aint heartily Sick of the Old Country Yet dont force him to Come to this Country Until he is, for he would Not Stay to take time to Make him A home.[9] But if he was As tired of the Old Country As I was he would think this A Glorious Country. As for My Indeviduel part I would rather die of Starvation in this Country than dig Coal for A Living in the Old Country, but there is no danger of that taking place. If David dont Come I would Like him to Send his And wifes Cards [photographs] but I woud rather See himself. If James Comes Let Me Know in time So I Can be prepared to Meet him.

Be Sure to Send My Instrument And peddle Stand. There Are two Songs I would Like him to bring Along Also: "The Lord Bateman Song" or "I am fond of A Lark with the Girls in the dark," And "Wholl be An Old Mans darling." Be Sure to give him Something to taste his Mouth Crossing the See. Also fetch the Song "Jolly Old Sam the farming Man." Perhaps You wonder At Me wanting So Many Songs but I will tell You: there is Little else Unless Singing & dancing done here in the winter time And

---

[9] He is referring to his brother David and implies that discontent with conditions in Scotland is a major factor in leading people to settle in Utah.

Unles You Can do Some of them You Are No Company. Thats the reasons.[10]

Me And Walter Lindsay & John Farrell Are working together At present digging Coal in Evanston Coal Mines. I have Not Seen Bro. Lot Smith for Some time but the Last time I Seen him he told Me when I wrote to Give You All his respects. I do Not know that I have Any More of importance to tell You. I Am enjoying the best of health And hopes this will find You All enjoying the Same Great Blessing. . . . Your Dutiful Son,

John McNeil

[PS]Please to Send Me A Balmoral Bonnet with A thissel on it.[11]

And Send One of those Cards with the insect Glasses or weavers Glass. It is very Useful here to Look At rock And See if there is Gold or Silver in it. If You Could Send Me A Couple of pairs of worked, worsted, drawers, Like what I brought I would like [them]. I want Some of the Girls to Send Me A Musical Album And there Likenesses in it.

John MacNeil to David and Ann MacNeil

Alma Station, Wyoming
12 March 1873

Dear Father & Mother,

I Sit down to Answer Your welcome Note, which I received A week Ago & which I Should have answered Sooner, but there was Some Little trouble About My work, & I did Not know how it would turn Out. So I delayed writing Until I Seed how it was Going to be. I thought we would have to Quit. We Got A hitch in Our place, that was what was the Matter, & they didnt want to pay Anything for it. I Am Still digging Coal in Evanston And doing pretty well At present. but how Long it May Continue A person dont know in this Country. I Am Enjoying the very best

---

[10]For a sampling of the kinds of songs enjoyed by John MacNeil and used by him in socializing with others, see the Appendix.

[11]The "balmoral" is a round flat hat made of wool and often worn with a thistle badge on it. It gets its name from Balmoral Castle, where Queen Victoria and Prince Albert helped popularize Highland dress and the wearing of tartan. The thistle is, of course, Scotland's floral emblem. Perhaps John planned to use the balmoral when he entertained friends with the songs he was sending for.

of health, Although I am working pretty hard Just Now. My Eyes Are All right Again.

I Am At present Batching. Perhaps you dont know what that Means Well Ill teell you: it is 4 Men of us Living in what we Call a dugout or hole dug in the foot of the Mountain, & Cooking Our own Grub. I Can Bake Bread, Make pies & Cook Anything As Good As Any woman Can. And for Sowing, you Should See Me At it. If Ann was to Come here, I think I would Go in partners with her in A Millinars Shop. I think we Could Make Money. Millinery & Dress Making is A pretty Good Job in this Country.

You Ne[ver told me] Davids wifes Name, where she Come from, who She is, how he Come to Get Acquainted with her, the Childs Name, Nor Nothing else. I am Sure It Must have been her that Sparked him for I dont think he Could Ever been so brave As to Spoke to A Girl himself. But I Give in beat, I hope its All for the best though.[12]

I had A Letter A short time Ago from Sessions Settlement & Sister Marshall is wholy recovered from her Sickness, And was At A dance with the Old Man A few Nights Ago. I have Not Seen Lot Smith for A Long time, Nor I have Not Seen John Hendrys Sister, being About 100 Miles from Salt Lake City At present, but I expect to See her when I go in the City. It May be About 8 weeks from Now, Namely the 1st of May. The work will get dull then.

I dont know whither I May Stay here till James Comes Along, or Not, but I Shall be in waiting As Soon As You Let Me know. . . .

You gave Me fits About Not describing things to Suit You, but I think You pretty Nearly As Scrimpet [niggardly] As Me with Your News. I want You to Send Me the Articles I wrote for, & I have request to Make yet. I have Got Some Songs which I would like you to try & Send Me. & I want All the Old Song books & Songsters that is in the House. . . . I Am going to Give You A List of Songs to Send Me.

1 Jolly old Sam the farming Man

2 I Never New A Maid So ficular so perticular

---

[12] David MacNeil married Mary Murray on 16 July 1872, at Dennistoun, Glasgow. Their first child, Ann Burnett MacNeil, was born 22 October 1872.

3 Miss Wobenson Song
4 wholl be An Old Mans darling
5 Lord Bateman Song or, I am fond of A Lark
6 I am A Jolly dog & I don Care a fig
 I Can do A double Shuffle or whistle A gig
7 Charming Flora Bell, the pride of Motherwell
8 O My Heart went pitety pat Sung by Harry Clifton
9 O My You Ought to See us going. or, we were A Couple
 of gay fellows Coming home from Brighton
Send Me Some Songsters & Song Books

John MacNeil to David and Ann MacNeil

> Bountyfull
> David Coy
> [Utah]
> 27 May 1873

Dear Father & Mother,

I received Your kind & welcome Notes bearing date April 27th & was glad to hear that You were All in the Land of the Living Yet. At Any rate, Your Letter with Likeness Enclosed found Me Enjoying Good Health & Spirits. I Have been Out Digging Coal At Evanston & have just Come in, the Slack time being the Cause.

I think I told You in My Last that Walter Lindsay & J Farril Were My Mates.[13] Well what I have Got to say About them is this: Walter Lindsy is A Mean Miserable Lying Unprincipled low God [damned?] skunk & Farral is a Deceitfull [?] Irish Muff.[14]

---

[13] There was a John Farrell at this time (three years older than John MacNeil) who seems to be the person with whom John had the altercation. He was a Scot from Ayr who joined the LDS Church in 1856, spent some time in Illinois c. 1857, and settled in Eden, Utah, in 1865. He was councillor to Richard Ballantyne in Eden from 1869 to 1874 and was appointed bishop of Eden Ward. He married a second wife, Marian Lindsay, in 1865. Jenson, *Latter-day Saint Biographical Encyclopedia*, 2:337.

[14] According to the *Oxford English Dictionary*, the expression "muff" is "a depreciatory term for a German or Swiss, sometimes loosely applied to other foreigners." John's use of it to apply to an Irishman is symptomatic of the hostility that many Scots felt toward their Irish neighbors and is repeated a number of times in these letters. This hostility is probably based on the perception that

My reasons for talking like this Are this: there was A Gentile working Along with us & When they were About to Quit they thought they would pay Me back for my kindness in Getting them work. So they told this Man A pile of lies which I had Said About him & Set the Man up at me. He went & Got drunk on purpose to have A fight with me. So we Met in butchers Shop & he Called Me Everything & Latterly Drew His hand to Strike Me & I Knowed there was no use Me tackeling him as he was A Man like Donald Diny.[15] Besides, Americans wont fight A fair fist fight. They Kick, bite, Gouge your eyes out & All that Sort of thing. So As Luck Would have it I hade a Deringer pistol in My pocket At the time, I pulled it on him & Stuck it Against his teeth & Cooled him down & backed him out, then we went After Lindsay & Farril & found them. I Accused them of it & they denied it & if it had not been for the Long Acquaintance we have had with Lindsays family we would have killed them but I thought they were not worth dirtying My hands on.

Farril is Bishops Councilor & he is deceitfull Enough for Bishops Devil.[16] They Are A Miserable Lot of Skunks that Cares No More About Mormonism than A dog does About his relitives. There God is Gain. They Are A Lot of Miserable Misers Like Old Colin Shaw Was. This is the truth.

If David is Going As Well As You Say he is I dont think there is Any Use in Me Sending him Money to fetch him here. He is As Able As Me to fetch himself. Besides, I dont think there is Any use in it for this reason: I think it would be Money threw Away, for if he is Making So Much Money there he would not Stay here two weeks. That is What I posted David Adamson & I dont think Our David has Got Quite As much Brains As Adamson

---

Irish settlers in Scotland took work away from the native Scots. The Irish were indeed often brought in to Scotland as strike breakers and as cheap labor. In 1861 almost 15 percent of the population of Lanarkshire was born in Ireland. The 1871 Census of Whifflet, Lanarkshire, reveals that the MacNeil home on Hamilton Road was virtually surrounded by Irish immigrants who worked in the mines and in the iron works. Alan B. Campbell, *Lanarkshire Miners*, 102–3.

[15] Donald Dinnie (1837–1916) was the world-renowned, champion heavyweight athlete of the Scottish Highland Games between 1856 and 1869. "At 6 feet 1 inch in height, he possessed a 48 inch chest and thighs measuring 26½ inches. . . . " Webster, *Scottish Highland Games*, 81–85. I am indebted to Betty Saunders and the late Bill Saunders of Bennion, Utah, for this reference.

[16] At the time, Farrell was councillor to Bishop Ballantyne in Eden, Utah.

therefore I think it would only be Money threw Away. It takes A Man to be Heartily Sick tired of the Old Country for to Stay in this One.[17]

I think I will turn My Attention to Making Me A Home for My Self & my Advice to You is to [sell?] up As soon As Convenient & Come here & leave them that dont Like to Come hear to Believe in those they like best & perhaps theyll want to Come When they Wont Have the Chance.[18] But it is Best to Let Such people find the Weight of them-selves.

I will be on Hand to Look After James when he Comes in. There has been more rain here this Spring than ever Was & A fair prospect of A Good Season for the farmers. I dont know that I have Anything More of Importance to tell You at present so I will draw to A Close. Marshall & Family are All Well & Send there Love to You. Give My Love to Brothers and Sisters and All inquiring friends. I remain As Ever,

Your Affectionate Son,
John McNeil

James B. MacNeil to David and Ann MacNeil

Bountiful
Davis Coy
28 June 1873

Dear Father & Mother,

I now write you these few lines to let you know how I got here.[19] I got on the Nevada all right and got down into my bunk all right, but you never told me that my old clothes were in the bag strapped on my trunk, so I had to wear my good clothes all the way. I got [across the Atlantic] without being sick but I lost

---

[17] John's estimate of his brother David's intelligence is another indication of his tendency to overreact to a given situation and to form a judgment about the character of others. Once again, there is the notion that dissatisfaction with the old country is a necessary condition for successful settlement in Utah.

[18] In subsequent letters we learn that David, Sr., wants to open another clothing business; John may be suggesting here that he dispose of what he has and come to Utah.

[19] James left Liverpool on the *Nevada* 4 June 1873 and arrived in New York on 16 July. This group of Mormon immigrants included 166 adults and 38 children. Liverpool Emigration Records.

my appetite. I seen a whale & some porpoises also a flying fish about six inches long.

We landed on the 16th in castle garden and were there till next day and they take advantage of greenhorns. It was all cents and no sense in it and wonder of wonders, i did not get shot when i landed, and greatest of wonders i did not lose any of my luggage. I seen some beautiful scenery coming up here, but this is the nicest place i have seen. I was nine days in the train.

I am now writing this with a revolver in each hand and a sword in the other, defending my life against, some flys and midges. I have been to the city, and on the way had a bath in the hot sulpher springs. I seen a man of the name of Crauford at ogden asking very kindly after you. Sometime president of the airdrie conference.[20]

I dont know that i have anything more to say at present until i look around a bit. If this does not reach you, you can let me know and I will write another epistle. I enjoyed Janets wine pretty muchly. Give my respects to brothers & sisters & all inquiring friends. I remain as ever,

Js. McNeil

[PS] plase xcuse the orthography

John MacNeil to David and Ann MacNeil

Bountyfull
Davis Coy
[Utah]
28 June 1873

Dear Father & Mother,

It Gives Me Great pleasure to tell You that I Shook Hand with My Brother on Thursday June 26th & he was in Good Health & Spirits. But I Shouldnt Have Known Him he is So Altered, & he Says he Shouldn't have Known Me Either if it Had Not been My Legs. He Says I Am A better looking Man Every way than

---

[20] John Crawford, another old family friend, was baptized at Airdrie on the same day as James Brady, March 16, 1848. There never was an Airdrie Conference. Crawford actually served as president of the Glasgow Branch in 1863 and came to Ogden, Utah in 1864. Jenson, *Latter-day Saint Biographical Encyclopedia*, 1:391.

I would Have been if I had been in the Old Country Digging Coal & I believe it to for I feel As fine As A cock, & Stout Enough for Anything.

James had a Good passage & would have Enjoyed it only he lost his Appetite for his food but he was Not Sea Sick. I think it would have been better if he had been Sea Sick for I could Eat As Much At one Meal As he Could Eat in A whole day, but I Expect to See Him Get Over it After A little.

I Have Done Nothing in the Shape of work this two Months but there will be Lots of work in A little All Over & we Are Not dependant on Any One for Our keep. I Have Got A Hundred dollars in My pocket, Yet I will Have More before thats done. I Have been trying to Get A job on the railway Firing But I don't know whither I Shall Succede or Not

Duncan Kelly Son of Old John Kelly Got Killed Last week. He was working At the Station At Salt Lake City & An Engine pushed A Car over his Legs Cutting them of. He died in A few hours After.[21] . . .

James Came Here with A Mishap only; he lost the keys of the valice & [music?] box but thats All the Misfortune Happened to Him. The boots you Sent Me was far to large. . . . Your Loving Son,

John McNeil

James B. MacNeil to David and Ann MacNeil

Evanston
[Wyoming Territory]
31 August 1873

Dear father & mother,

It is with pleasure i now take up my pen to let you know how i am getting along. When last i wrote to you i was in Sessions settlement. We stayed there about a month looking after work on the railroad, but could not make it. It is very hard to get along here if you have not got some freinds to take you by the hand. We

---

[21] Duncan C. Kelly was born 31 August 1847 at East Muir, Scotland, came to Utah in 1869, and died 11 June 1873. Liverpool Emigration Records; Salt Lake City Cemetery Book of the Dead.

started for cottonwood with a roll of blankets on each of our backs. We traveled until it got dark then opened our blankets and squatted down among the brush. Got up next morning, got our flitting on our backs & started of, but we could not get work. So we started down canyon till dark, & spread our blankets, lay down among the brush. We got back home after five days travel among the mountains. We stayed a week & started again for cottonwood but could find no work to do. We went to brother [Hamilton] Park. He got us work. John to make an embankment with stones, me to work in the tithing yard at two dollars a day each, one quarter in flour another in cloth, another in store pay & the remaining quarter in money.[22] But we skinned & made for evanstone. We got there and are doing the best we can.

It dont agree with my constitution packing blankets twenty or thirty miles in a day. I have never layed on a bed but twice since i levt home, and that was on a hay stack. Farming in this country is a pretty easy life. They can raise as much in the summer as will do them all the year round. Brother marshall is pretty comfortable here. It is a hard life a miner [has] in this country. You may get pretty constant work for a few months, but you pay six or seven dollars for board each and then lay idle for a few months. No, not idle but travelling about sometimes with a roll of blankets on your back. sometimes without, and all the time paying away money for railroad. A single man in this country dont commence to have the comforts that a marriad man has. We are going to look out a place this fall. If we suceed at the mines, we will settel down.

You say you think about coming next spring.[23] I wish you to bring along the manchester science lectures, also murdochs poems. I want Ann [to] try and get some of the glees and songs i

---

[22] At the tithing yard in Salt Lake City, unemployed church members could work on "socially useful" projects and receive some remuneration. Park was Brigham Young's business manager at this time and might have been able to use his influence to assist his fellow Scots, but they didn't give him a chance. Neither John nor James seemed interested in mundane work; they wanted the more exciting, and potentially more rewarding, work in the mines. As single young men they were probably more interested in cash than in flour and other payments in kind. For a contemporary description of the functions of the tithing yard, see the *Deseret News*, 19 July 1884.

[23] David, Sr., has apparently accepted the advice of John to emigrate in the spring of 1874.

heard at the singing school: craiglee, the cristain mariners hymn, the old old home. daisy deans, hail smiling morn, larney o'flaningins cortship and tis lifes glad moments that quickly fading glows and all the glees and songs she can get. John wants you to send along some of the best of brudder boness lectures, and going of to brighton.

I have seen a great deal of the handy works of the lord here. It is a rough country and it makes the people rough, but they are a kindly people withal. In fact more kindly than i expected. There is exceptions but this is the general rule and a more cortoes people to strangers you could not find. I have been to see Lot Smith.[24] I had my bloat of apples from him. He has a spledid house and orchard. I never seen more fruit on any trees in my life. This is a splendid country for raising fruit of all kinds.

Tell david he need not come here unless he is prepered to stand a great deal of hardship and good patience to with it. I have had diahrea a good few times. I have been off work two days with it but im all right now.

Brother [Lot] Smith and [Hamilton G.] Park sends their kind love all off you. They would like well to see all off you out here. I dont know i have anything more to say at present. Give my kind love to grannie, to brothers and sisters and all enquireing friends. I remian as ever, nae maer at present. Frae your neer do weel Son

timothy grahoun[25]

[PS] please exquese the orthography.

I have just been away angling and brought home about four pounds of trout for an hour. I have caught as much as eight pounds in an hour and you can get all the shooting you want, prairie chikens about the same as a partrige, sage hens, the same as a hen for size part. Then there is lots of wild duks, and rabbits & hares by the score. I want you to get John Whitten to get me to casts of good strong gut, not salmon gut, but strong round gut. And a dozen night flys well tied. Also some good rounds bend hooks for trout.

---

[24] Lot Smith had a home in Farmington, six miles north of Bountiful.

[25] "Granny" was grandfather James Boggie's second wife, Mary Waite Boggie, who lived in Edinburgh. In signing himself "timothy grahoun" James may be playing on the fact that he had just been hunting and thus had been acting as a "greyhound" — a swift hunting dog used in racing in Scotland.

There is trout caught in this Bear River from one to twelve pounds.[26] They angle here with a piece of ham cord and a hook on it, no gut bout it. Send them in the inside of a news paper. Rawp the flys and get up in a piece of paper or an envelope. Dont forget. I will send Joseph a dollar the first chance i get.

[James MacNeil]

John MacNeil to David and Ann MacNeil

Almy Station
Evenston
Wyoming Ter
17 December 1873

Dear Father & Mother,
I Sit down Once More to drop You a few Lines in Answer to Your welcome Note bearing date Sepr 28. We were Happy to know that You were All well As this Leaves us at present. We are working At the Coal Mines Evenston At present but doing No Good whatever. The Country is Nearly damned with Chinese who works for A doller & ten Cents per day & they Can be kicked & Cuffed About Like dogs so they Suit Masters better than white Men.[27] This Country is played Out for white people Unles You have friends to take you by the hand. This is the worst Season for work I have Seen Since I Come to Utah. Nothing Doing Unles for Chinese. The poor Emigrants who Have Come in this Season Are running All Over the Country Nearly Crazed Looking for work &

---

[26] The Bear River rises in Utah's Uinta Mountains and passes through Evanston, Wyoming, on its way to the Great Salt Lake.

[27] John is reflecting the common assumption that Chinese immigrants were depriving "whites" of work. This perception led eventually to the passage of laws designed to exclude Chinese from the United States beginning in 1882. Utah's *Ogden Junction* argued in an editorial in January 1879 that such laws were necessary because there were more workers than work available. Under such conditions "to divide what little there is with the inferior and alien race, is not a good nor a just policy. . . ." No consideration was given to the fact that the Chinese also operated important businesses which helped create more jobs and that very often local people were not willing to do the hazardous jobs the Chinese took. See Don C. Conley, "The Pioneer Chinese of Utah," in Papanikolas, ed., *The Peoples of Utah*, 260–61.

Cant find it. I dont know what it will Come to. There is Hundreds of Stout Able bodies Men running Around who would be glad to work for there Grub. We are digging Coal for Our Grub At present & Glad to Get that to do & Living Like dogs in A Hole in the Mountain, what we Call A Dig Out & Cooking Our Own Grub.

James thinks it is pretty rough for A Start but he is Not So badly Out of patience with it as I am. But perhaps things will take A turn. Suffize it to Say we are working hard & Making Nothing. You Can See by this few Lines whats the Cause of the Scarcity of work: it is the Emmense Emigration of Chinese & Mormons together.[28]

You Seem to be very Anxious About A description of the Country & things which I dont count worth describing. Evenston is North East from Salt Lake City About 87 Miles & on the Line of the Union Pacific Railroad. It is A City of Stables & pighouses with A Humain population Living in them of About two thousand people. All Lumber Houses fit for Nothing but pigs. The Coal Mines Lays About 3 Miles North from Evenston City.[29] There is a branch Line into it & the Coal, As I told you before, is 28 feet thick & Just Sticking Out of the foot of the Mountain. We work ten feet in the Centre of it which is Comparitavely Clean Coal. It is A Strong rough Coal to dig. All Blasted Just Like quarying. We use All Churn drills & dig About four ton Each which Makes us About 4 dollers Each.[30]

It is Mostly Scotch & English people that is Conducting the Mines & Mormons At that. If You want to See the beaters of Sanny White You Have Nothing to do but Come to Utah & You Can find Men with Several wemin who Has been through the

---

[28] John blames both Mormon immigrants and Chinese for the shortage of jobs, talking as if he were not a recent immigrant himself. A major cause of the problem was the nature of the mining industry. While Utah's general economy was less affected by the national economic depression of 1873 because it was more independent of the national scene, mining was part of the national economy and consequently suffered the reverses that John and James describe in their letters. Dean L. May, "Towards a Dependent Commonwealth," in Poll, et al., eds., *Utah's History*, 237.

[29] The mines were located at Almy, Wyoming.

[30] A "churn drill" is a heavy chisel-edged percussion drill for drilling vertical holes in rock during shaft-sinking operations. By lifting, rotating, and dropping the drill repeatedly, the rock is shattered and the hole is sunk. It was also used for coal mining.

House & received their Endowments who Can beat Sanny White Hollow, & Come to Meeting on Sunday, get up behind the Stand & Hollow & preach the word of Life & Salvation to the very people whom he has been robbing all week.[31] That [is] the prevaling principle with Mostly All Mormons. If the gentiles Want A finished Scoundral they Hire a Mormon. There is More rascality in A day in Connection with Mining or Any other thing that A Mormon Has to do with then there is in A week in the Old Country & Scotch Men is the worst of them All. The Owners of the Coal bed is Just a Company of Speculators who Has Shares in the railway Also.[32] We are Enjoying Good Health with it all. James Eats Like A Horse.

Decr 17 discharged Again from work to Make room for Chinese. James is Acting the fool & Vexing Me More than I have been Since I left the Old Country. He wont take No advice from Me about Nothing & I am afraid to Let him go about his business & do what he has a Mind to do for I know he would Not Live Long. His Impudence would Get him self Shot Amoungst Strangers in double Quick time. He has gave Me Enough of

---

[31] Mormons who receive their "endowments" are interviewed regarding their "worthiness" as faithful members of the church, and it is this fact that seems to be causing John MacNeil some trouble. He is disturbed that, although they have been endowed and are therefore considered worthy, they still do things that are at odds with his perceptions of righteous living.

[32] Although he opposed silver mining, Brigham Young encouraged coal mining because of its direct benefit to the community; wood for fuel was severely limited. In the 1870s the main developer of the coal fields in Utah and the adjacent areas of Wyoming was the Union Pacific Railroad. In the early 1870s the Rocky Mountain Coal and Iron Company controlled the mines at Almy, Wyoming. The LDS Church and other private interests tried to compete by opening mines at Coalville, Utah. Scots with expertise in mining could have been involved in the management of any of these companies. As of 1880, there were 152 miners in Utah who were born in Scotland. Of these, nineteen identified themselves as Mormons on the census returns, seventy-eight as Gentiles, and the rest were undesignated. The latter two categories were often in fact Mormons. Kenneth Davies of Brigham Young University estimates that probably half of the Scottish miners in Utah were members of the Mormon Church (letter, Kenneth Davies to author, 25 September 1987). The extent to which individual Mormons managed the mines is unknown. During the nineteenth century British capital flowed into the mining industries (and railroads) of the West in "significant amounts," and one traveler described the mines in "Mormon land" as "more British than American." Cited in Spencer, *British Investments and the American Mining Frontier*, 223. See also Alexander, "From Dearth to Deluge," 327, and Sims, *History of Almy*, 3–6.

Misery Since he has been here to drive Me Out of the Country Quicker than Hunger. I would rather Stand Hunger & Cold than Have a Tantelizing, Querrelsome disagreable person around Me. I thought when [I] Left Whifflet that I had Seen the Last of Contention, but I found the Same Spirit with James as Soon as he Come here.

We are Idle at present & Cant find work to do. We are Living on the Charity of Our friends or acquaintances rather, but I Shall Either Leave the Country where he is or Get Married & Let him Act on his on Conceit & do the best for himself. I am Sorrow to have to Say So About him but I Guess You know Something About it. He Seems to have the Ability to Make Enemys but no Single friend whatever. As regards doing Me good he is An injury rather. He is to Stubborn to be any good to any One or to himself. It is Not in his Nature to pull At one End of the rope with Any person. I dont think he will do any good in this Country.

I had part of this Letter wrote three weeks ago but for reasons which I wont Say, I had occasion to Lay it one Side for a Little. We are well at present & Staying with an English family of the Name of Cooper from Nottingham Shire.[33] I have Nothing More of Importance to tell You So I will Draw to a Close. Marshall sends his kind respects to You. . . . Your Affectionate Son,

John McNeil

Editor's Note: While John and James MacNeil were attempting to wrestle a living from mining in Utah and Wyoming, their half brother, John Thompson, had established his family in Illinois. Since last writing, his family had grown to four children and he too was facing economic hard times, but he was able to rationalize that he was rich in spiritual things. He and his wife were laying up "tresuers in heven."

---

[33] The home of Millizzer Robinson Cooper, widow of William Cooper, who died in 1868. It was in this home that John met his future wife, Annie Cooper Warrilow, the widow of John Warrilow.

John Thompson to Elizabeth Thompson

West Belleville
St Clair Co.
[Illinois]
28 January 1874

Dear Sister,

. . . We have Moved from Caseyville Since i Wrote to you last as you will See from the Abouve heading which was the Cause of Our Not Receving your letter Sooner. We was over at Caseyville on New years But did not Call at the Post office as i was Not Expecting aney letters to be there for Me.

Dear Sister, i thought that you with the Rest of the fameley had forgot to writ to us as it is the way of the woreld at the Present time, Out of Sight out of Mind or at least to a Great Extent. But i hope you will writ oftener in the futuer then you have in the Past.

Dear sister, as Regards to our Prosperety in woreldey things we have not Increased Much. Our Eferts at Farming ware a Sorce of lose to us and not Gain So far as Acoumulating this worelds Goods is concerined. But i Gained Some Experince that May be useful to Me in the futuer. I May Also State hear that we are trying to Acoumulat in Good works or in Other words to lay up tresuers in heven where Nether Moth Nor Rust Doth Corrupt nor theves Brack through and Steal. Thank the Lord for the aid of his Spirit to Assist us in Our Eferts to leren the Paths of truth and walk there in. The lord has Said that those that Seek me Earley Shall find Me. He has Also Said take My yock upon you which is Esey and my Burden which is light. He Also Said that he that heareth My Sayings and Doeth them i will licking him to a wise Man that Bilt his house on a Rock and when the winds Blue and the Reins Desended and Beat upon that house it fell not. Dear Sister, Pray that the Spiret of Iserals God may be with you to Gide you in the Pathes of Truth and Righteousness and that all the Famley May have the Same influence to Be there Gide.[34]

---

[34] It should be remembered that John Thompson was now a member of the Reorganized LDS Church. The MacNeils and Thompsons were then getting three different interpretations of the LDS experience: from John, who seemed very skeptical and was determined to do his own thinking; from James, who was

Dear Sister, you Say in your letter that you have hard of the Bad times that we have in America. Well thay have Being verey hard with Some Peopel Espacly in the Large Citys But we have not felt them Much Altho it has caused a dulness in our traid as well as in all others. I thank you for your kindness in Ofering to Assist us with what Means you have. But we dont Need it at Present.[35]

Dear Sister, i am Sorrow to hear that Wileys Joney is not used Right By his step father but hope he will Be abell to Bear it till he can Do for himself.[36]

Dear Sister, i Would licke to See Mother & all the famley But i have No Chance at Present. We have a Leittel Famley that will Require my Attention for Some time to Come. We have four Children now — Elizabeth, Joney, Robert, & Anney. Old Mrs Haig was well when we was over at New years But is Goning fast Doun the hill. The Rest of the famley are well. Jane had a Son About tow Weeks ago. Betsey Says that Aney is Just like hir antey ann. She is Nearley 17 Months old. I will now Close Give our love to Mother, David, Ann, Margret, Husband & famley, Janet & Husband, young David & Wife, Williams famely, and Anty Mergret and Except of the Same for your Self.[37] Your Brother,

John Thompson

---

on his way to becoming a "true believer" and who gave his allegiance to Brigham Young; and from John Thompson, who rejected mainline Mormonism and opted for Joseph Smith III as his prophet. No record exists of how these divergent streams of thought were received by the family in Scotland, except that David, Sr., liked what James had to say, while the mother and the daughters were impressed with John MacNeil's perspective.

[35] The national economic depression began in September 1873 and lasted until almost the end of the decade. It marked the end of the "boom" economy stimulated by the Civil War and was in part caused by overspeculation in western railroads and the collapse of a number of eastern financial institutions. It was also influenced by the general European depression, which caused foreign investors to unload their investments in North America. Hicks, *American Nation*, 77–78.

[36] Reference is to his brother William's son, John Thompson, who eventually came to Arizona in 1882. This boy's father, William, was killed in 1863.

[37] Note that John Thompson refers to his stepfather as David rather than as "father."

James B. MacNeil to David and Ann MacNeil

Bountiful Davis Coy
31 January 1874

Dear Father & Mother,
. . . when Last I wrote to you I was at Almy [Wyoming] to
the coal mines working with John. But everythings dull all over &
the coal mines was no exception. I come here in a bad time, work
has never been so dull Since the Utah Mines Started.

You will be wondering why I did not write before but I had
no good news to tell So I delayed writing untill John got Anns
letter.

You talked about this being the place for Tourists. The Scenery in northern Utah has no equel. Up Cottenwood Canyon you
can See water fall nearly a thousand feet & make a natural tunnel
for a couple of hundred feet through granite. When we were out
the coal mines we went down the river to Randolph a new Settlement thirty miles from evanston. If we can make a raise this Summer we intend taking up a place there as John is going to get
Married on the 2nd of next month. I think it is the best he can do.
Dont laugh. It is a widow with to little girls, english: comes from
nottingham, Annie Cooper by name.

I have got to know a little of the world Since I left home. I
have been Studying human nature a little Since Ive been here & I
fancy I have learned a little. An unsophisticated youth like me
coming into this country Soon gets to know Summat [something].
I have traveled a hundred & five miles by myself without a Single
cent in my poket & got one meal on my way. But they tell me Ive
got to get thrashed but I am enjoying better health than ever I did
in my life. So I am content as far as that goes.

We intend Starting out next week for little Cottenwood.[38]
Tell David if he intends coming out here he must make up his
mind to Stay here. A married man in this country after he makes
A raise can live a great deal easier than in the old country. You
Can raise enough in four months as will do you the rest of the

---

[38] Little Cottonwood Canyon is located in the Wasatch Mountains fifteen
miles southeast of Salt Lake City. Its granite was used in the construction of the
Salt Lake Temple, and at Alta there was a roaring silver mine camp, to which
the MacNeils now repaired in their search for work and reward.

year. John intends going into Stock raizing. It pays better than farming if you are in a country where there is plenty of feed for them.

I have been to See Brother [Hamilton G.] Park Since we ran away & he felt hurt about us acting as we did. I have also been to See Brother Lot Smith & Stayed with him a couple of days. He treated me the best kind & asked very kindly after you & all the rest of the family.

You talked of me learning the Fiddle. I have never got a chance yet. You must not think that this country is the Same as the old country. There are few here that are learned by note & the few that are learned by note it takes money to buy their learning.

Ann talkes of the Whuttons Stopping their Custom but I think with gods help you can get along without them. I want you to write & tell me if the widow Wadell is married yet to that neer-do-weel, & Tell me how Ann & Johnnie Waddel is making it. I was very Sorry to hear of Andrew Beards illness also of archy w illness. I think they were two good boys.

You may think greatly about me being changed. I am in some respects but I am Still as fond of a laugh as ever. It is quite a different Sort of life we lead to what we did in the old country. It goes all by seasons & you have to work while you can get it. But I have only worked about a month Since I come here.

We have very little amusment here, we have got to make our own. I have Never heard a good Song Since I have been here. The only amusment is dancing here. I am learning to dance. I can go through a cottilion now. But we weary awfull, So I want you to Send along all the new Songsters you can get, & you can Send brudders boness lectures & the Songs I sent for.[39] Also the Free & easy comic Songster. I got the Flys but you did not Send the gut line. We are both well at present, me being 167 pounds, hoping this will find you all enjoying the great blessing. . . . I remain your affectionate Son,

J[ames] B. B. McNeil

---

[39] The "brudders boness" lectures were part of a series of stereotypical comic readings published by Cameron and Ferguson, Glasgow. The one James was requesting was probably "Brudder Bones' Stump Speeches and Burlesque Orations; containing also Humorous Lectures, Negro Drollerie, and Comic Recitations."

James B. MacNeil to David MacNeil

Bountiful, [Utah]
4 February 1874

Dear Father,

It is with none of the best of feelings that I now Sit down to
write to you. I have Just been to the post office & received your
letter. John was not at home, Him & wife went away yesterday so
I took the liberty to open your letter. So I take the liberty to write
an answer. A story is none the worse for being told twice.

When we were to work at almy Coal Mines the work was
dull & we did not get on very well. Have patiene & read it, Father.
It is probable the last. We did not get on very well & it made us
both ill tempered. We quarreled one sunday morning. It was while
we were batching. I cooked the food & John procured it, that is
went errands, I having a sore foot at the time. So he agreed if I
would cook the food he would go the errands. So on Saturday
after work was over he felt to tired to do any errands. We had
enough for supper so on sunday morning we had nothing to eat
until he went for some. When we got up I washed me & put on a
clean Shirt & he wanted me to start & clean the guns while he
went for some breakfast. I said I wanted something to eat first, so
he said he would not go untill I said I would clean the guns while
he was away. High words passed between us & John struck me. I
went & got my shoes & cap & went. John asked me where I was
going to I said i did not know. He [followed] me & offered me
some money but I would not take it. He told me if I was going I
was not to come back.

I had not one cent when I left him & went over to evanston
but could not find anything to do. By this time it was two oclock
in the day. I Started for bountiful a distance of one hundred &
five miles. I got one meal when I was about half ways from a man
that took pity on me. I traveld the last 4 miles with one shoe
under my arm. I arrived at Johns wifes mothers & got my supper
there & went on to brothers Marshalls about 2 o clock in the
morning. I wrote to John to send the keys of my trunk so I could
get my blankets. He wrote an answer & asked me to come back.
He said he was sorry for letting his temper get the better of him. I
went back as he said things were very brisk there.

When I got there I could not get any work to do. I stayed there a week & at the end of it John got his discharge with nearly all of the white men. So John Said I would better go to coalville about 60 miles from almy. So I got my blankets & sent to echo station by express (the nearest station to coalville 42 miles from Almy). So me & another man started out on monday morning about 9 o clock, John Saying he would Stay & see if any work turned up there. I was to write & let him know if there was any work & he would come along. We started out & traveled to echo Station 42 miles & the only thing I got to eat was a piece of bread which my partner had brought with him, & that was froze so hard that he had to break it with his heel. We got to echo Station about 12 oclock [Conclusion of letter is missing]

[James McNeil]

John MacNeil to David and Ann MacNeil

City Bountyfull
Davis Coy Utah
6 February 1874

Dear Father & Mother,

It is with pleasure I Sit down to drop You A few Lines in Answer to Your Kind and welcome Letter which I received on the Second day of Feby. I was Married on the first to a Mormon Girl & a widow with two Children. Her Maiden Name is C. Annie Cooper and is A Native of Nottingham Shire England. I Should have wrote Sooner but I have been Sick Since I was Married through Getting Cold when I went through the House and received My Endowments before I was Married.[40] We are Living with her mother who is also a widow.

---

[40] John and Annie were married by Daniel H. Wells in the Endowment House in Salt Lake City "for time" only on 2 February 1874. Annie had previously married William Warrilow on 2 September 1864 and was sealed "for time and all eternity" to him on 2 February 1869, six days before his death. Endowment House Record Book. According to Mormon belief, this means that in the "next life" her husband would be William Warrilow rather than John MacNeil. The fact that the endowment does involve a "washing ceremony" lends some credence to John's complaint about getting sick. In addition, the initiatory temple rites included baptism. Latter-day Saints believe that complete immersion is the only acceptable form of baptism, but February in Utah was not a particularly good time for this experience. Given his frame of mind, getting sick as a result

Neither Me Nor James has done any work Since I wrote to you Last. James is getting as fat as a hog & Stout & powerfull. He has Just gone down to the water to get Baptized today.[41] I believe James disagreable disposition Hurried My Marriage on a Little but I hope it is all for the best. At Least I Cant be no worse of than I was.

James read that Letter and also Seen the Check and he was as Mad as A bitch wolf. He Sat down right away and Commenced writing & Looked as black as Hell at me to that Extent that My Wife Commenced Crying. [She] thought they had Offended him Somehow and God knows he Couldnt be treated with more respect At home if You was able to try Your best. Everybody is trying to do him kindness. My Wife & Mother runs after him, dancing his attendance Just the Same as Mother used to do & Yet he is Neither Contended Nor agreable. He Seems to have No property only to Make Enemies to himself & Me and Out of his friends to. I will write you a Long Letter pretty Soon Give You all perticulars. I am A Little Sick Just now & dont feel Like writing much Just now.

I am thankfull for the Use of that Money Just now Until I have an Opportunity to pay it back.[42] I will have our photographs taken pretty Soon & You Shall See how My Little family Looks.

I received a Letter from Ann but I am to Sick Just now to answer It but I will do So pretty Soon. We all Join in Sending Our Loves to You & wish You all a happy & prosperous New Year. My Wife Says She will Bless You all the days that She Lives for raising Such a boy for her. . . . Give My respects to brother and Sisters. Also My Wifes as I have No Other way of Introducing her to You at present.

Your Affectionate son,
John McNeil

---

of participating in the endowment ceremony must have done little for his perspective on the rites.

[41] No record of a previous baptism for James could be found in the Scottish Mormon records.

[42] Since the family was able to offer money to both John Thompson and John MacNeil, this may be another reason why those in Scotland may not have felt the need to come to Utah. Glasgow and the West of Scotland were experiencing some economic depression also, but perhaps it became a matter of "better the hard times you know, than those you don't."

John MacNeil to Ann MacNeil and Elizabeth Thompson

Bountifull [Utah]
11 February 1874

Dear Sisters

It is with pleasure I Sit Down to Drop You a few Lines in Answer to Your kind & Welcome Note which I received A week ago but Owing to me being Sick A Little through Getting Cold I have Not been able to answer Your Note Although I was very Happy to See it. I managed to write a few Lines in answer to Fathers Note which I received a few days after Yours, but did Not feel well Enough to answer Yours. But I am better now And A Married Man which You will hear by Fathers Letter.

I have done No work for two Months. Nor James Either. We have Not been Able to find work unless We work for our Grub to people that has plenty but Intends to keep it. I Like this Country for the freedom a person Enjoys, but what is freedom Going to do for You if You have Nothing to Eat. The fact is there is two Many Men and two Little Labour and as regards working for my Brother Mormons I might as well be in Hell with my back broken, for to get Money for Labour out of A Mormon is an Impossibility.[43] They would Lye, Cheat, Steal, Swear and Everything Else before they would part with a doller in Money. There is Some very good people Here but they are the Exception Not the rule. Mormons will pay a poor person money for the reason that they would Not get them to work to them for Nothing. A Man to get Money has to Go out and work to the Gentiles Somewhere & when he Comes in they are after him for his tything.

It is No place to raise a family Unless You want to raise a parcel of dull Heads and proflegates. It [is] getting to be as wicked as any place in the world for its Size. There isnt very much whoredom Carried on but drinking & the Mormon boys Can beat the world for Swearing. They are very Ignorent, Caused through Suffering hardships, being deluded through Mens' talk, and Not

---

[43] John MacNeil's complaint that Mormons did not pay their workers in cash probably refers to the practice of using "scrip" because cash was scarce. However, this practice was not limited to Mormons, but was widespread throughout the West. For a discussion of the advantages, disadvantages, and abuses of scrip, see Allen, *The Company Town in the American West*, 134–38.

being in a position to be able to afford to pay School fee So that they Could Learn anything.[44]

Mormonism here is Just the Same as Catholicsm Nearly in the Old Country. The rule is: them that is Ignorent keep them Ignorent Or they will Cause trouble. A man that wont work to them for Nothing and goes out & works to the Gentiles he is thought Nothing of. It is worse than the Old Country if You Stay in the Church, for all the wealth of the Country is Monopolized by a few of the Old Speck drawing Yankies and they will Not Assist the poor.[45] They Make A Speculation of the trafic of poor people to this Country they are anxious for them to Come here to do there dirty work for Nothing. They will Make it there boast that they will have White Slaves Enough to work for them for Nothing when the Emigration Comes in. They will be poor Enough & Hungry to work for Something to keep them alive.[46]

If I was to tell You all You would Not believe that people Could be deluded to Such an Extent. I Could not tell You all I know about that but I am going to write a Long Letter to Father & tell him the truth & the hole truth. The truth will Out, and if he Chooses to Let You See it all right. I knowed that if I had wrote

---

[44] Free public schools were not available in Utah until 1890. In 1874 only about 40 percent of the school-age population attended the district schools, which were supported by local property taxes and tuition fees. Mormon resistance to public schools was ideological as well as economic, and many non-Mormons charged that the church was opposed to free schools because it wanted to keep its people in ignorance. Whether it wanted to keep the people "ignorant" is debatable, but it is clear that the Mormons did *not* favor a school system based on secular, non-Mormon values. See Buchanan, "Education among the Mormons" 440–41, and Peterson, "The Limits of Learning," 65–78.

[45] The expression "speck drawing Yankee" is a mispronunciation of the Scottish term "sneck drawing," which John uses in denunciation of Americans in his letter written 6 March 1874. According to the *Scottish National Dictionary* a "sneck" is a small door bolt, and to "draw a sneck" is therefore to open a door. When used figuratively, it can mean to "insinuate oneself into an affair surreptitiously, to let in in a crafty stealthy manner." This meaning is what John seems to intend in his stereotypical characterization of the leadership in Utah.

[46] A common charge brought against Mormons was that they imported poor immigrants for economic purposes. John is reflecting some of the national exposés about the "white slave" trade among the Mormons. There may have been some exploitation by Mormon entrepreneurs, but cheap labor was at most only one of several reasons for the church to sponsor immigration to Utah. Overall it was probably much less important than gathering for religious purposes to create and build Mormon communities, which was viewed as an expression of the physical Kingdom of God. Taylor, *Expectations Westward*, 87–112.

what I knowed about things he would Not believe Me, but I dont Care Now Ill give it to him & he Can believe in it or Not. I Should Not have Stayed in this Country if it had Not been My woman that atracted Me to the place & My Fathers words when I Left the Old Country. He Said he would rather hear tell of the Ship going down with Me as to hear tell of my backing Out from this Church. Well I have Not backed out of the Church but I back Out on all Scoundrels that I find wearing the Cloak of religion & God Nows there is to Many of them hear. I have Got Married Now & I have Got to do the best I Can here Now. James is as fat as a hog and Stout. We are Living with My Mother in law and doing Nothing in the Shape of work. . . . I remain Brother as ever,

John McNeil

11 February 1874

Dear Brother David,

I take up My pen to drop You a few Lines I want to tell you that I Have took Me a wife & a Widow at that with two Children, two Little girls. When I Can Get an Opportunity I am Going to Get Our Likenesses taken & I will Send You a Card. I thought I would Not Let You beat Me to Bad. I was very well pleased with My knife and hankerchief which you Sent Me and will return the Compliment Some day Soon. I will write to You a Long Letter pretty soon. I am Enjoying good Health and So is James Likewise. I remain Your Brother,

John McNeil

John MacNeil to David and Ann MacNeil

Bountifull City,
Davis Coy [Utah]
6 March 1874

Dear Father & Mother,

It Gives Me pleasure to drop those few Lines as I promised I would. We are in Good Health At presant and Hope this will find You all Enjoying the Same Great Blessing. We are doing no work as Yet but Expects to Soon.

I promised I Should tell You the truth, the whole truth & Nothing but the truth So heer Goes. To Commence with, You See the best of Mormonism in the Old Country. [In Utah] it has No resemblance to what is talked up in the Old Country. I dont want You to take A wrong Meaning Out of My words because I dont Mean Mormonism all together. Its the people. The Sweepings of Hell is gathered here. I have Got to find the first really decent person Yet. It requires A person to Come here themselves & See & heer for themselves. If I was to tell You all I know You would Say I Lied. That is the Cause of My None Descriptiveness. The principles of Mormonism May be all right, I dont know, but the Amount of rascality that is practiced by Men is Standing in the Church Leaves A doubt in the Minds of rational thinking persons in regards to it.

I have been through the house of the Lord & received My Endowments, but I believe there is a great deal of hokeypokey About it. People that went through in Nauvoo Say it has No resemblance to the Same thing. My Wife was through Several Years ago but had to go through again with Me and She Says its Altered all together Since she went through before.[47] They are altering it all the time and the very persons that Conduct the affairs of that place are No Examples. Every person that Goes through there is told they Must Not Cheat Lie or Steal and the Consequences in Connection with it. But directly the position holders in this Church Get out of the house they are at all of these practices & they have the Yankie Impudence & Adosity to get up in a Meeting and preach on that Same Subject while there is people Sitting in the Same Meeting who know them to be Unprincipled Swicks [cheating rogues].

---

[47] John MacNeil's wife, Annie Cooper, received her endowments 2 February 1869, when she was "sealed for time and all eternity" to William Warrilow. According to her there had been changes in the form of the endowment since 1869. The endowment ceremony was initiated at Nauvoo between 1842 and 1845, and there have been changes in the ceremony's form, if not its purpose, over the years. In mentioning the historic changes that have taken place in the ritual of the temple as a basis for his having doubts about the validity of the endowment, John MacNeil may be reacting to the commonly held misconception that there have been no essential changes in the temple ceremony (or indeed in Mormon beliefs) since the beginning of the church. See David J. Buerger, "The Development of the Mormon Temple Endowment Ceremony," *Dialogue* 20 (1987): 33–76.

You thought it took an awfull Amount of Music to Keep a Mans Courage in Its right place but I will tell you Something, when I Came in here the only Means of Amusement was private dances: You Invited Me to Your House & I Invited You to My House. But the Idea Struck the position Holders & Moneygrubs to Have dancing halls put up & of Coarse they were the only One that had Means & Liberty to do it, So directly they were up Orders were Issued, No more private dances, on perl of being Cut of the Church. You Must go to Our halls & pay a doller a dance. Fetch Along Your Money & Your wheat, if You Must have amusement & we Shall take Care of it. You dont know how. That Club Consists of the Bishop his Council, & a few More Sneck drawing [crafty] Yankies. You dare Not Invite a few friends to pass the Night Singing a Song or a dance, without first going to the bishop [and] Slipping him five dollers, then its all right.[48]

Brigham himself Issued orders for the people to Sell there Hogs, Eat No More pork, & he turned to & bought them up. Pork rose to an Enormous price he sold [and] Cleared thousands of dollers. There is No Such a thing here as rogery. The term for it with the uper Class Mormons is Financing.[49]

Before going through the house to get Married & Your Endowments You have to get a recomend from Your Bishop but the bishop did Not know Me when I went to ask him for a recomend (me being away out at work out of the Settlement Most of the time). He Said I had ought to have payed tithing & poor Silly Me did Not know what he Ment, but the people told Me I had ought to Sliped him 5 dollers & It would Matter Nothing whither I was in the Church or not.[50]

---

[48] Dancing has always been viewed by Mormons as an important part of community recreation. John interprets Mormon attempts to keep the Saints free of non-Mormon influences in their entertainment as motivated by financial considerations, but he may be reading more into this than is warranted. There were attempts to regulate contacts between Mormons and Gentiles, and putting dancing under the control of the ward bishops and charging for admission was one way of accomplishing this end. For an example of the conflict this policy created see Anderson, *Desert Saints*, 420–22.

[49] The writer has not been able to find any evidence for Brigham Young trading in pork. John MacNeil may be repeating some of the grist of the local rumor mill, which was often stimulated by exposés printed in the national and local non-Mormon press.

[50] John's growing skepticism about Mormonism may have been coloring his perceptions of Mormon practices; he accepted without question the exagger-

You talk about preast ridden people; we are worse than any Catholics Now. Its Money, Money, Money, & keep them Ignorent. You have got to Swear You will Spend Your Money in the Co Operative Mormon Stores which Consists of the big Mormons or Else Not go through the house. They will Not Sell as Cheap as the Small gentile Stores Nor as good articles & getting thousands of dollers for Every five dollers a gentile Store gets.[51] But the greed of Money is So great they Seem to want to Make as Much as they Can before the gentiles gets to Numerous and pulls the Scales of the deludeds Eyes.

You Must Not believe all that is in the Star there has been & is Lies told in the Millenniel Star. You have an Idea that Co Operation is a good thing. Well, It is where its honestly Conducted, but the big bugs kicks the poor bugs Out with their few dollers as Soon as it proves a Success. Thats Financing here. We was told in the Millennial Star that the Mountain Meadow Massicar was Committed by Indians but It is known by Everybody here to have been done by Mormons & Brigham Calls down the deed & Calls it a heartless butchery but harbers the very Men that did it and there is One if Not More of them Bishops.[52] Joseph Smiths Basterd daghter is Living in this Settlement You perhaps

---

ated claim that bribery was all that was needed to get into the Endowment House.

[51] The cooperative movement was designed to make Mormon Utah self-sufficient. Another effort to realize a just economic society in Utah was made by Brigham Young in 1874 when he launched the United Order. Many Mormons did not accept Brigham Young's innovations with enthusiasm, and after his death Mormons accommodated more and more to the prevailing American economic system. Arrington, Fox, and May, *Building the City of God*, 110, 136–37.

[52] The Mountain Meadows Massacre occurred in September 1857, thirty-five miles southwest of Cedar City, Utah, when 120 immigrants from Missouri and Arkansas were killed by a band of Indians and the Southern Utah Mormon Militia. Although Brigham Young may not have actually "called down the deed," as MacNeil says, the fiery preaching of many Mormon leaders contributed to the antagonism that many Mormons felt toward the immigrants, who in turn had been expressing anti-Mormon sentiments. For many years Mormons denied any complicity in the tragedy, but in November 1874 John D. Lee, the Mormon in charge of Indian affairs in southern Utah, was arrested for his part in the massacre and was executed in 1877. Before his death, Lee implicated Brigham Young and other Mormon leaders as being indirectly responsible for the killings. See Brooks, *Mountain Meadows Massacre* and *John Doyle Lee* for a dispassionate treatment of this tragic event. Reports of this massacre may also have influenced the thinking of John MacNeil's half brother, John Thompson, as he was contemplating moving west (c. 1857) from Illinois.

dont know what that Meens. I will tell You: whilst in Nauvoo Joseph Sent A Brother on a Mission to the Old Country & whilst he was gone he Seduced his wife and that is known to be part of the Cause of Joseph Smiths death. The Man Come back [and] found his woman about to have a Young one. He held a pistol to her head, forced her to tell who the father was, So She told it was Joseph Smith.[53] There is people here who is Stiff Mormons that will testify that it was a part of Mormonism wherein the Bible Says the Cattle on a thousand hills are Mine. So Saith the Lord & they Counted themselves the Lords people. So they went into the field & butchered Gentile Cattle in Nauvoo. I am acquainted with A Man who Says he killed Many & Many an animal for beef in the Night & he has been through the house of the Lord Several times.[54]

Its Like all Other religions to. You wont get two Men of the Same opinion about It. There is a Score of different Ideas all about the One thing preached from the Same Stand Every Year. But I dont want You to get the Idea that its the religion altogether, its the people. I dont know for Myself whither Mormonism is right or Not. I Consider myself an Example to any thing Ive Seen or found in this Country in the Shape of a Mormon with the Exception of A few whom I know Nothing about. I quit this for this time, but will give You a few More Items Some Other time.

Bro. Marshall has gone right back on Me Since he found Out I was Not goin to have his girl.[55] Any friends I have found in

---

[53] The number of plural wives Joseph Smith reportedly had ranges from none (the official stance of the Reorganized LDS Church) to forty-eight — see Brodie, *No Man Knows My History*, 434–65. Linda King Newell and Valeen Tippetts Avery list evidence for at least sixteen (see *Mormon Enigma*, 143 and 333). There are reports that his plural wives had children by him and that they were living in Utah, but these are difficult to verify.

[54] There was a great deal of tension mounting between Mormons and non-Mormons in 1846, and there is some evidence that bands from Nauvoo were involved in raiding and stealing of property in the country around Nauvoo. The Mormon-dominated Nauvoo courts did not prosecute them as severely as non-Mormons wanted. Berry, "Mormon Settlement in Illinois," 88–102.

[55] John Marshall had hoped that Ann MacNeil would marry his son John, and now it appears that he may have been trying to arrange a marriage between his eighteen-year-old daughter, Eliza Jane, and John MacNeil. Eliza Jane eventually married Chancy West in 1875. Whether the relationship cooled because John rejected this offer cannot be determined, but there does not seem to have

this Country are Mostly Summer friends. Friends when You dont Need them. I Cant Say but Bro. Marshall treated Me very good but I paid for all the kindness, & It was all done with a double Motive which time proved. . . .

Your Affectionate Son,
John McNeil

John MacNeil to David, Jr., and Mary Murray MacNeil

Bountifull City, Davis Coy
16 March 1874

Dear Brother & Sister David McNeil,

. . . I thought perhaps You would Like to Know Something about the Country & the people & all that Sort of thing. I want to Have Some Intercorse with You, that is, I want You to write to Me, & tell Me how You Get along & all the News. If James Sharp is Near You give him My respects & Let Me know how he gets along in his Married Life also Yourself. How You feel about it.

I got Married a few weeks ago which I expect You know all about before this time. I Only regret Not Marrying Sooner. Its differet in this than In the Old Country in regard to Marrying. Its an advantage to be Married in this Country. If a Young Man was Making a fortune Every day he wouldnt have a Cent to bless himself with. You have to Give 6 dollers per week for your board & It takes nearly all You Can Earn to go along. A woman Can Make More than a Man keeping borders here. I Have done No work for about 4 Months & got Married in that time also & have No prospects of work. Yet this is a very good Country when a Man gets a Start but it is pretty difficult to get Started unles Your a Little Lucky, which I Never was. Although I have had Chances If I had been Married which I Could have turned to good account.

Mining here is a Somewhat different Life than in the Old Country. Its a rough Life Unles a Mans Married. James thinks he would Like this Country if he Could find Sufficent work but the

---

been much contact between the two families after John married Annie Cooper Warrilow the month previous to the writing of this letter.

Chinese is raising Hell with this Country. They work for a doller per day & Stands kicking & Cuffing around to any Extent.

The people here are Just the same as at home. Some very good people, but the Majority is both Mean & wicked Like every other place. Religion dont Make No difference to A Natural Scoundrel. Heel Still remain a Scoundrel & religion Affords him a Cloak for his practice. Mormonism May be right & it May be rong, I dont know. There is One thing I do know, the Mormonism of the Old Country has No resemblance to the Mormonism here.

Theres No Amusements here unles You Make it Yourselves & then the Authorities in the Church wont allow You Unless You pay for the priviledge. Its Like all the rest of the Churches, its pay Money, pay Money, all the time & dont ask where it is going or Your an apostate directly. The Mormons of Old times or Nauvoo Mormons, are Men that Wouldnt Stand any hardship they Could get Out of. They have all the Mean qualities of any Irish Ever You Seen has the Yankies. Especially Mormon Yankies.

I Could tell You Lots of My Experience which would be profitable to You but I will Only tell You One Little thing that is this: Never Let religion Stand betwixt You & prosperity. I find "Man Mind thySelf" to be the Leading Principle amongst Men Every where & More So amongst Mormons than any other people. Religion Makes no difference in Men. [Moromonism is] Only a form Like all other religions & a Cloak for the knowing deceiver. Enough Said Just Now.

Theres any amount of Snow here at present two feet deep & Still Snowing. Every persons after Self Interest, religion or No religion.

Your Loving Brother,
John McNeil

Editor's Note: John's frank and negative assessment of Mormonism in particular and indeed of the human condition in general had reached the stage where for a person of John's stubborn disposition there could be no turning back. The following poem was found among the letters sent to Scotland. Although it is not dated and the writing is not that of any of the MacNeils, it is included at this point because it reflects John's developing perspective as of 1874 and also his later membership in the Socialist Party in Utah after 1900.

The Modern Creed and Commandment
(From Yankeedom)

If a man's down, give him a thrust,
Trample the beggar into the dust;
Presumptuos poverty is quite appaling,
Knock him over and kick him for falling.
But if a man's up lift him still higher,
For your soul's for sale, and he is a buyer!
Dimes and dollars, dollars and dimes,
An empty pocket's the worst of all crimes.

I know a poor but honest man,
Who strives to live on a Christian plan;
But poor he is, and poor he will be,
A scorned and hated thing is he.
Abroad he leadeth a leper's life,
At home he meeteth a starving wife.
They strive against fearful odds.
Who have not worshipped the modern gods.
Dimes and dollars, dollars and dimes,
An empty pocket's the worst of all crimes.

So get your money, no matter how;
No questions are asked at the rich, I trow;
Steal by night or filch by day—
But do it all in a legal way!
Join the Church—oh, never forsake her,
Can't turn up your eyes and insult your Maker!
Be hypocrite, liar, or knave quite cool.
But dont be poor. Remember the rule—
Dimes and dollars, dollars and dimes,
An empty pocket's the worst of all crimes!

James B. MacNeil to David MacNeil

[Bountiful?]
[Utah]
[After 20 April 1874]

Dear Father,

It is a pleasure to Me to Sit down to answer your kind &
welcome letter which I received on the 20th of april. I was Sorry
to hear of your ill health. I hope it will be better next time you
write.

You have asked me a deal of questions which I find hard to
answer, not because they are hard to answer, but because I may

not be beleived. But I am Satisfied with the conclusions I have arrived at. You Say John has mixed So much amongst apostates & the like. Well I dont know much about that, but I will tell you what I beleive in & also what I dont beleive in. In the first place I beleive in Mormonism & it is going to take a bigger Stone than John has tumbled over to Shake My belief.

You want to know if it was through Need that I got babtized [etc]. My folks Must think I am a low, degraded, contemptible Skunk. No I will never be forced into a thing such as Mormonism if I have not faith that it is right. I am not So easily led as all that. No, I have the Means of getting along better right here in utah if I was not a Mormon. There is A great deal of apostats & nonmormon here.

I dont Say John is not A Mormon, but Father, I would rather ten times See him out of the church than See him act the part he does. He has told me A dozen times that he does not beleive one thing in connection with it. And this after he was babtized in the old Country & twice here, & also been through the endowments house & received his endowments & got Married & wears garments every day.[56] You will naturaly think there is Some thing Curious in Connection with this. I will tell you what I think is in Connection with it, it is this: A womans apron Strings. That is all the Conclusion I can get at in respect to that.[57]

As to the ignorance of the people, the rising generation, I find very much ignorance amongst them but I deny it being the fault of the authorities of the Church. No it is their own folt. The Schools is there if they want it & there are Some here that are as well learned as you will find anywhere, & I defy anybody to find More Convience for learning anywhere than their is here. I have been in Settlements two years old & found a School even there.[58]

---

[56] After Mormons have been endowed, they are supposed to wear specially marked undergarments as a constant reminder that they have made serious vows of obedience, sexual purity, and commitment to serve God.

[57] James may be suggesting that Ann MacNeil had a negative influence on her son John's religious development. Note too that this letter is addressed only to his father and makes no direct mention of his mother. The "apron strings" comment may mean that John was only going through the forms of Mormonism to please his wife. He had been a skeptic before he went to the Endowment House.

[58] Here James differs with John over schooling in Utah; if one really wanted schooling, it was available. And indeed it was, but it wasn't as readily

But it would be good for John if he would look to home A little more. He would not find So Much to talk about abroad but he looks at the dark Side of the picture all the time. I do not deny but that there are Some men in the Church that are liars, cheats, backbiters, filling offices. But dear me, that dont alter the truth one particle in my opinion.

Regarding your Coming out to this Country I have only to Say please your Self as to that, but if you do you Must Make up your Mind to Suffer a little at first. But depend upon it, You will be better of in the long run & you may depend upon it I will do my best to halp you if you do come.

I have Sat & listened to apostates & I have found Some truth in what they Said. But I found Some damnable lies in what they Said as well & the latter was the majority.

You Say you had a dispute with Gaven Findley & he Said that Brighamism was all Apostacy. Well, if [Joseph Smith III] has got authority to reorganise the Church, why dont he do according to the plan laid down by his father. It was his father that first revealed polygamy & practised it & yet he Says he dont beleive in it & yet he Says he beleives in everything that his father revealed. Hell is full of Such beleivers as he is.[59]

I will tell you a circumstance that happened to [David Adamson] while he was here. He rented a nice house when he come here & hung up his venetian blinds on the window. One day he was sawing Some wood for the fire when along comes a fellow that knew him & told him, Says he, "Davy, youl have to take of your Coat if you intend Staying in zion" & I think that was a death blow to Mormonisn in David's Sight.[60]

---

available or as widely distributed as Mormons have claimed — there were pockets of excellence and also pockets of ignorance.

[59] Gavin Findlay was a member of the Reorganized LDS Church who had apparently returned to Scotland as a missionary for the "reorganization" movement. See comments about him in John Marshall's letter of 26 February 1871 and John Thompson's letter of 5 February 1872. The major difference between the two Mormon groups at this time was the RLDS contention that Joseph Smith never taught or practiced plural marriage.

[60] David Adamson was apparently a Scot who had defected from the LDS Church in Utah. James's account of the reason for Adamson's defection is perhaps a way of saying that some people abandoned the church for trivial and absurd reasons.

I want you to tell Me what was the cause of seperation between David [MacNeil, Jr.] & his wife next time you write. I was Sorry to hear of David being idle. There is prospects of this being a very brisk Season in the Silver Mines.

John took Sick about a week ago & went down home. He is getting better last time I heard from him. You Say [you have] little Spirit or energy Since Johns letter came. If you are So easily discouraged as that I am afraid you will make a poor Show in utah. When you get knocked down here at anything you have got to get up & bump at it again until you Succed. It dont do to Sit down & cry over it. It dont pay that nowhow.

I have nothing more to say at present. Give my kind love to David, Lizzie & all the rest. . . . from Your loving Son,

James McNeil

[PS] The reason why young Joseph does not beleive in Polyligamy is he finds it is deal more palitable to the peoples taste to have that out. Give my kind love to Grannie & tell Me how She is getting along next time you write. . . . write soon. I want you [to] tell me has young William rodger come back.

John MacNeil to David and Ann MacNeil

Bountifull City, Davis Coy
14 May 1874

Dear Father & Mother,

. . . [I] have been More or Less Sick Ever since I Got [your note] & Not very Able to write. We was at work in Cottonwood Canyon At the time it reached us. James is Suffering a Little from Cold. Will Soon be all right again. James is up in the Canyon Just Now. I am at home at present Convelescent After being Leaded while I was At work. I payed the Hospital fee So I Got a free Line to that place. I am pretty nearly well Now.[61]

---

[61] "Leading" or "lead colic" is caused by inhaling poisonous fumes or dust. James explains it in his letter of Fall 1874. John was probably treated for lead poisoning at St. Mark's Hospital, founded by the Episcopal Church in April 1872. Miners paid one dollar per month into an insurance plan. Tuttle, *Reminiscences of a Missionary Bishop*, 397; Allen and Alexander, *Mormons and Gentiles*, 110.

I dont think [John] Marshall wants to be troubled writing to you any More.[62] All you have Learned has Not brought You to the School door Yet, Compared with what Youll Learn if Ever your Spared to Come to Utah. You Accuse Me of writing to You & Adressing My Letter to the Girls. Well there is Certainly Some Mistake About that because Any Letter I Wrote to you I think I adressed it to You. But You have heard the Last from Me You Are Likely to hear on that Subject.

Anyhow I knowed from the first whenever I wrote that Side of the Question It would Not be Swallowed but the Other Sliped Over Like New Potatoes. Well that is the way with Fanaticism. You accuse Me of Either Lying before or Now. Well You was Not here to know the position I was in. I was Influenced by parties who wished Me, well to write Cheery News and tell them the best Side. It will do No Good to write bad News they wont believe it anyhow. You want Me to Explain A whole Lot of Items to You & at the Same time You would rather take the news paper reports than My words & destinctly tell Me I Lie. Well I am Not going to get Mad about it. All I have to Say is Come here & prove it.[63]

Our Late Member to Congress Namely Captain Hooper has Given in his Name to be Cut of the Church also Wm. Jennings another big poste in the Church & Teasdel also.[64] They have Just done Like all the rest of them whenever they Made their pile or Stake they Shell Out of it for fear of some trouble. Thats the

---

[62] As far as is known, the last letter written by John Marshall to David MacNeil was the one of 10 October 1872.

[63] One might think that all newspaper reports of this period sensationalized events in Utah, but there was also a growing awareness on the part of the press that there were at least two sides to news coming out of Utah. David O. Calder traveled 1,500 miles throughout Scotland in 1872 attempting to give the Mormon perspective to editors, merchants, ministers, "and others of the middle classes" and found considerable admiration for the Mormons in his travels. *Millennial Star* 34:475. In time this early public relations effort may have led to a more balanced treatment of Utah and the Mormons.

[64] William H. Hooper, William Jennings, and George Teasdale were all deeply involved in Utah's economic, political, and religious life. However, as far as this writer has been able to determine, they were in "good standing" in the Mormon Church in 1874. Teasdale became an apostle and Jennings was elected mayor of Salt Lake City in 1882. MacNeil may have been responding to hearsay in the community. All are listed in Jenson's *Latter-day Saint Biographical Encyclopedia*; apostates or malcontents were usually not listed in this publication.

kind of Leaders the Mormon people are to follow and put to flight Six times their Number through their faith.

Well I am here & you are there. You know what You know & I think I do the Same. I have been Endowed with Some little Sense & Judgement of My Own which I believe was Given Me to Use & I intend to use it Just as Much So as any of the Authorities of the Church. No More On this Subject. Them that wants to Satisfy themselves about the truth or falsety of My Statements Can just Come here & try.

I am Intending to try & Make a home here if I Can. I like the Country well Enough. I will refund that Money Just as Soon as I am able. This Sickness So Shortly after My Marriage has threw Me back a Little. Perhaps You dont want Me to Mention Any Ones Name only Yours in Your Letters. Ill do that if that is what You want. I have No More News of Importance this time.

The Order of Enoch is all the rage and talk here Just Now but how Its Going to Succede is doubtfull.[65] I have No More this time. Write again if you think I am worth it but Ill have to get along anyhow.

John McNeil

James B. MacNeil to David MacNeil

[Salt Lake City, Utah]
[23 June 1874]

Dear Father,

I take the pleasure of writting you a few Lines Simply because I want to Say Something to you. It is a Subject that I cannot approach without a feeling of Diffidence but I feel compelled to Say Something to you. It is in regard to the Gospel of the Living God. It is a great Many years Ago Since you came to a knowledge of the Truth and there is no doubt but if you had wanted to obey

---

[65] The United Order of Enoch was established by Brigham Young in 1874 and had its roots in the efforts of Joseph Smith to establish a communitarian economic system. Like the earlier efforts of Joseph Smith in the 1830s, the United Order lasted only a few years. It was generally abandoned after Brigham Young's death in 1877, and none of the communities organized around the principle survived beyond the mid-1880s. See Arrington, Fox, and May, *Building the City of God*, 136–37.

the Servants of that God in their teachings you could have been here years ago. But you have never been anxious to come Father. It Seems to Me and to everyone that knows you that you have a Dread of the hardships attendant upon your Migration here. And if so you are unworthy of being Classed amongst what is known as Latter Day Saints.

It is of no use Saying that it was because the Family would'nt come. You know better than that and even if it was so, you should have come. He that will not lay aside all Family Ties for Christs Sake is unworthy of Christ. But I dont think you would have had to make that Sacrifice if you had Shown any anziety to Come. But that was never manifested to My knowledge that I can remember of. You know that you do not attend the Meetings. Your life is a Lie, for as Such you are living it.

I have got proof Enough to Satisfy Me in regard to the principles of Life and Salvation and I intend to act in accordance with them or as near as I can come to it. If you have not received confirmation you will never get it Living as you are. No, you Must follow the Teachings of the Church and then you will receive a knowledge. But you know it already and still Live in direct opposition there to. That is what I term "Living a Lie."

President Young Said today they that are not of this Church and kingdom, be they Father, Mother, Sister or Brother are nothing to Me, Nor do I want them.[66] Now I would like to see you here but if you dont choose to come I cannot help it nohow. I must follow the Course that My convictions point out to Me and leave you to do as your judgement dictates.

I intend to Marry Next winter and Settle down to obey the Teachings of the Gospel of Christ as Near as possible. I will have to look out a ranch Somewheres and take My living from the Soil. I cannot live a pure life and follow Mining for a living. That is an impossibility in this country. If I intended to follow Mining

---

[66] James wrote this letter after attending a service in the Third Ward Meeting House in Salt Lake City on Sunday, 23 June 1874. On that day Brigham Young gave an extended discourse on the need for religious commitment and chided the Latter-day Saints for being too worldly and even idolatrous. He commended those who had come from foreign lands and had left husbands, wives, children, and parents "for the sake of our religion." This apparently made a strong impression on James and helped shape his admonition to his father. See *JD* 18:235–49.

in this Country I should never marry. I know this to be true and you cannot blame Me if I direct My Life accordingly. Nor do I care whether you do or Not.

I care not what anyone thinks of me when I know I am doing the will of God. That is paramount with Me. I know the work that I have to do and to lay aside those old Superstitions that were ingrained into My Nature for Eighteen years will nesecesstate A Struggle on My part to overcome, But I go into [it] with a Strong Self reliance and Faith in God, for God helps them that help themselves. Now I said what I have to Say and being done will Stop. May God bless you is the prayer of your Son,

Jas. B. MacNeil

John MacNeil to David and Ann MacNeil

Alta City,
Little Cottonwood
25 August 1874

Dear Father & Mother,

. . . I received Your Letter A week ago but delayed writing for want of Something to Say that was of any Importance. We Lay Over All winter Nearly doing Nothing & had Our board to pay when we worked. We Are working in Little Cottonwood Canyon at present & we have Got Out of debt and are working Steady.[67] I have my woman up here Likewise and James is Staying with us & working in the Same Mine with Me. I got Over My Sick Spell all right & am well and Strong Again & we are all well & hope these few Lines will find You all the Same. I have Not Much News of Importance to tell You.

All the talk Just Now is the Order of Enoch, but the people dont Seem to Care About it. Three fourths of the people will have Nothing to do with it. The rascality of the Affair is to palpable. It

---

[67] Alta in Little Cottonwood Canyon and Brighton in Big Cottonwood Canyon, situated in the Wasatch Mountains southeast of Salt Lake City, were the sites of extensive silver mining in the 1870s. The latter place took its name from a Scottish settler, William Stuart Brighton, who told a visitor that the canyon "minds me of my ain hame in the Hielands." Codman, *Mormon Country*, 116. British interests invested heavily in the mines in these canyons, including some with their headquarters in Glasgow. See Jackson, *Enterprising Scot*, 188–89.

is to Make positions for the Sons of the big bugs. Bro. Brigham has put Nothing into it himself. He Says he has Nothing to put in. His family has it all & they Need it & Orson Pratt is preaching to the people to Not Join Until Brigham does it. It Looks to Me Like this, if they Ever had the right thing amongst them there overreachingness & Love of Gain has drove it from Amongst them.[68]

I Sent You A Utah Humming bird in an News paper Some time ago & I am Going to try & Send You Some Specimans of Ore pretty Soon. We are all well at present, Struggling along, knocking Life out to keep it in. This Country has its faults Like all Others. If it isnt One thing it is an Other. I would Like if You Could Send Me that Negro burlesk book, brudder boneses Songs & dialoges. . . . I have Not Seen Marshall Since I Got Married. Let Me know If he Still writes. No More. I remain as Ever Your Loving Son,

John McNeil

James B. MacNeil to David MacNeil

[Bountiful, Utah]
[Fall 1874]

Dear Father,
. . . I was sorry to hear of the State of your Health & also the State of things in General there, but I hope to See Some of you out here next year. I am at Bountiful just now. Came down to get Some winter Clothing & other things that I want to Spend the winters up there.

You say Mother & the rest were well pleased with John's letter. Well, if they are well pleased with his very wise reasoning let them be So by all Means, & if they are displeased with Me I think they will remain So. All I have to Say is there was no insult meant, but if they think they will make me discard My Religion that I have taken up by fowlloing that course, they are utterly Mistaken. They Must recollect that My faith is Not based on the Jennings or Hooper or any of the other of the magnates. My faith

---

[68] No evidence could be found that Apostle Orson Pratt opposed Brigham Young's plans for the United Order.

is based on Something more Substantial, that is the word.[69] I respect my mother & sister as Much as ever I did.

I am at work just Now & I feell happier than when I last wrote to you. I am working at the Victoria & Imperial Mines just Now.[70] I receive 4 dollers per day. You ask what John means by being leaded. Well, when you are digging ore there is a sulphur Comes from it which Carries arsenic with it & your bowels gets bound. You have no appitite & there is a weight lays at your Stomach & that is lead.

You Must excuse My delay in writing. I will write oftener Now. I want you to Send Some Songs. You May think it Strange that I should ask for so many songs. Well there is very little amusement here unless you want to go to the bad. There is plenty beer Saloons, whore houses, hurdy houses & gambling houses any amount that is up in Alta City. But You Must Not Suppose it is that everywhere. There is no branch of the Church here in Alta.[71] I want You to Send My Gennology when ever you can find time to do So. I want you to Send the auld Scotch Sangs. When we were at the schule My friends. No more at Present. Give My kind love to all and tell David to write. . . . I remain your affectionate Son,

James MacNeil

[PS] Write soon & excuse this hurrying Scribble.

John MacNeil to David and Ann MacNeil

> Alta City, Little
> Cottonwood
> 6 January 1875

Dear Father & Mother,

. . . I received Your Kind & welcome Letter, date I dont Know what, but I have Just Got it Now On Account of A Little

---

[69]"The word" could be interpreted to mean the Bible, the general principle of revelation, or simply Jesus.

[70]This mine was located in Alta, Utah, and was one of the many owned by British (including Scottish) investors, who owned eight companies in 1871, fourteen in 1872, and twenty-one by 1878. Jackson, *Enterprising Scot*, 189.

[71]It is remarkable that in the 1870s there was no organized Mormon Church branch in Alta. Perhaps the leadership felt that to establish a branch in the mining community would legitimize mining as a desirable occupation. See Arrington, *Great Basin Kingdom*, 241–43.

Smartness of One of the Brethren of the Same Name as Me. He Lives in Sessions & is an Irish Man, a thief & a Scoundrel. He has took Several of My Letters & Kept them Sometime. He Kept this One Over a Month & took that piece or article You refered to Out of it & to[ok] it to the Meeting & Spouted on it.[72] That is Just the way things is done in Utah. You Must Adress John. B. B. Mc Neil to Make A distinction.

You Never told Me Whither You Got the Humming Bird that the Little Girls Sent You. They want to know.

I am working in the Silver Mines in Little Cottenwood Kanyon & I have My Wife & Family up here to. My Wife had a Daughter on the 18th November So I proclaim You Grandpa & GrandMa to a Live Yankie.[73]

I have been working Steady for Six Months at 4 dollers per day. James has been working at the Same place & the Same wages 5 Months but is Idle Now but Could Get plenty of work if he wanted it. He has bought Some [livestock]. He has Gone down in the Valley with $180 dollers but what he is going to do with it I dont know. He dont tell Me None of his business. He seems to want to do things on his Own Hook & at the Same time take any Kindness or assistance that I Choose to Lend. In fact he is to Selfish for Me to have anything More to do with him. He Seems to want to pull at the Opposite End of the rope from Me all the time. He is to big Headed to Learn anything from the Like of Me & if I Should Save him anything by advice or assistance he would Only Spit in My Face & tell Me it was No More than I Should do. So I have Got tired of that Sort of d——d Nonsense. He wont take Advice from No person. He knows to Much for any person to Learn him. So I Made up My Mind to Let him Learn the practicle of it. He Can find any Quantity of Friends where he is, So Long as he has plenty of Money. The Old Story (You know).

He is in Good health & So is all the rest of us Crowd & we hope this will find You all the Same. We wish You all a Happy New Year & More Means & better Health throughout.

---

[72] The other MacNeil in Sessions Settlement was probably John C. MacNeil, who was born on the Isle of Man, 10 January 1823, and died in the Mormon colony of Morales in Mexico in 1909. Given John's disposition to be critical of the church, this incident did little to endear him to his Mormon brethren.

[73] Ann Eliza MacNeil, who later married Alfred Henkel and became the mother of Gladys Henkel Thorne.

Thats all a Hox about Brigham Dying. They print anything to fill up a paper in this Country Lies or anything. We Get the papers all right but Not the Letters.

I think James has an Idea of Marrying pretty Soon & paddling his own Canoo & I think he is playing fool big but I dont know. Only I Can hear things About him & I know that he Goes down there with [Money] & Comes back without. no More at present. Never Mind Boneses book. . . . the babys Names Ann. I Cristened it Myself.[74] No More Just Now. I am as ever, Your Affectionate Son,

John McNeil

Adress John H. Mc Neil

James B. MacNeil to David and Ann MacNeil

Bountiful
Davis Coy
14 January 1875

Dear Father & Mother,

. . . You Must excuse My Not dating My last letter. I was in a big hurry at the time I wrote that & as for getting Material for writting purposes I can get all I want but it is Not that that keeps Me from writing. Here You cant always find the time & place Suited So that is the reason & No other.

I dont say that a Man works any steatier in this Country than at home. On the contrary he does his business if he works half as Much, but that is all that is wrong with it. You cant get working Steady enough. But still when you are in work You have got to work right along at it every day Sunday & all if You wish to keep Your Job unless You are ill. In that case they will keep Your work for You that is at the Silver Mines.

I had to quit work there about the Middle of December & I had a bad cold & so I thought I would come down to the valley for a little while. They reduced the Number of hands at the Mine

---

[74] In spite of his criticism of the church, John was still willing and able to christen or bless his first child. He did not, however, christen or bless his next three children, an indication, perhaps, that he had become inactive in the church. See North Kanyon Ward, Record of Children's Blessings.

I was at So there was Not enough work for Me So I got payed off & came down here.

You ask Me whether it is Shin Plasters or Coin I get payed in. Well it is Neither of the two. I get payed in Greenbacks. Shin Plasters is out of date Now.[75]

A Man, iff he works 5 Months in the Year he Can live right well the other 7 Months. For instance I done No work from beginning of December 1873 till the Middle of March & I got work [in] Cot[ton]wood in Aprile & I had to pay My board bill from Dec 1st till Aprile 1st So I payed it the first Money I earned. Well I only worked 6 Months out of 14 Months & I bought a Mare & three Milk Cows & have got a little to Spare Yet to. If you want $50 Sent to You Just Say So. When you come, them critters they are here for you.

I think You can earn a good living here. Education is a great thing here. I find the want of it keenly & depend upon it I will do every thing in My power to help You. You will Never want for the Nesusurias of life as long as I have health & Strength. I would like to See all My folks out here & Father it is the dearest wish of My heart. I think we could all be a great deal happier if we were all here together.

You dont like the idea of me being So far removed from a branch of the Church. Well I am doing all for the best and You Must Not be uneasy on My account. I will keep as far right as I possibly Can, depend upon it. Father I think a great deal too Much of Mormonism for to get disgusted at it through some of them cheating Me & depend upon it I will never turn My back on it because Some great Magnate or other turns his on it. It is a grand Mistake to depend on Some Man or other taking You to heaven in his breast pocket. All Such will find out Some day the truth of the Saying: every tub Must Stand on its own bottom, & then they will be like a Man I have read of, they will find that they were ten Minutes too late in finding it out. I Sincerly hope it will Not be So with You. As for My being as well at home as I am

---

[75] According to the *Oxford English Dictionary*, a "shinplaster" is a piece of privately issued paper, especially one poorly secured and depreciated in value. The reference here may be to the Mormon practice of issuing such notes ("scrip") in payment for work done on church and civic projects. Scrip was still being used in the 1870s in church-related enterprises. See Arrington, *Great Basin Kingdom*, 189–90, 312–13.

here I would rather be here. I am Not all the time in Cottonwood as you see from My letter.

I was glad to hear that David was living with his wife & Struggling on Manfully. Give him & his wife My kind love. Tell him I will write to him ere long. I would like You to tell Me how John Hendrie is getting along & I would like You to find out about little Jonnie Thomson & tell me all about it.

When I came down from Cottonwood the Bishop was advising all the young Men that were worthy of it to go through the house & receive their endowments. So I thought on it a little & went up to visit Lot Smith 8 Miles North from here. I Stayed with him three days & he treated Me the best kind & I asked his advice on the Matter. So he adviced Me to go & receive My endowments. So I got a recomend from the Bishop & went down & got My endowments & I Seen old John Lyon, alias the Lion of the Lord.[76] I Made Myself acquainted with him & when I was coming away he told me to give you his best respects. Father, he give Me a good advice I can tell You. So I wear My Garments Now all the time & I think it done Me good & I only wish You were here too go through as well.[77] I hope you will be ere long & all the rest. I will start for Cottonwood in a few days & I hope the Next time I come down it will be to Meet You.

I want You when You have time to trace My Geneology & Send it.[78] Lot Smith Sends best respects. He will write to You. I think I gave him Your adress. You want to know if I get the Nespapers. I get them pretty regular & I am very thankfull to you.

I want You to give Me a rough estimate of what You owe. You Say D. Adamson was Bankrupt. . . . he will Continue going

---

[76] John Lyon of Kilmarnock joined the LDS Church in 1844, was active in missionary work in Scotland in the 1840s, and came to Utah in 1853. He served as a writer for local Utah newspapers and church journals and was Territorial Librarian. He undoubtedly knew David MacNeil at the time of his conversion in 1847. When James received his endowments on 6 January 1875, John Lyon participated in the rites. Endowment House Record Book.

[77] Part of the rationale for gathering to Utah was that only there could people have the endowments performed. Not until the 1950s did the LDS Church begin building temples outside North America, which encouraged members to stay in their homelands and build up the church there.

[78] John wants his genealogy so that he can have his ancestors baptized by proxy, an important rite in Mormonism since 1840. Allen and Leonard, *Story of the Latter-day Saints*, 168–69.

down & all Such. You Must enquire what it will take to convey a box of goods to Salt Lake City. Tell Me & then I will let You know whether it will pay. I want You to write & tell Me all about how Jonnie McLean & Janet are getting along. Give them My kind Love & Lizzie & Ann My kind Love. Also tell them I havent forgot them Yet. & I wish You would tell me how Grannie is getting along & give her My kind love. . . . I dont know that I have anything More to Say. In the Meantime May God Bless You with health & Strength & understanding that You May be enable to Come to a proper understanding of the Lords works & purposes. I remain Your affectionate Son.

James MacNeil

James B. MacNeil to Elizabeth Thompson and Ann MacNeil

Bountiful
Davis Coy
27 January 1875

Dear Sisters Lizzie & Ann,

I was Sorrow to hear of the dull [Shape?] of trade but it is as you Say everybody has a struggle of Some kind. Some Less Some More. But if you were here I think Your troubles would be a great Deal Less. You Must Not think there is Nothing but Mormons here because there is Most every Kind of Denomination here Right in Salt Lake City. So You Must Not Suppose You have got to be Mormons if You Come here. I am getting along very well at present.

You Say You Never did nor Said anything that Could Make Me disrespect You. Well I want you to understand that My affections & resolves was Not Depending on a word, Nor even A Deed because we are all lyable to be Misled or to err at one time or another. You Say that if I am right in my beleif You would be Glad if one of You had Such Light: Supposing it Left you in Darkness: Well, Sisters, You Must Not Scoff at the Light that is given unto you if it is not exactly to Your Minds. Remember Gods ways are Not as your ways & they that do Not receive & obey Such Light, but rather Scoff at it will Most assuredly inherit the Scoffers portion, and that Light being from God there is quite a probability of your being Left in Darkness if you do not receive & obey Such light. I hope you will See & obey Such Light.

I was very gratefull to you for Sending all the home News. I was very Much Surprised to hear of Rob Hays Marriage as I thought he was a Confirmed bachelor but wonders will Never Cease. Not as long as oor Jock Sells Yule & Yule Ye Ken he Mun Sell.[79] I was very Much gratified to hear that grannie was Still to the fore. May God bless her in her old age. Give her My kind Love. . . . May God bless you all with health Strength & understanding that You May be enabled to See & do his will. I remain as ever your affectionate Brother,

James MacNeil

[PS] Excuse this hurrying Scribble. A longer one next time. Write Soon.

James B. MacNeil to David and Ann MacNeil

Evanston
[Wyoming]
[c. April 1875]

Dear Father & Mother,

I again take the opportunity of writing a few Lines to Let you know how I am sliding. Since Last I wrote to you I got into a Stumpy patch as the yankeys put it, but I am begining to get into [clear] thatches agin.

Things has went a Little agin Me Since I Last wrote you So that I have Not been able to keep my promise to you & that is what has Delayed My writing to you. I thought It Might brighten up a Little So that I could keep My promise to you but it Seemed kinda Slow So I thought I would write to you & Let you know how I was placed So that you would not think that I had forgot you. I dont often Let you out of My Mind rest assured. You Must Struggle on a Little longer & depend upon it I will do every thing in My power to help you out of it as Soon as I can & I think it is Not far distant either. But then things Dont count in that way, it

---

[79] By "Yule" James probably means "yill," the Scots word for ale. The complete expression means that miracles will never cease as long as ale is being sold.

takes greenbacks, but you know without hope there would be No Life Much. I think there is a prospect of Me getting a Little ahead of times before Long.

I was Sorrow to hear of the State of your health & it would have give Me Much pleasure to have been able to assist you, but I have had it pretty tough this Last Little while. But then I will get over it.

We have a branch of the church here Now & they have had Me up bearing My Testimony to this work & I have got to live a Little Straight Now. I have got to pay My Tithing & all of that Sort a thing but I feel a great deal More blissed & More contented & I sincerely hope the Lord will always keep Me so.[80]

We have the gifts & blissings, the power of performing Miracles. I have seen it Myself although I Never had any worked on Me. The Lord has always blessed Me with good health but I have faith if I Needed it he would also grant Me that confirmation. It is a poor one & happily I dont Need it. The reason I Say it is a poor one is, he that is confirmed in that way generally dont Last Long because at Some future time when they think that Such a blessing is Needed, the Lord May See that it is Not wisdom to grant such a blessing. Moral: the Lord will Not give his children poison even if they do ask it. Depend upon it he will Not grant what he in his far seeing wisdom sees will be a curse even if they think it would be a blessing. But there is a great deal depends upon a Man Living his Religion. Of course the More obeidient a child is to its Parents so Much More will those parents Like their child. And so Much More favours will be granted to that child. That is My idie on that particular point, but I suppose this is rather Musty reading for such as you.[81]

---

[80] James was probably attending church in Almy, Wyoming, where in the early 1870s regular Mormon meetings were being held. In 1878 a Mormon ward was established there. He had been involved in a "testimony meeting," at which members are encouraged to spontaneously express their belief and knowledge of the truth of Mormonism. Such meetings serve as a means of reinforcing publicly the faith commitments of the Latter-day Saints. It appears to be the beginning of James's conviction that Mormonism was for him.

[81] James is referring to the Mormon practice of anointing with oil and laying on of hands for the blessing of those who are ill. Of course, sometimes healings occur and sometimes they don't. However, according to Mormon belief, it is God who ultimately determines whether the healing should take place. James is reflecting the notion that one should not depend on miracles as the basis of

"The ring" is on its Last Legs. Governor Woods has been removed & Judge Mckean has also got the kick & he is practising at the bar where he was Judge for an attorney.[82] Governor Axtel in Woods's place & Judge Lowe in McKeans place.

I have just got up from Salt Lake City where I was getting My Naturalization papers. I stayed with Brother Hamilton Park & he treated Me very kind. So I got my papers & Now I can go & take up Land or anything. I was with Lot Smith part of the time. He Says he wants you to send your photograph by yourself. Lot Sends his Love to all the Folk & so does Hamilton. He wishes you were all here.

I wrote to sisy but I Never got an answer. I also wrote to David but received No answer. So I think they will "blink bonnielie" the Next one they get.[83] Father I have enough to contend with without their foolishness. . . . Your Loving son,

James MacNeil

John MacNeil to Ann MacNeil or Elizabeth Thompson

Alta City, Little
Cottonwood
4 May 1875

Dear Sister,

. . . Ive been on the Eve of Leaving this place for the Last 3 weeks but Cant Get My Money for 4 Months work which I did

---

one's faith. In describing his attempt at "theologizing" as "musty" compared to his father's knowledge of Mormonism, John suggests that his father had knowledge of Mormon thinking, on this subject at least.

[82] "The ring" refers to the non-Mormon federal officials who were perceived by the Mormons as attempting to undermine Mormon authority in Utah. Chief among these officials was James B. McKean, who was appointed Chief Justice of Utah by President U. S. Grant in 1870. McKean clashed frequently with the Mormons over interpretations of law and how much power the territorial government should have. He was also embroiled in conflicts with influential Gentiles, which hastened his departure as Chief Justice in March 1875. See Alexander, "Federal Authority versus Polygamic Theocracy," 86–100. George L. Woods was governor of Utah Territory 1871–74, and he cooperated fully with McKean in his campaign against polygamy. His successor, Samuel B. Axtell, had much more congenial relations with the Mormons.

[83] "Blink bonnilie" means that his brother and sister will be astonished (their eyes will open wide) if they ever hear from James again.

and I didnt want to write Until I Moved. But I havent got My Money Yet So I Concluded to drop You a few Lines anyhow. It isnt So Easy getting Money Out of Yankies Even when You work for it. There Natural Instinctive Swindlers. The real Yankie Possesses all the Mean traits of the Irish and his Own besides. So Much for Yankies. I would have done very well this Last Eight Months if I hade got My pay for My work but there is a dub at Every door[84] & So It is.

James has done well Since he Come here Considering the amount of work he has done. He hasnt worked half time Since he Come & he has Got 3 Cows & 3 heffers that will be Cows Next Year & a good Mare worth $75 dollers & he has Some Mining Claims also that Might Make him wealthy Yet if he perseveres.

I have Nothing Yet Except A Wife & a Lot of Young Ones but I am Contenteder than I was in the Old Country. We have always plenty of good grub to Eat. We Eat a whole Stear Ourselves this winter So You Can See we have beef Enough. I havent got a house of My Own Yet but hope to Soon. I have a Little piece of Land in Bountifull, 8 Acres, which I Intend putting a house on it this fall or perhaps Sooner. . . . [85]

Whatever My Father May think About My Opinions I Cant help. I am here & know things he dont. Nor wont, Until he Comes here & then he will perhaps be Like Some More of the honest in hart that has Come here. Heel Die with Chagrin & astonishment. But I have Nothing More to Say about it to No person. You Can all Come here & find Out for Yourselves & then Youll believe.

The Mormons Claim that Every Man has a free Agency that Comes on Earth & Yet they are as Much priest riden as the Catholics dare be but Youll find Out for Yourselves when You Come here. No More this time.

---

[84] Dub — a puddle — an obstacle at every door.

[85] John's name does not appear on the land deeds of Davis County, but Annie MacNeil is recorded as having bought 6.56 acres from Luther Burbank for seventy-five dollars on 21 May 1875. However, John is listed as the owner of this land on the Assessment Roll of Davis County and paid $2.28 as taxes in 1880. It was apparently sold to Malcolm MacDuff for four hundred dollars around 1880. The property was located east of Utah Highway 106 and west of the present Bountiful City Cemetery. Davis County Record of Deeds and Tax Assessment Rolls, Books D and F.

James Sends Kind Love to all of You. & accept the Same from Me & My Wife & Little Ones. Little Lizy the Second Oldest girl Says She will Catch a humming Bird for her Scotch Aunt Lizy & She Aint agoing to Let her Sister fall on it this time & Kill it, as She did before.[86] She Says Shes going to Send her Scotch Aunt Lizy a Live One. They were both at the Catching of it and they Scrambled for it & killed it betwixt them. . . . We are Your Loving Brother & Sister,

John & Annie McNeil

John MacNeil to David and Ann MacNeil

Alta City
Little Cottonwood
29 August 1875

Dear Father & Mother,

I take up my pen Once More to Write You a few Lines to Show You that I havent forgotten You altogether. Although I have ben long in Writing My Excuse is this I wanted to Get Moved before I wrote. Ive been fixing Me a home that I have Not had Leasure Enough to write but Ive got that Job done Now So Ill have More time to write. Ive built Me a good Loghouse, granery, Seller, Chicken coop & pig pens & bought Me two Cows & they have two Nice Calves. I have got a big Steer that will Make My winters beef & Ive got 8 acres of Land which Ive payed the Government for. So I Can Sell it or do what I please with it. So You See Im worth More Now for the 16 Months I been Married than all the rest of the time.

Ive Just got back to work again in the Silver Mines of Little Cottonwood & Left My wife & family below in the Valley about 45 Miles from Me which Makes it a Little unpleasant but it is the best we Can do at present. I Expect by Next Spring to be in a position So I Can be at home with My family More. After that I May Can assist You a little. We are all well & hope these few lines will find you the same. My Wife & Little ones Send there kind

---

[86] John's two foster daughters were Elizabeth (b. 18 June 1865) and Amberzine (b. 23 February 1868), daughters of Annie Cooper and her first husband, William Warrilow.

Love to you all & So does Lot Smith and accept the Same from Myself.

James has done Nothing for Nearly 3 Months but he is working Now & Ive been down in the Valley for over three Months building Me a home. So that Ive Earned Nothing for that Length of time Yet theres No Such a thing as having Nothing to Eat here. We have always plenty of provisions to do us a Year at Least & we Live better than we done in the Old Country. James is well and Sends his best wishes. I believe You wouldn't know him Now he has grown So big & Stout. He is 6 feet one inch & Lacks about 2 pounds of being 13 Stone wight [180 pounds].

There is great Excitement here about the Mountain Meadow Massacre. They are having the Supposed perpetrators tried but it isnt decided Yet.[87]

I Just Come into the Mountans two days ago & I Havent found work Yet but I Expect to Soon . . . write Soon & Let me know how your getting along & give me all the News. . . . Your Loving Son,

John McNeil

Elizabeth Haig Thompson to David and Ann MacNeil

Caseyville,
Illinois
20 September 1875

Dear Father & Mother,

It is with Sorrow i write to you to inform you of the Death of my Husband, your Son John Tohmson. He was Killed on the 30th Day of August by a fall of Coal. About 200 Bushels in one peice fell on him & Killed him dead but I Trust in god he is in a better place.[88]

---

[87] John D. Lee's trial began at Beaver, Utah, on 23 July 1875.

[88] According to the *Belleville Weekly Advocate*, 3 September 1875, John Thompson was killed in a fall of coal at the Wenona Mines near Belleville, Illinois. I am indebted to Mrs. Jane Shelley of Edwardsville, Illinois, for this reference. With the death of John, Ann Boggie MacNeil had lost all of the four sons she had by her first husband, John Thompson.

I hope you will excuse me for not writen Sooner. I have been Sick ever Since his deth & Elisiabeth, Johney and Robert have all had the fever and Ague every Second day So i could not get a minet to spare from attending to them. Please to write & Send me Johneys correct age.

Some of My Brothers will write to you in a week or two and give you an account of Johneys Death and Curcumstances.

Hopping this will find you all in better health and Spirits [than] it Leaves myself and the Children. I hope you will let Johneys Sisters Know of his Sad fate.

I can say no more but trust to God to give Strenth and suport to my Dear Husbands Mother that She may be able to bear the Sad news that this Letter brings to her. I Remain your Daughter,

Elizabeth Thompson

James B. MacNeil to David MacNeil, Jr.

Alta City
14 October 1875

Dear Brother,

. . . I have been very busy of late that is the excuse I have to offer for not writing Sooner. I am out of work just now owing to the Mine Shuting down that I was working at. The Superintendent Says I will get the first Shour but I dont want to work for nothing and board myself. I cant get what I have already worked for, for quite a while yet. So I will try to get A job Some otherwhere. It is Conference time just now & and I would like very much to go to it but owing to what I have already mentioned I cant go.

President Grant has been here. He came on Sunday and left the City on tuesday morning. This is first time that any of the Presidents has been out west and he didnt go any farther than Salt Lake City, didnt go to California at all. I think his reasons for coming here was to Satisfy himself as to the State of affairs in utah There has been So many lies told about this country and this people, the one conflicting with the other, that he thought he would come and See for himself but he did not Stay long enough to make true observations.[89]

I See by Fathers letter that you are living there So I will direct this to him. David, A Miners Live in this country is a hard one but he has A chance to Make A raise Sometime in his life, whereas A man may work all his life there for a bare living. Some makes it in no time, others it takes years. There has been a time when I thought I had it. Last Spring I thought I had Sure but it Slipped Me. Nothing More of interest this time. I am as ever your Loving Brother,

James MacNeil

James B. MacNeil to David and Ann MacNeil

[Cottonwood Canyon]
25 December 1875

Dear Father and Mother,

I have just received your very welcome letter dated Nov 30th [and] was glad to hear from you. Times are pretty dull there just now. It is so here likewise. It seems as if there was no money in the country just now but hope for better days.[90]

I took a contract three weeks ago to run fifty feet of tunnel for a california company. It is chance worke whether I make at it or not. I have 18 dollars per foot for it. Men were plenty and I had to take it cheap to get it. It will keep me in work for a while any how. I sent for John and he is working on it with me. We have a thousand dollars worth of work to do altogether and I think it is likely I can rustle a few dollars together in the spring and if David wants to come out here all he has to do is to Say so.

---

[89] Although President Grant was paid much deference and honor during his visit, on his return to Washington, D.C., he continued the "get-tough" policies that had characterized his administration. Like many other federal officials, he was determined to eradicate polygamy as a threat to moral law and order. In December 1871, Grant's annual address to Congress referred to polygamy as "a remnant of barbarism, repugnant to civilization, decency and the laws of the United States." Cited in Alexander, "Conflict of Perceptions," 36.

[90] The depression that set in during 1873 lasted until 1879, and the United States went from being perceived as a land of economic opportunity to a land of economic gloom. In the words of one historian, "the apostles of pessimism reigned supreme." Hicks, *American Nation*, 77-79.

But I want it to be under-stood that he does come here he must not say that I seperated him from his wife. I dont want any of that in mine.

I have about three hundred dollars owing to me now but I cant get it. You say you would require fifty Pounds to open your new place. Father I dont mean to hurt your feelings but if it was only fifty cents you wanted to open it I would not let you have it. I thinke that is a losing game and has been from the beginning. If you want to come out here I will do everything in my power to assist you but I begin to doubt whether you want to come out here. But it is a thing I wont do is to work hard in the mountains to get money to distribute amongst a lot of rascals and cheats. I know your foible Father to well. Any other purpose on gods earth rather than that. I have said enough on this subject to let you know what I mean; that is that you shall come out of that abominable hole if you want too.

I was down town last night. Had to wade to my breast in snow to get there and just a few hours before three men were killed by a snow slide. Their bodies have not been found yet. One of them I was well aquainted with. There is other Seven missing.[91]

Tell David if he wants to come out here in the spring to be prepared. It gave me very sad thoughts when I read of Johnnie Thomson deaths.[92] We had a very dull Christmas, I can tell you. Just got your letter day before. I will draw to a close by wishing you all a happy New Year. As ever your Son,

James MacNeil

[PS] Lot Smith wants to know why you have not wrote to him. Sends his best wishes to all. Write soon please.

---

[91] The men killed in this snowslide in Gladiator Gulch were James Moore and John Douglas of the Highland Chief mine and John Gustason of the Gladiator Mine. Moore and Douglas were on their way to Christmas dinner with a friend when they triggered the slide. The unusually warm, spring-like weather at Christmas 1876 may have also contributed to the avalanche. See *Salt Lake Tribune*, 23 and 28 December 1875. In December of the following year a slide at Alta killed all seven residents of the B. H. Wellington boarding house. See *Deseret News*, 1 January 1877.

[92] He is referring to the death in Illinois of his half brother, John Thompson.

5

"Confident of Sucess as Ever"

Letters from James Brady MacNeil, John MacNeil, Elizabeth
Haig Thompson, Ann MacNeil, Jr., and Allen Hendry

1876–85

Most of the letters in the period 1876–85 were written by James
Brady MacNeil as he moved from Alta in Big Cottonwood Canyon of the Wasatch Mountains to the banks of the Gila River in
Arizona. The other letters are mainly from John, who was farming in Bountiful and trying to make ends meet through mining. In
addition to the notes written by Ann MacNeil, Jr., and her father
David, Sr., we briefly meet Allen Hendry, a friend of James, who
informed Ann MacNeil of her brother's death. There is also a
single letter from the widow of John Thompson, Betsy Haig
Thompson, in Illinois, which tenderly described the close relationship she and her husband had enjoyed.

Even though James and John attempted to work together
mining silver at Alta, Utah, the partnership did not last and the
two brothers separated. For a short period John followed James
to southern Utah where James mined for silver at Silver Reef.
However, by 1881 James had moved to Arizona Territory, where
he acquired enough money in bossing at a mine to allow him to
settle as a farmer in Graham County. For the next few years everything went well for him, and he settled down as a farmer. James
even hoped to return to Scotland on a mission for the church.
Predictably, John felt that his young, idealistic brother was building castles in the air.

During this period, the letters also give us some insight into
the attitudes of the women in the family. Ann MacNeil, Sr., simply refused to consider going to America, and it is obvious that
she and her children Ann, Elizabeth, and David, Jr., do not accept

the Mormon message. In his moralizing manner, James chastises his mother for not obeying her husband as she promised at the altar. He also calls his sisters to repentance and to acknowledge the light of the Mormon gospel, which had become a beacon to him.

David MacNeil, Sr., was not a particularly stable individual. Around 1878 his second drapery business was sold at a public bankruptcy auction. At about the same time, he left his wife for another woman. James blamed his father for the family's departure from Mormonism — his failure to control his passions had set a poor example. But despite his shortcomings, his sons still felt some sense of obligation to him and made vain efforts to get him to the United States.

Because David, Sr., no longer lived with his wife, most of James's letters are addressed to his brother David and sisters Elizabeth Thompson and Ann MacNeil. By this time David, Jr., had six children and he and his family were thinking of emigrating. However, neither moralizing nor "a stoot hert tae a stye brae" (a stout heart to a steep hill) could compensate for the harsh realities that had to be faced when James MacNeil died pursuing his dream in Arizona.

As this group of letters ends, we find John MacNeil 1,000 miles from his home and family taking care of his brother's business affairs in Arizona, where John reveals once again his tendency to suspect the worst of people. In his letters to Ann and Lizzie he engages in virulent criticism of the Mormons among whom James had settled. One wonders if anyone could ever meet the high standards John MacNeil sets for others. Nor, perhaps, could he ever meet the high expectations he had of his own life.

According to his family tradition John MacNeil stopped wearing temple garments at some time in the late 1870s, a sign that he no longer considered himself part of the Mormon community. One factor in this decision may have been the actions of his Mormon neighbors in Bountiful, who are reported to have cut his fences and allowed their cattle to graze on his land and crops. However, it is also reported that he would not allow his children to criticize the leaders of the church in his home. His wife, Annie Cooper MacNeil was a very committed Latter-day Saint and contributed money to the LDS Church out of her meager resources. As far as can be determined, his children remained in the church.

Apparently John MacNeil did not go out of his way to undermine their commitment to Mormonism.[1]

To the very end, both brothers played out roles that seem almost predetermined. Indeed, their responses to life were perhaps part of their genetic and social inheritance—for James the Hopeful, one must bump at life until one succeeds; for John the Skeptic, one is incessantly faced with a "dub [puddle] at every door" which makes success well nigh impossible.

John MacNeil to David and Ann MacNeil

Alta City
Little Cottonwood
23 January 1876

Dear Father & Mother,

I take up My pen after due Consideration to drop You a few Lines to Let You know how I am getting along at present. We had a dull Christhmus, Our baby being Sick.[2] It has been Sick Eight Months Now and Circumstances Uses Me rough generaly although thats the Only Sickness Ive had to trouble Me in the family. But theres Such a Multiplicity of Men in this Country Now, that works Scarcely to be Got. You have to be well acquainted to get a Job Now & wages are Small Likewise. But we have always plenty to Eat, thank God. If I get two Months work in the Year I Can Live Now with My Cows but its hard to Get hold of Money.

James talks Some of Sending for David in the Summer but hees afraid heel blame him for parting him from his wife. Me & him are working together on a Contract in Little Cottonwood Kanyon. We are running 50 feet on a tunnel at $18 dollers per foot but its pretty hard & James hasnt the bottom required. Hees too anxious to do it all in a day and it Cant be done. He Cant Make it fly like Coal & it gets away with his patience Not having None.[3]

He also builds two Many Castles in the air. He has his Calculations Made what to do a Year or two ahead. Hees going to

---

[1] Interview with Mrs. Gladys H. Thorne, 28 December 1984.

[2] The baby referred to is Ann Eliza MacNeil, who at this time was fourteen months old.

[3] The reason it would not "fly like coal" is that most of the rock in Alta is quartzite, commonly referred to as granite.

take You all out this Year & hees going to bring Johny thompson & David & hees going to Marry pretty Soon & hees Going to Arizona and God of Heaven knows all that he is going to do this Year.[4] If he pays what he Ows this Year & brings David, heel do very well.

I think in the Coarse of another Year Ill be able to help a little but Ive had to Look to home first. I hadnt 10 Cents in the world when I got Married and three people to Look after and a home to Make, and only worked 5 weeks this Last Eight Months Until Now. This Job will do about 2 Months I Expect, after that I dont known what Next.

Lot Smith has been Called to go down South to Arizona to Open Up a New Country, an hostile Indian Country to.[5] There is a Croud going. James Was going to go to if he hadnt been Engaged to the Contract. His Minds runs Every ways. Its what they Call the Summer Complaint thats the Matter with the Young One.

Ive been very healthy Myself Ever Since I Come to the Country or it would [have] been hard with Me Many a time. Its a rough life Mining in this Country it takes a Man to be in proper health . . . I was sorrow to hear of the Death of Johny Thompson. It Made Me think a Little. Give kind Love to Leezy & Ann & Janet & Mother & Maggie & David & all Inquiring Friends. . . . Your affectionate Son.

John McNeil

Elizabeth Haig Thompson to [Elizabeth Thompson?]

Belleville
[Illinois]
9 April 1876

Dear sister,

I take the pleasure of answering your kind and welcome letter and i was glad to see from it that you was all well except

---

[4] Johnny Thompson was the son of William Thompson, the MacNeils' half brother. He came to Arizona through James's assistance, c. 1882.

[5] Lot Smith was called by the Mormon Church leadership to help establish Mormon colonies in the lower valley of the Little Colorado, Arizona, early in 1876. Eventually Smith presided over the Little Colorado Stake of the LDS Church—the equivalent of a bishop's diocese in the Catholic Church. His colo-

mother. I did not expect that she would be well. I know that it was a great trial to her.

Dear sister, i would have write sooner but the children and myself has been sick. I have not been verry well since John death. Weer are all well at present. Thank god for his goodness to us. You want to know how i was getting along and the childerns ages: Elizabeth is 10 years, John is 8 years, Robert is 5, george is 17 mounths. The county gives me 5 dolars a mounth and that Just pays the rent and i go out a washing to help and my Brothers dose the reast. There is two sisters in the church has been verry good to me but the most of the Brenethen is poor in the church.

It has been a great trial to me. Stil i know that the lord is good to his children and i know if i live faithful to the end i shal meet with him again for he did live and die a fathful Brother in christ. I had 10 years of a happy married life. He went to the greave [without] ever giving me [an] angry word. He verry often said to me, "I wonder if thear is man and woman as happy as we are."

He had large funeral. Thear were 23 carragas and a herse. The coal diggers marched and the sunday scool children marched three miles to the graveyard. About his age, he was 38 this last december 27. I have his age in the house. My Brother Robert wrote that letter and i was in so much trouble he never asked me. That was his reasens for askning you.

Work is verry dul here at present. They dig for 2 cents a Bushel.

I live about 9 miles from mother. It is much healther hear and a good Branch of the church. You know my folks is verry much aganst the church. . . . The children send love to their grand-mother and to you. They say they wold like to see you Both. No more at present but reamans your sister,

Elizabeth [Thompson]

[PS] Be sure and write soon.[6]

nizing activities are detailed in Peterson, *Take Up Your Mission*. See also Peterson, "A Mighty Man Was Brother Lot," 393–413.

[6] Although other letters from Betsy Thompson may have been written to her husband's family in Scotland, none have survived and little is known about the Thompson family in Illinois. As the widow of a Civil War veteran, Betsy applied for, and was granted, a pension of eight dollars per month under the provisions of the Pension Act of 1890. In an affidavit in support of her claim to

James B. MacNeil to David and Ann MacNeil

Salt Lake City
12 October 1876

Dear Father & Mother,

You perhaps think I have forgotten you but it is not so, believe me in this particular at least. No doubt you think you have a very undutiful Son in me. I have no doubt it do Seem that way to you, but pray do not think too hardly of me. God alone can judge the heart. I have been unfortunate and I did not wish to crowd my misfortunes on my parents and so I shut them up in my own bosom. I asked no one to Share them With me and So I kept Silent that is the reason I did not write Sooner.

The Last time I wrote to you I told you I had got a Contract and had taken My Brother John in with me. John wrote and told the truth of the matter I Suppose. At least if he did not inform you he did it here, that is was only an ambuscad prepared for his ruin. The Contract did not pay. We could not make wages at it, the rock changed so much. My name alone was Signed to that Contract So you will See what amount of Skill was displayed in making that ambuscade for my unwary Brother. It is needless to Say we quarreled often and Sometimes hard words passed between us Brothers but did ever I write to you blaming my Brother John for my misfortunes. Read my correspondence and answer.

That Contract was finished and accepted and John had two hundred dollars coming to him for work done on that Contract, the wages I aggreed to pay him, after he drew out of the Contract. Which two hundred dollars I paid him when the Contract was finished. I was out my work on it. And was two hundred dollars in debt two the provision Stores besides. Now I ask no favour what ever. All I would wish is Justice in your feelings. Weigh the pros and cons of the matter and I will accept your ultimatum what ever it may be. This I must tell you, John and myself

a pension, her neighbors Joseph E. Betts, Sr., and Mrs. Mary Groom stated that her only income was earned from "her own daily labor in washing and ironing clothes and house scrubbing and cleaning . . . she is poor and very dependent and in actual need of a pension." Another affidavit simply stated, "She has had a hard struggle since her husband's death." She died at Belleville on 8 May 1918. Military Service Records of John Thompson and Declaration for Widow's Pension submitted by Elizabeth Haig Thompson, National Archives.

can never be Friends, and Brother in name alone. This is not a conclusion come to in the heat of the moment. No, I have thought over it a long time and I have come to the conclusion that I can never forgive in this world for the words he used in talking to me at that time and his utter disregard for my feelings.

I was Sick for awhile after my contract was finished then I started to work but was hardly commenced untill I had to quit owing to a sore finger, the middle finger of my right hand. It turned out to be the whittle.[7] I have been off ten weeks with it. I had it opened and the bone taken out of the first joint. It is getting well now.

Father Dear, if you can only Struggle on a little longer I will try to releive you soon. And mother Dear, keep up your heart. I wont forget you, depend upon it. Father, I know the world better than I did and learned to face difficultys which at one time I would have pronounced insurmountable. Such is the effect of being sent out into the world and thrown on your own resourses. It is good for a youth to be knocked about in the world because nine tenths of the Sum total of youths enter life with a Surplusage of Self Conceit. The Sooner they are releived the better. If in measuring themselves with wiser and older men than themselves they discover that it is unwarrented and get rid of it gracefully of their own accord, well and good. If not, it is desirable for their own sake that it Should be knocked out of them.

This world is great public School and it Soon teaches a new pupil his proper place. If he has the attributes that belong to a leader he will take his place as such. If not, whatever his own opinion of his abilities, he will have to back into the rank and file by the time he as found his legitimate position in the world, be the same high or low. The probability is that the disagreeable traits of his character will be softened down and worn away. Most likely the process of abrasion will be rough perhaps very rough, but when it is all over and he begins to see himsel as ithers See him and not as reflected in the mirror of Self conceit, he will be thankfull he has run the gauntlet and arrived though by a rough road at knowledge.

---

[7] James was suffering from a whitlow (or felon), an infected inflammation of the finger, especially around the nail.

No matter what Loving mothers may think to the contrary, it is good for a young man to be knocked about in the world "it makes men of them." As Burns Says,

> And even should misfortunes come,
> I here wha Sit hae met wi some,
> And thankfu for them yet,
> They gae the wit o age to youth;
> They let us ken oorsel;
> They mak us See the naked truth
> The real good and ill:
> Tho losses and crosses
> Be lessons right severe
> Theres wit there, ye'll get there,
> Ye'll find nae ither where.[8]

I heard Bro Brigham preach a sermon a few sundays ago. He spoke with great force. I thought a great deal of it. It is curious the different ideas that are afloat in the world. America is a country of free thinkers and it is astonishing how far men will go when left to themselves. Clever learned men Seeking to come to an ultimatum in regard to God and religion through Science. But tis of no use their trying, because truth will come through the channel of truth alone and that is God.

> But this world is wise with wisdom Slowly culled,
> And men grown bold like well trained hunters leap
> From crag to crag of truth with sight undulled
> Oer precipieces Steep.[9]

Seemingly without a consideration as to what they are doing.

Is David living in Glasgow just now Father and how is he moving along with his wife if I may ask. And is Sister Ann married yet. There is Some good men here although I dont know whether She could find her ideal here amongst them or not. I wrote to Lizzie but she never answered it, so I guess I wont write

---

[8] From the seventh stanza of Robert Burns, "Epistle to Davie, A Brother Poet."

[9] The source of these lines could not be determined. The Brigham Young sermon to which James refers was given at the Third Ward in Salt Lake City on 8 October 1876. At this meeting Young talked about the superiority of religious revelation over science as a way of knowing about God. *JD* 18:257-64.

any more to that Sister. One Slieght is plenty for me. I would like
to know how grannie is getting along and if she has enough to live
on. . . .

I will ask you once more to hunt up my geneaology and
post me in regard to it. I would like to know very much if you will
be so kind. The Endowment house has been moved to the temple
in Saint George three hundred and Sixty miles South of here.[10] I
have an idea of going down to Arizona next fall. Lot Smith is
down there trying to make a Settlement in that country and it is
up hill work. A hard country it is. There is lots of people coming
back from the pioneer companys. If I can get my bussines Settled
up here I will try to dispose of my claims in cottonwood next
Summer and if I can I will go down there.[11]

I had a letter From Brother Lot A little while ago. He Sends
you all his best respects. Father, I think you slighted Brother Lot
a little dont you think so. He is very good man. A Sterling man I
think. He fully expected you to write to him Father. He has been
a true Friend of mine and as such I will continue to respect him.
He is a better man than those you think more of, not Saying who
or which. However Suit your own self Father.[12]

If you need a hundred & fifty or two hundred dollars I can
get it for you but if you can get along without pinching yourself I
will try and do better next year. But if you need it write immedi-

---

[10] James is referring to the fact the Endowment House in Salt Lake City
was closed for a few years in order to promote use of the St. George Temple for
vicarious baptisms and endowments for the dead. I am indebted to M. Guy
Bishop of the Seaver Center for Western History Research, Los Angeles, for this
insight.

[11] That Lot Smith was writing to James at this time suggests that he may
have been trying to influence him to go south, but no official church statement
linking James to the Little Colorado mission could be found, although James
later says he had been called on a mission to Arizona. James was correct about
the large numbers who abandoned the mission. Smith himself acknowledged
that most who went originally "got weak in the knees or back" and went home.
Cited in Peterson, *Take Up Your Mission*, 59.

[12] None of Smith's records about his mission to Scotland have survived,
and the present letters give no indication of the cause of David MacNeil's alienation from Lot Smith. Perhaps David was simply falling away from the faith
and didn't want to be confronted by such a strong-willed person as Lot Smith. It
is clear, however, from the number of times he is mentioned in the letters that
Lot Smith held a special place in the thoughts of the MacNeils — especially James,
who seemed to admire the red-headed, volatile "Brother Lot."

ately and let me know. If I had what is owing to me I could make you a nice present but I dont expect it now.

How is Sister Janet and Johnie [McLean] making it. Tell me all about my old aquaintances how they are getting along. I will draw to a close now hoping this will find you all in good health and Spirit. I remain your Faithful Son,

James Brady McNeil

[PS] Enclosed find two photographs. Brothe and Sister Lawson Send you their respects, tailor Lawson of motherwell branch.

John MacNeil to David and Ann MacNeil

Alta City
Little Cottonwood
16 December 1876

Dear Father & Mother,

I take up My pen Once More to drop You a few Lines. It is a Long time Since I tried it before and perhaps Ive Learned how to write truths Now. So Ill try at any rate.

You May See by My Letter that I am Not at home Nor am I very often. There is Nothing to do for a Man in the Valley. It is all farming and they Mostly do there Own work. So I have to be away from home Nearly all the time. It is rather Unplesent but it is Nothing in this Country. It takes Me Scratching to get along on account of work being So hard to get. This Country is Overrun with Men and a Man Cant do Much farming Without a Span of horse and a wagon. He has got to have a Start. Theres No Use talking, it takes time & Money to accomplish it. If God Spares Me Until Spring I am Going to try & get Me a wagon & horses So I Can do farming for a Living.

This Mining in this Country is to rough a Life for A Man to Stand Long No Matter how Stout he is. It is beginning to wear Me Old already & Ive been as Stout & tough as any person You Ever Saw. Since Ive been in this Country I Can Stand Up to work that would kill James in two Months, but Ive got five to feed & Cloth Now. But its an Easy Matter to get plenty of Eat in this Country provisions is So Cheap but theres Other things besides Eatables Neaded.

You Can Judge it a Curious Country when I tell You I am doing Blacksmithing for a Living at One of the Mines. I thought I Could do Nothing of the kind in the Old Country but in this Country You Must Say You Can do anything. There is No Such thing as Cant do and dont know in this Country. You Must Say You know Everything and Can do Everything. Even if You dont know Your behind from a hole in the grund.

I will be in a better position when I Can farm for a Living. Then I Can go to the Mines in the winter a Month or two and Ill Make More headway then. Ive got to have $325 dollers to get Me a team wagon and harnes, but if I have Luck to Stay at work till Spring I Can accomplish it Nicely.

Ive got a very Careful Saving woman but She dont turn out Nothing but girls & that Makes it bad for John, for he wanted a boy to do the ploughing when he Started farming. But She Says its My fault & I Say its hers, So there the Matter Stands. . . .

James is working here also but Not at the Same Mine as Me. He is in good health Now but he has had very bad Luck for Over a Year. He had a Sprained arm, then boils, then pluricy, then the whuttle in his finger. He Lost One Joint, and one thing after another Like that for Over a Year, & to tope [it] of took [on] a Contract that didnt pay. But hees getting Over it Now.

My Wife Gives Me Hell three times per week for Not writing to You, but My hands are So big & Stiff & Clumsy that I hate to take a pen up, but Il try and write a Little Oftener. James Sends respects to all.

I would like if You could Send Me a real good rasor & prooning knife by Hamilton G. Park when he Comes hom. . . .[13]
[PS] Adres as before
J. H. MacNeil, Davis Coy, Utah.[14]

---

[13]At this time Hamilton G. Park was serving his third mission in Scotland.

[14]John added an initial "H" to his name and changed the spelling to "MacNeil," probably to distinguish him from the other McNeils in Bountiful. John regarded them as Irish, although they were actually from the Isle of Man. There is a persistent myth among Scots that "Mc" is Irish while "Mac" is Scottish, but "Mc" is used in contracting "Mac" (meaning "son of") in both Irish and Scottish names.

[PS] Write Soon whether I write or Not & tell Ann to write to Me also. Excuse bungles, Fur I am John.

James B. MacNeil to David MacNeil, Jr.

Alta City
5 August 1877

Dear Brother,

I take the present Opportunity of Answering your welcome Letter . . . the reason of My delay in writing to you was I was Not in a Settled State and did Not know where I Might go to. I have Not done anything for three Months. Could Not get anything to do times was So dull. I have got Started to work Now but wages are So low that one can't Save Much and what I have I have been in Such difficulties for the past two years that it has taken it all to pay My debt and have Not got clear yet. "But a stoot heart to a Stey brae [A stout heart to a steep hill]". I wont be long in getting all right Now.

I get two Dollars per Day and board. I work ten hours per day but it is Not very exausting. Dont work Near So hard as they do in Coal Mines but it is Not So healthy. However, there is as good wages paid here as anywheres in America that I know of. There are Some that do very well here and every Spring that I have been here there has always been two or three poor cusses "Struck it" and Made their little pile and it May Come My turn Some Spring. If it does come you May be Sure that I will remember you. Nothing would give me So Much pleasure as to have you here on a farm. . . .

[this part of the letter is damaged, but James seemed to be bearing testimony to his brother that Mormonism is the true religion]

But dont go anywhere with the idea that you are going to get Everything your own way. You will find it very different from that No Matter where you go. As Soon as I get Enough to bring you I will give you the chance. . . . Your Affectionate Brother,

James B. McNeil

[PS] . . . I will be glad to get the Photograph of your Boy. I have Not got any Song that you Sent me.

James B. MacNeil to Ann MacNeil

Bountiful
8 May 1878

Dear Sister Ann,

I got your letter last Night and hasten to reply to the Same.
I am glad to hear that my Folks are well as this leaves Me at
present.

The Subject of your Letter is rather painful to an honour-
able Minded Man to contemplate. This I will talk plain over. That
is my Style. In the first place, My Mother done wrong in refusing
to come here. It is a wifes place to lover honour & obey her husband which She vows Solemly before God at the Alter to do. And
the Woman that has Not Made up her Mind to do that Same has
no right to Marry untill she finds a man that she can Love, honour,
& obey. My Father done wrong there is no doubt of that.[15] My
Sense of Honour and right would condemn him because there is
no circumstances that can justify a Man or woman in doing wrong.
They have a right to do right, but no right to do wrong. You Say
you dont know what might happen Should My Father and David
Meet. Well it would Not Faiz David Much to do My Father an
injury in any case. If he can look back upon his own life and find
it is without a Stain let him be carefull to keep it so. But he will
find out Some time that he has Exceeded his position and authority if he Ever takes upon himself to judge and inflict punishment
upon those that are older and wiser in every way than himself. So
that he had better go Slow.

If my Father thinks he can begin life in this country and
live right controlling his passions, I should advise his coming here.
He will find plenty room to do right in this country if he wishes so
to do. But he will find there is less inducements to do wrong than

---

[15] Although this letter gives no details regarding the actual wrong that
David, Sr., had committed, apparently he had left his wife for another woman.
James seems to partially justify his father's actions by blaming his mother's out-
right refusal to leave Scotland. It was not unusual for families to be split in this
way. For instance, in 1866 Mary Murdoch Mair of Gaswater, Ayrshire, left her
husband, James, and a son in Scotland and took her other son and two daughters to Utah when James refused to "gather to Zion." For years James left the
door unbarred at night in the hope that she would return. See Nicol, ed., *James
and Mary Murray Murdoch Family History*, 90–91.

where he come from. It is a big country but not big enough to hold him if he ever done wrong.

If he chooses to come here. I will send money Enough in two months from Now to fetch him. In the Meantime encourage him to Earn an honest Living until that time.

I am going down South. I Start tomorrow. You can Show David this letter. . . . I remain as Ever your Brother,

Jas B. MacNeil

John MacNeil to David MacNeil, Sr.

Bountiful
Davis Coy
20 April 1879

Dear Father,

. . . I recd Yours of Jan. 31st all right but have been knocking around the Country hunting work and the Letter hunting Me. You have very Little Idea of this Country & I wouldnt try to Convince You that I am Capable of telling the truth about anything. I want You and Everybody Else to come here & Convince themselves.

I have 4 Children. Besides my Wife I had five. One Died Jan 22d.[16] I Cant Complain about having plenty to Eat but Money is hard to get hold of and Clothing & Shoes are high in Comparison with the Scarcity of Money. Its a hard Country for a Man Like Me with No Education, but a Man Like You Can Make Money. Even Yet, Ill bet all Im worth. If You had Come here in place of John Thompson You would have been Wealthy today.[17] The doller is the Salvation Every bedys after here.

My reason for Not answering Davids Letter, it was a tirrade about You runing away with a woman & So forth & I thought he Ought to have talked Last, or in Other words, took the Mote Out of his Own Eye before he began picking Someones Else. This is the reason.

---

[16] His first son, John, was born 22 December 1878 and died 19 January 1879.

[17] He is referring to his half brother John Thompson, who left Scotland in 1857.

If You think You would Like to Come here I will Ensure You of plenty to Eat any how & if You would Like to Come here Now Your down, Let Me know & I and James May be Able to Scratch up Enough to fetch You if You wish it.[18] Theres No use Me Denying it, I have a hard Strugle with the Crowd I have to keep going. I have been putting Myself in a position to get a Living without Mining and it Costs Considerable to do it. Namely to get two horse, a wagon, plough, Harrow Cultivator &c &c and at the Sametime keep My Family and buy My Land to. My hands had been pretty full but I think Ive Nearly Mounted the hill. My Little boy Dieing this Season Set Me back also but if You wish to Come here Let Me know Soon as possible & Ill See what we Can do towards it.

This Country is in a bad State Just Now to, but it gets Over it quicker than the Old Country.[19]

I havent quite Lost all feeling of Humanity Yet, although Ive had It dulled Considerable. James assisted it and I had Enough of trouble of My Own without borrowing any. Ill always do My duty to My Family First and them that [are] Nearest & Dearest Next. I dont think Youll find Me Altered a bit as regards principle. All the difference there is in Me is I think for Myself Now and give Everyone the Same Privilege.[20]

The Last I heard of James he was in St George Living with Your Uncle Archie. It is 350 Miles from here. He was Mining for himself & Uncle Archie then. That is Nearly two Months Ago. He was well then. . . . The Children Say they would Like to See there Scotch Grandpa. . . . Accept Our best wishes for Your Weel Meantime.

> I remain Your Affectionate
> Son,
> John H. MacNeil

---

[18] The reference to David, Sr., being "down" may refer to the fact that he lost his draper's business in 1878. According to a "Bankrupt Stock" broadside among the MacNeil letters, David MacNeil's drapery business was sold by "Public Roup" at Wishaw 22 April 1878. This may have been a contributing factor in his leaving his wife; at least the two events — the trauma of bankruptcy and leaving his wife — are closely related in time.

[19] The United States was in a severe economic depression between 1873 and 1878.

[20] This statement may be seen as John's declaration of independence from the Mormon Church.

John MacNeil to David MacNeil

Bountiful
Davis Coy
18 July 1879

Dear Father,

I take this Opportunity of answering Yours of May 15th. You No doubt think I Might have wrote Sooner but Circumstances alters Cases. I was 70 Miles from home when i Recd Your Letter, working in the Mountains & twenty Miles from any Store & had No writing Material along. I Come home on the 1st of July & found harvest ready. The grain was ripe, the Hay ready to Cut all at one time & I had to waltz in & help So as to get help Myself with My Own & it was helter Skelter for a few days.[21] The grain ripened so fast this Season all in a day or two we have had Such dry winds. We had to work Night & day to Save it & I Can tell You it [is] hard work in the hot Sun. It Nearly kills Me Yet.

I have heard No word from James Yet. I write to him today. I havent got a cent of pay Yet for that work I done in the Mountains when I got Your Note. Nor dont know when if Ever but Ill try to rais the Money Someway although I dont know how Just Now.[22] Crops is very Light this Season on account of the drought. Everything Nearly burned up. The worst Season for 15 Years. They have had Still Enough to Eat. I think Ill have Enough to bread us anyhow & potatoes Enough & the winter before Me to get the Clothing & Shoes & groceries [etc]. So if I Can Only rais the Money to fetch You I think we can get along.

The Young Ones has Great talk about their Scotch Grand pa Coming. . . . I will write pretty Soon again I am So tired & unstedy this time You Must Excuse Short letters. Your Affectionate Son,

John H. MacNeil

[PS] Write Soon please

---

[21] He is referring to the rural cooperative practice of mutual assistance during the harvest period.

[22] David, Sr., has apparently requested assistance in coming to Utah. However, he remained in Scotland until the fall of 1889.

James B. MacNeil to Ann MacNeil

> Silver Reef[23]
> Washington Coy,
> Utah
> 15 September [1879?]

Dear Sister,

I received Your very welcome Letter tonight & hasten to reply. In the first place I was glad to Hear from Home, and in the Next place I was glad to Have You write Me a letter that I can realize was written from the Heart. There is Nothing dark or Misterious about that & I can understand Clearly.

You Say that Mother grew very anxious about Me. I am Sorry that I gave Her any uneasiness on My account. Tell My Mother that Her boy Can take care of Himself, dont fear, & if You were all Here I could take Care of You all Just as Easy as I can take Care of Myself. Because what it Costs to board Me would keep A family Very Comfortable & None of You Need want for any thing if You were only Here.

You Must think fearfully Hard of Me to think that I would let You want while I had it or Could get it. That is Not what My religion teaches Me at all. Quite the reverse. It teaches Me to Love all & to Help those in Need and I will be willing to be judged accordingly by the great judge of all.

Now the reason that I did Not Send You any Money in Your Hour of Need was this. I had No Money to Send to You. The first 5 Years Earnings I Spent in prospecting trying to find A Mine. Well I did Not Suceed. Consequeently the 5 Years Labour went for Nothing. Then I thought that I would quit Mining & turn My attention to Farming & I done So & just about this time the crash Came at Home & for 10 Months I had Not twenty five

---

[23] James was working at Silver Reef, eighteen miles northeast of St. George. According to Nels Anderson, "Silver Reef was a shack town, its main street lined with saloons, gambling places, and other conveniences for sinners. St. George was a moral family town, where the humble domestic virtues were glorified." For a vivid comparative social analysis of these two towns at the time James was mining there, see Anderson, *Desert Saints*, 428-34. In the surviving fragment of an earlier letter to his brother David, James noted that he was working in a silver mine twenty miles from where his father's "comparitivly rich" "Uncle Archie" MacNeil lived. Their Utah kin wished that David, Jr., would come to Utah.

Cents because I was working for Trade & Could Not get Money for My Labour. Money is very Scarce amongst the Farming Class.

If I cannot Make You beleive in My inability to Help You at that time the only thing that I Can do in the Matter is to prove to You in future My Love for My Mother, Brother & Sister by giving to them when I Can. I will Make any Sacrifice in My power to prove to You My regard, & if You Say Come Back & do as You done formerly I will Come Back & do so. But it would Break My Heart to live there as I done Formerly & I dont think that I Could do as well by You all there as I Can Here. . . .

I concluded to try Mining again So that I could get Money to Send Home & that is what I am working for Now and just as I get it I will Send it to you. That is the best I Can do. I thought that I would Save the Money that I Earned & buy a place for a Home for You then Send Money & bring You Here & put You in A Home of Your own where the Cares & anxieties of life would be lessened. I Could Have Saved Enough by Next Spring to Have bought Such A place in A quiet little town Close by Here Called St George, the Nicest town in Utah. There is where I would like to Make My Home & that is where I would like to be along with You all. But if You rather that I would Send My Earnings Home I shall Certainly do So.

You thought that Simply because My Religious Convictions differed from You that I would Not Help My own Mother when in Need. John Differs from Me in that regard but He is welcome to all that I Have whenever He Needs it. Just last Night I Sent Him 50 dollars So that He Could fix His family & Come Down Here as I think that I Can get Him work Here. John bought A New farm this last Spring and I guess He is tight run just Now. If it Had Not been for Helping Him I Could just as Easily Have Sent You A Hundred dollars but this $50 that I Send to You is all the Money that I Have at the present.

Now the reason that I Had Come to the Conclusion Not to write to You any More was this, I Never could get an answer in any reasonable time. I Have a Very retentive Memory and I wrote to You and You Never answered it for a Year and at the Same time You were writing to John and Sending Him little presents. Now I want only to be Considered good Enough to write to. I wrote to You in the Month of November and Just Exactly 10 Months Elapsed when I received an answer.

Now in regard to the Money that You Sent to John to releive us in our difficulties. I did Not Send for any Money Nor did I receive any. I knew that John got Some Money from Home but How Much it was or what He done with it I do Not know anything at all about. You Can rest assured that I Never will accept anything in the Shape of Help from Home. If I Cant give anything I wont take any. The difficulties that I was in at the time You Speak of I Settled Shortly after when I got work. As regards Your asking any Help from us it was your Right & Your Duty to ask for Help and it was our Duty to Help So far as lay in our power.

Now in regard to My Father, You Should Not wonder that I did Not Mention His Name after what A wreck He Has Made of the Family & the way He Has led Your Minds into Error in regard to the Gospel of Christ. My Fathers Life So far as I know Has been A Lie, pretending to beleive in the Gospel and perverting it to gratify His passions thereby Causing You to turn Your Hearts against the work of God. Such A thing would Not be tolerated Here & I presume He knows it.

If You were Here You would alter Your Mind Very Materially in regard to My religion I can assure [you] of that. It is Very Very Different from what you Suppose it is Here. Nor Can I blame You in A measure for thinking as You do with Such an Example Set before You. But if You Can find any fault with the Gospel as it is taught and practised Here let Me know it. I feel perfectly Satisfied. If I Could only be beside You for a little while that I Could eradicate all the faults You Have Conjured in Your Mind as belonging to My religion, the religion of God.

There is one thing that I wish understood, that is, if My Father Comes Here that No Such going ons as He Has been indulging in will be Successful Here. That Course will Meet with Summary punishment I Can tell Him. My Love & respect for My Father Has been lessened I am forced to admit but Still He is the author of My Existance and as Such Claims Consideration that I Could Not refuse, & if He would do right when Here He would Have My assistance as far as Lay in My power.

You Say that You Have an idea that it Must be A Very Hard Country to get on in. Well Ann it bears No Comparison to the old Country in that regard. For if I Have My Health I think that I can Make Myself independant of working for anyone in three or four Years. But You See that Most of My time Here Has been Spent in following a willowisp as I Stated to you before. Still I Have got A few Horses & A few Cows withal My Misfortunes. I Have Had a fearfully Hard time but it Has left Me as Hopefull for the future as ever, & More So because I Have gained Experience that will Help Me in future. You know our Burns Says:

> Though losses & Crosses
> Be lessons right Severe
> There is wit there Ye'll get there
> Ye'll find Nae ither where.[24]

I am Sorrow to Hear that David is Having Such a Hard time. If He was Here I think that He would do well as A Married Man always gets along better than A Single Man Here. But David Made His bed Himself & Has only Himself to blame for it if it chafes His bones. He will be Here as Soon as I Can get Him Here that is the best that I Can do. You see Ann that I remember the High Handed Manner that He used to bear to Everybody around Home.

In regard to writing to My Sister Lizzie the last time that wrote to Her I received No answer So I Came to the Conclusion that She did Not want to write to Me any More. Sister Lizzie Should know that She was always My Favourite. She is as Dear to Me as My own Self and I would be only to Happy to Correspond with Her if She will write to Me. I dont know Her adress. I am just as fond of reading as Ever & would be glad to Have You Send the papers to Me. I am glad to Hear anything that pertains to Home, all about Everybody that I used to know. I will draw to A close Hoping that you will write soon. I remain Your Loveing Brother,

Jas. B. McNeill

[PS] Enclosed You will find a check for 50 dollars. More Anon. Jamie. I like punctuality.

---

[24] Burns, "Epistle to Davie, A Brother Poet."

John H. MacNeil to David MacNeil, Sr.

Alta City
Little Cottonwood
3 October 1879

Dear Father,

I take My pen in hand Once More to Let You know how I am getting along. We are all in good Health at present although I have been pretty Nigh killed twice Since I wrote You Last with One of My horses kicking Me Once in the belly & Once in the Mouth.

As regards My prospects of being able to Send for You this Season Ill say they are very Slim. I tried all I Could to rais Money Enough but Couldnt. Almost anytime but Just this Season I Could have assisted You but if You Could weather it till Spring I think I can do Something then if all goes right. That is the best Encouragement I Can Give You in the position I am placed at present.

My Wife would have been More than glad if I Could have raised the Means to Send You So She Could have Some Company this winter while I was away at work but I Couldnt Make it & James Couldnt assist Me. At present he is in St. George Staying with Your Uncle Archy but he dont write Often.

We are having the dryest Season here we have had for fifteen Years. Its horrible. We dont know what [rain] is Since Early Spring but hope wont Let us give up. . . . No More at present from Your Loving Son,

John H. MacNeil

James B. MacNeil to Ann MacNeil

St George
[Utah]
15 November 1879

Dear Sister,

I take the Opportunity offered of Answering Your letter and I will be Candid with You & tell You that I had Come to the Conclusion that I would Never write to You Again. But I Have relented. I find it is Hard to give up all Family ties.

I would like to See You all here and doing right. I Have looked at it almost every way and I Cant See that life is worth Living without the beleif of the existance of A God & the Knowledge of How to Serve Him Acceptably. I Must either deny the Existance of A Supreme Ruler or beleive in the principles taught by Jesus Christ while upon the Earth and the Same that Joseph Smith taught before He was Martyred like His predecessor.[25]

I cannot disbeleive in the Existence of a God, So I took the pains to investigate and find out for Myself the true way to Approach and Serve that God. I Have proven it to My Satisfaction & I think that I Could prove it to You in A Short time if You were Here. But Mormonism So Called is A practicle Religion. It is Not the letter of the Law Denying the power thereof but is the word of God with the power.

I am Sorry to Hear that You Have been So unlucky as You Seem to Have been for a Length of time and to Hear of Your ill Health and How things were running. But I think that it is all for the best and we Must admit that God plans it all for the best if we could only See into His purposes and act Accordingly.

My Father Seems to be A little out of His Head as far as I Can Learn. He May Have gone astray but I Must Not judg least I be Judged. I would advise You to let Him take His own Course for A time and do the best you Can under the Circumstances and keep up Your Heart and cheer Mothers life as Much as possible.

I was greived to Hear of Grannies Death. I recognized in Grannie the best Friend that I ever Had & I Shall do Every thing that I Can for Her.[26] It is Some thing that we all Must Expect to Come to Sooner or later & I Hope that we will all be fitted & prepared for it when it does Come.

You think that I forget You all at Home, but You are Seldom absent from My Mind. I Never forget & I Love You all More

---

[25] James's approach to religious belief reflects a common Mormon perspective which holds that if Mormonism is not true, then it would be difficult to believe in God at all. This attitude may have led his brother John to turn to agnosticism once he had decided that Mormonism was a sham.

[26] James's "grannie" was his grandfather's second wife, Mary Wait Boggie, who died at the age of seventy-six at Edinburgh on 3 June 1878. The promise to do "everything I can for her" probably refers to the LDS belief that one's relatives may be baptized by proxy in a Mormon temple. No record of a proxy baptism for Mary Boggie was found in the Family History Library.

than I Ever did & I would like to See you all Here and living Happily together as we ought to be. It is getting late and I Must draw to a Close. Give My Love to My Mother, to David & His Family and to Lizzie & Janet, & Rob and Maggie [Paterson] and the Boys. I wish to be remembered to all My relatives and Friends.

I Have been Called to go on a Mission to Arizona & I am on My way Now.[27] It is late So I bid You all an affectionate Guid Nicht. From Your Loving Brother,

James B. MacNeill

[PS] Adress Bountiful, David Coy., Utah.

John H. MacNeil to David MacNeil, Jr.

Alta City
Lit. Cot. Wood
10 August 1880

Dear Brother,

I thought I would take the Liberty of dropping You a few Lines to Let You know how I am getting along at present in America. I Understand from Father You would Like to Come Out here Now. Well I would Like to assist You if I Could but I have My Own troubles to Contend with here. I Could have helped You better any time Since I Come to the Country than Just Now. I have Just got in a Law Suit & May possibly Lose all Ive Made Since I have been in this Country.[28]

I Understand James has been talking Some of helping You Out here. Well I hope he will. If he will I will do all I Can for You when You get here. But I Cant rais Money Just Now to fetch You here.

But its a preferable Country to the Old Country although people has there troubles here to, but theres a chance for a poor Man in this Country but None in the Old.

If it hadnt been this Suit I Intended to give You and Father a Chance this Season but if James dont I will do My Endeavours

---

[27] No trace of any official call to James B. MacNeil to serve a colonizing mission in Arizona was located in the LDS Archives.

[28] John seems to blame his legal problems on James. Perhaps James left John owing money as a result of the mining venture in Alta. No reference to the lawsuit could be located in the Utah State Archives.

Next Season. Its Not Much trouble here to get Something to Eat but it is hard to get Steady work So to Save a Little Money. If James does help You it will be the Only good he has done for himself or any Other person Since he Come here. But it May be all right if it dont End in talk. Thats all he has amounted to Yet, but I hope it will be all right. He has brought Nothing but trouble to Me Since he Come here. This is Some of his troubles I am fighting.

Now You Neednt to give Yourself any trouble about having to be a Mormon to Live here because theres Scores of people here that isnt. Im No Mormon Myself now.[29] There is Lots of Men Comes here & Leaves there families in Care of Some person and Earns Enough to Send for them after they get here. Its all on to Your Luck in getting work.[30]

I have got Six besides Myself to keep in Shoes & it takes Something in this Country I tell You. If James does Send for You Let Me know So I Can prepare Some place for You. If he Cant fetch You all and Could You alone I would take the Chance.

Tell Me about Mother and Ann where are they What are they doing please.

If I Could find Some place to Leave them till I got the Means to Send for them. You Can Just as Easy Send Money to keep them from this Country as You Can keep them there. And the three of us Could Soon get them here but James Never would pull at No End of a rope Since he Come here So I Count Little on him.

I am working in the Mines Now but I think of Quiting Next Season & Going to Farming. Ive got a hundred Acres of Land I intend to work Next Season. I will write You again pretty Soon but dont Let it prevent You from writing. We are all well & hope You are also. Your Brother,

John H. MacNeil

---

[29] It may not have been intentional, but John's "disaffirmation" with respect to his religious beliefs follows immediately on the heels of James's stirring affirmation. Thus the brothers continue to pull at both ends of the family's religious perspectives.

[30] According to Tullidge, although most of the British immigrants were originally artisans and manufacturers, they turned to agriculture in Utah as part of the church plan to promote community success rather than individual success

John MacNeil to David MacNeil, Jr.

Silver Reef
Washington Coy
Utah
15 November 1880

Dear Bro[ther],

I recd Yours of Sepr 18th all right & was Sorrow to hear of Your bad Luck but will try to assist You Out of Your troubles as Soon as it is in My power I Can assure You. But the world has Used Me rather Rough Myself of Late. I Lost One of My Children also about two Years ago and I have been having a run of bad Luck Ever Since I have Left Cottonwood Canyon & gone 350 Miles further South. My Family are Still in Bountiful.

I am beside James Now in Silver Reef but he has quit work & is going of further South about 300 hundred Miles further but he Says he will do all thats in his power to get You Out here Next Season. If I get Steady work here for a half Year I May Can help You Some Myself but I Sold My house & ground where I have lived So Long and got an Other piece of Land for it. I have a hundred acres Now of good Land but I am Strugling to get Means to build Me a house on it or Otherwise I will have to rent & that would Keep My poor for Ever.

I am Earning $4 dollers per day Just Now and if I get Steady work for a few Months I will Come Out all right but things is very Uncertain in this Country & Especially Mining, Lively today & dead tomorrow.[31] So You Cant Count on it a Month ahead. But I will Live in hope & keep a trying. I had a Cow Die a few days ago. That is $20 dollers gone but One thing is Standing by Me that is My health that is good also the Most of the Family to. Nothing to Complain of in that regard at present. . . .

---

as wage earners. However, the MacNeils simply could not or would not break out of the mold of being wage earners. Tullidge, *History of Salt Lake City*, 670.

[31] 1880 was a boom year for Silver Reef, but the companies decided to cut the pay rate from $4.00 per day to $3.50 because of fluctuating market conditions. A strike ensued and a Mormon posse from St. George was called in to arrest some of the strikers and convey them to Beaver for trial. This event essentially marked the end of the Silver Reef's boom, and it may have convinced James and John to leave the area. If John witnessed the Mormon posse breaking the strike it might have further confirmed his disposition to see the church as a conspiracy against workers. Anderson, *Desert Saints*, 432–33.

We Must keep trying though and hoping for better Luck I have five Children besides My Wife to get Showes for & it takes a Little to keep them going but if I had One Year More in I will be in a position So it will Cost Me Nothing to keep the family there. I Can Save Something. My Farm will rais their Living & I will Stay at work Until I have assisted all that wants to Come to this Country of Our Family.

I Can hire a boy to work the Farm. I have got a Span of Mares & two good Colts & wagon & harnes to Start with on the Ground but No house to Live in. I got Out of that Law trouble easyer that I thought for but Still it Cost Me $50 dollers besides Loss of time. . . . Give my regards to Father & Mother & Annie & all the rest of them. . . . Your Loving Brother,

John H. MacNeil

John MacNeil to Ann MacNeil

Silver Reef
Washington Coy
Utah
21 November 1880

Dear Sister,

After Long deliberation I take My pen in hand to drop You a few Lines to Let You know how I am Suceding in this Country. I have had rough Luck and the harder I fight against it the worse it is. It hangs Over all Our Endevors Like a fate of Some kind, both Mine and James & try as we May Something turns up to Frustrate it. I have Such a Family it Nearly takes Me all My time to keep them going because a Man Never Can get Steady work here.

For the Sake of getting work I am 350 Miles from My family Just Now. Until You have a piece of Land that You Can farm for Your Living it is very uncertain. I will have that pretty Soon Now I think if My health Stays with Me. Then I Can do Some good for the rest I think, but it takes time in this Country as well as the Old if You do it honestly.

I Must Own I got a Little Out of patience with all of You when Father Cut that Caper up. I Suffered So Much from Jameses Mule headedness I got disgusted at the whole Lot. Father had it in his power to Come. David had it in his power to Come here. Neither done it & We kept telling them it was a better Country for a poor Man but they was Making Money then (that is all on that Subject).

I am beside James at present but he is going of again 700 hundred Miles further South into Arizona. He got Out of work again.

My Family are well Last I herd from them & Me also. Only Im getting a Little Older Annie (that is my wifes Name to and [my] little girls). I have 5 Children 4 Girls and one boy & One boy Dead. We are always well of as regards Something to Eat in this Country, but Money is hard to get because work is hard to get. A Man is in Luck to Snatch 4 or 5 Months work in a Year. Well Annie, we Must keep hoping. Give My Love to Mother and Lizy and Janet and Maggie. I would Like to See them all in this Country Yet. So You See I hope. . . . Your Loving Brother,

James H. MacNeil

[PS] Write Soon please

James B. MacNeil to Ann MacNeil

Mesa City Maricopa Coy
[Arizona]11 January 1881

Dear Sister,

When I received your welcome Letter Dated Oct 22 I was at that time Making ready to leave that part of the Country & I did Not know where I Might Stop, for that reason I did Not write on receipt. My reasons for leaving there was I got knocked out of work. There is quite an Emigration from Utah into these Parts So I thought I would Move South also.[32]

I Started out on the 7 of Dec [1880] & arrived Here on the 18 Dec, 500 Miles in South Easterly Direction from Starting point. We come by team across the Country. It is a Barren Volcanic

---

[32]Mormon settlement in Mesa, Arizona, began in October 1878 and was a logical extension of Mormon settlements in Utah. Other Scots had preceded James MacNeil as pioneers; the first president of the Maricopa Stake, organized the year James arrived, was from Perth. He was Alexander F. Macdonald—"a sturdy, lengthy Scotchman, a preacher of the rough and ready sort and of tremendous effectiveness." McClintock, *Mormon Settlement in Arizona*, 220.

Country that we passed through Coming Here. At one time it Must Have been A very Hot place. Of course it Has all died out Centuries Ago but it Has left its Mark indelebly Printed on the face of Nature. In Every direction that you turn the Eye rests on Numberless Extinct Volcanic Craters & Miles of Molten Lava beds, untill the Barren Desolate aspect pains the Eye as You gase around You. This is the Case with the Country through which we travelled. There is No farming Land untill we get into the Southern portion of the Territory.[33]

The First Valley of any Note is the Salt River Valley in which I am Staying intending to Make A permanent Home & in which I Hope to See you all Settled Soon. This is the finest valley that I Have Seen west of the Missouria. There is Millions of acres of good land. The River from which they take the water to irrigate the land is about the Same Size as the Clyde at the toll Brig.[34]

They Can grow any thing almost: grapes, oranges, peaches & grain does Splended. You Can buy grapes Here at 7 Cents per Pound. It is just 9 Years Since the first white Settlers Came into this Valley. There is about 8 thousand inhabitants in the Valley Now. It is being Settled very fast. There is a railroad within 28 Miles of this Place & it bids fair to be the garden of the Territory. I Have No doubt land will be Very Valuable Here in a few Years. The beginning is worst of it but the worst of it is Not very bad & then You know You are working for Yourself & will get the benifit of your labour & in a few years I will be independent of Days labour.

I was very glad to Hear that you were all doing as well as you Say. I was anxious to know your financial Condition. I Had a letter from David just after I got Yours. I am Sorry for David Seeing the fix that He is in. I shall do My best to get Him out of His difficulties as Soon as I can, but it is just as I Have told You before, there is Nothing Certain about Mining in this Country. Cannot tell when You May get knocked out of employment.

---

[33] James was traveling over the geological formation known as the Colorado Plateau Province, which consists of numerous volcanic cones ranging in height from a few hundred feet to 5,700 feet above the surrounding countryside. Henry P. Walker and Don Bulkin, *Historical Atlas of Arizona*, 4a.

[34] If James is referring to the Garrion Bridge that crosses the River Clyde two and a half miles south of Wishaw, the Gila River would be approximately two hundred feet wide.

You say I Should write what I Have to Say bout David by itself So that He wont get offended. I Have this to Say, if David Cant bear to Have the truth told about Him, He Had better go into training until He Can Control that Morbid ignorant Pride that Has always Stood in the way of advancement intellectually. I Have Suffered from it before Now, as You probably know. Scenes that Can Never be Erased from My Memory, but which I Have long ago forgiven. But the Sooner He realizes His Legitimate Social position the Sooner He will be respected as A Man Capable of Controlling Himself & Consequently Capable of Controlling others.[35]

I Shall Secure land Enough for David if He Concludes to come Here. If He Concludes to go into the Country where John is, it will be all right any how. I Shall take up 160 acres for David. If He dont Come it will be all right.

I Have lost Lizzies address. Give My Love to Her. Tell Her to write to Me. I Hope to Hear from You Soon. My warmest Regards to all My Friends. My Mother I Hope to See Soon & prove to Her My love. Your Loving Brother,

James B. McNeill

[PS] I Have Not got a Photograph of A Single Member of My Family John Having Claimed them. Please Send Me pictures of all My people.

James B. MacNeil to David MacNeil, Jr.

Pinal City
[Pinal Co]
3 May 1881

D Mc Neill Jun

Dear Brother,

I Suppose You will Have thought by this time that Your Brother James Has thrown of on You by My Not writing to You Sooner. I will tell You My reasons for Not Doing so. The Place that I was in when You wrote Me last I thought I would Have

---

[35] It is unclear what James means by saying that David must recognize his "Legitimate Social position" before he can make any advancement. Perhaps he is suggesting that David thinks of himself as more important than he really is.

Steady employ Ment for A few Months & I knew that I Could send Money Enough to bring You out if I could get steady work for 6 months. But I got knocked out of work & I Had to travel. So I Concluded Not to write to You untill I got to My Destination 550 Miles from Utah.

When I got Here I waited thinking that I would get into work So that I could give good News when I did write but it is up Hill work when You aint acquainted. I Have been Here 2 Month doing Nothing. So You May judge How I am fixed. If I dont get into work I will Not be able to bring You & Family out this season, but if I get work I wont be long untill I send for You. There is one thing You Can depend on that is that I will Devote My time & Energies to that object.

It is Not So Very Much the sum but luck is against Me. Keep up Your Heart David. I will get You out Never fear for that, then I am Coming Home to See My Mother. I am pretty Sure to be Home Next Year Some time. I Have been longing to See My Family of late Very Much. How old are Your Children?

The fare from Liverpool to Salt Lake City is £14.18.2 for one person. I wrote to My Sister Ann A long time ago but Have received No answer as Yet. I Hope My Folks are well. . . . Your Faithfull Brother,

Jas. B. Mc Neill

P S let Me know all You Can about Brother Wills Boys John & Tom. See if they would Not like to come out to America.

James B. MacNeil to Ann MacNeil

Globe City
Gila Co
A[rizona] T[erritory]
26 September 1881

Dear Mother,

I suppose You are wondering what is the Matter with Me that I dont write to You, but dont give Yourself any uneasiness on My account. I am all right thank God. The reason of My Contin-ued Silence was this: I Have been traveling a great deal the last 10 Months & did Not know Exactly where I would pull up at. You See I am in a Strange Country Not knowing any one or any one knowing Me & it Has proven up Hill work beginning & I only got Started a Month ago. I Have No doubt but that I will work My Self into a better position after a little. I am Boss of Some Copper Mines just Now & I am doing Moderatly well Considering I Have only been in the Locality 2 Months. To get Any position of Trust You Must be known, for this Territory is one Half theives & Murderers & outlaws just as it is in all New Frontier Countries. They are gradualy forced Back as the tide of Civilization, Law & order approaches.[36]

Thank God I Have been able to preserve My record clear of Blots or Stains all through My wanderings & therefor I Can look adversity Squarly in the face & with Moderate Composure. For I Have Nothing to fear Having done the best that I Could under the Varied Circumstances in which I was placed. I am clear of the Vices that Seem to be the ruin of So Many in this western Country & especially amongst the Mining Class. In Mining Camps there are but few women Compared to the Number of Men & what few there is are of the Loose Stamp. Gin Mills & Gambling Dens are in the ascendant, So You See there is Not Much Choice Society to Move in in A Mining Camp. I Have been in Camps of from 3 to 5 Hundred Men & only 2 or 4 woman in the Camp. Of Course You will Meet in with good Men in Mining Camps but they are the Exception Not the rule.[37]

You will perhaps Say why dont He leave Such places & I will tell You why. I know this Business better than I do any other & So I Stay at it untill Such time as I get Enough of Means for to Make an independent Living at Something More in accordance with My tastes. . . .

Sister Ann was Mistaken in regard to this Territory. It belongs to the U.S. instead of Mexico. It did belong to Mexico but the

---

[36] According to Bancroft, outlawry and banditry in Arizona reached their apex in 1880–82 with numerous stage robberies, attacks on towns by cowboys, and the lynching of robbers. Sheriffs and their posses often met armed resistance in their efforts to enforce some semblance of law and order. Bancroft, *History of Arizona and New Mexico*, 575–77.

[37] For example, in Silver Reef, Utah, in 1880 there were 680 males and only 173 females, compared with 298 males and 347 females in the Mormon town of St. George. The disproportionate ratio of men to women was one reason Mormon leaders discouraged their people from becoming involved in the social life of the mining camps. Anderson, *Deseret Saints*, 432.

U.S. purchased it from the mexicans, though there is quite as Many Mexicans in the Territory as there is whites.

My partner & I own land on Salt river.[38] He is running the Team, for we own A Team between us & He Freights with it, but we Have Had A Very wet Season Here & the rivers were Swollen So that we Could Not do Much. But they are going down So that we will do better in Future with our Team than we Have been doing formerly.

I wrote to Salt Lake to Mary Hendry but My Letter was returned from the Dead Letter office So I Have Lost track of Mary altogether. I expect She Has got Married by this time. If So I wish joy May attend Her. By the way if Some of You Folks dont come out Here pretty Soon & keep House for Me I May be tempted to do Something Desperate Myself. So You Had better Hold a Pow wow & Send Somebody along Here if You dont want to See Me Sacrificed & led like a Lamb to the Slaughter.

I thought when I Met in with Mary that I could palm Myself of on Her but She could Not take a Hint Nohow. So I am Still Living in single blessedness & More Single than blessedness, Cooking My own grub & doing My own washing. You would Have A hearty Laugh if You Seen Me buckle up My Sleeves & go in to do a Months washing. You would be Saying to Me its changed times My Laddie. And There is quite a Marked Difference Sure Enough but I Hope it is for the better.

I wrote to Brother David but I guess He Has taken the Huff as I Have Not received an answer Yet.

You Said Something about My Grandfathers watch. I would like Very Much to Have it only for a keep Sake. I Have So little Now to remind Me of My Boy Hood, only My Memory but that retains its power. Sister Ann, I wish You to remind Sister Lizzie that I am over the water & would like to Hear from Her & all My relations the Same . . . So Now good Night Mother. Your Affectionate Son.

J. B. McNeill

---

[38] From a later letter we learn that James's partner was Sam Alger (b. 1858), a native of Payson, Utah. Alger went with Jacob Hamblin to build a road from St. George to the settlements on the Little Colorado in 1876. He lived in Arizona between 1880 and 1884. See Jenson, *Latter-day Saint Biographical Encyclopedia*, 1:798.

James B. MacNeil to Ann MacNeil

> Globe City
> Gila Co
> A[rizona] T[erritory]
> 29 December 1881

Dear Mother,

I Have just received Your welcome letter & Very glad to Hear from You I assure You & to know that You were well.

I Had A letter from Johnnie Thomson yesterday & He is in Kansas.[39] He rather Surprised Me Calling Me Uncle. I began to feel Old & wise right away. He was asking Me My opinion of the Country, where I thought was the best place to go to. I advised Him to Come Here as I think this is about as good a place as I Have been in, that is for a workin Man. In fact this is the best part of America for wages & I Have been pretty Much all over the west. I think He Could do better Here with Me for I can give Him work at 4 Dollars a Day & post Him in regard to the Country. I will assist Him all that I Can as I am in a position So that I Can help My Friends just Now. Maybe I will See Him Soon. I Hope So. He Dont Seem to like the place where He is at present.

I am Sorry to Hear that You are Necessitated to leave Overtown on account of Trade.[40] You Must find it difficult Moving Now. I think You Had better Make a good Move while You are at it & Move out Here. If You will Come Mother I will begin preparing a place for you So You will be comfortable. You Need Have No fear of lacking the Comforts of life when You get Here. I think I will Send the Money to bring David Here in the Spring or Summer. I Had Enough a few days [ago] to bring [him], but knowing that He would Not want to come in the winter time across the Sea, I put the Money into A Team. That is I bought A Team. I think that I can Make Some Money out of it. I will try any how.

---

[39] Johnnie Thompson is the son of James's half brother, William Thompson, who died in 1863.

[40] It is not always possible to determine where the MacNeils were living in Lanarkshire, but apparently since 1860 they had lived in three locations: in Whifflet (near Coatbridge), Overtown (near Wishaw), and now in the 1880s they were in Wishaw.

I get one Hundred & fifty dollars per Month in the Situation I am in just Now. You Need Not give Yourself any uneasiness about My Matrimonial proclivities. You See I will be 27 years on this Mundane Sphere, as the Yankie expressed it, pretty soon & to be Candidad with You Mother, I am almost over the Hasty impulsiveness of Youth. I am more Settled in My convictions & resolves than I used to be. I take time to Consider Now before falling Head over ears into that Boiling Cauldron Called Love. I Have been about 40 times in Love as I thought but it dont Stay with Me like Nothing.

I will send My Sister Maggie a present pretty Soon for Her kind remembrace of Me & David. Also I will probably See David Next Summer if He wishes to Come to this part of the Country. I Dont think that He Can do better but He Can Suit Himself where He goes.

I had A Letter from John A while ago. He is Never Satisfied with the Part of the Country that He is in but family ties Holds Him to it. Well as one Makes & Shapes So the bed feels.

It is almost Neier Day [New Years' Day] So I will wish You all A guid New Year with Many Happy returns. "And let us Hope our Years May be as guid as thae Hae been, And trust we Nier again May see the Sorrows we hae Seen."[41]

I intend Savings My Money up to Send to David but if You Need any thing let Me know & I will Send it to You. Wish all A Happy New Year for Me. Ever Your Loving Son,

Jas. B. McNeill

[PS]

Hail Land of My Nativity, & Learnings guiding Star,
With feelings of Base Slavery, thou ever wert at war.
Hail Land of rugged Scenery, Hail Mountains Streams & Vales,
My Heart was warmed in boy Hood, listening to thy Battle Tales,
Of How His Countrys Saviour fought against Tyrannic Hate,
And Secured thy independence though His life Blood was the stake.

---

[41] James repeats the first lines of the last verse from the song "A Guid New Year" which concludes:
> And let us wish that ane an' a', Our friends baith far an' near,
> May aye enjoy in times to come A hearty guid New Year.
> Chorus: A guid New Year to ane an' a', An' mony may ye see;
>   An' during a' the years to come, O happy may ye be.

Miller, arr., *Forty-Seven Popular Scottish Songs*, 56. I am indebted to Jean H. Kelly, Salt Lake City, for this reference.

Home of Science & of Arts, Home of Social Honest Hearts,
Thou Hast given birth to great Men, Men of Genius & of worth,
Who will Live on Historys page while Learning Has A Name
And Future Generations pay Homage to their Fame.

My first Effort
His Countrys Saviour is
Borrowed from Rabb [Burns]

James B. MacNeil to David MacNeil

Globe City
Gila Co
A[rizona] T[erritory]
21 February 1882

Dear Brother,

I have just received Your letter Dated Jan 15. . . . You Say that You want to Come out as far as I can glean from Your letter & there is 6 of You altogether. Well David it will take A good bit of Money to fit You out & bring You Here. I dont Suppose that it will take less than 80 pounds to do it & I Have Not got a Cent of it Now, Having Sent the last Money that I Had to Johnnie Thomson. He asked Me to Help Him to get where I was. He Said that it would require $100 to bring Him out. I sent $85. That was all I Had at the time but that would More than pay His fare. Since I sent the Money I Have Never Heard from Him. I dont know what Can be the Matter with Him.

Now David I dont want any funny Business because I am Not finding the Money that I get & I want to get a foot Hold in the Country Myself. You know that I am getting along in Years & it is Most time that I was doing Some thing for Myself, but at the Same time & I would Not See any of My people in want. I Can Send You the Money, that is 80 pounds, about the first of June or Maybe Sooner.[42]

---

[42] For years James had been trying to convince David to come and that he would help him all he could, but now when David says he is ready to do so, James seems to be putting conditions on his coming. It can only be conjectured as to what he means by "funny Business." Perhaps he means that David must be serious about coming and seriously intends to make a go of it in America, or perhaps he's saying that he wants the money he sends spent only on fares.

You will Come accross the Sea with the Saints & the returning Elders will direct You as to the route. I Cannot tell You any
things about it unless You want to go where John is. In that Case
You would Stay with the Company all the way through. You See
I am away from where there is any railroad & So I Cant find out
any thing about it. You would do well to recognize Yourself with
the Saints if You Have Not already done So.[43] John is talking of
Coming down Here but it is a quite A walk, being about A 1000
Miles from where He is & He does Not like to leave His family &
Has Never been accustomed to knocking around, So Maybe He
wont Come. I wrote to Him Stating that I could give Him work if
He Come. You Have Not given Me Your adress So I will Send
this to Ann & She Can Send it to You. . . . Im a thourough old
Bachelor . . . your Brother,

James [MacNeil]

James B. MacNeil to Ann MacNeil

Globe City
Gila Co
A[rizona] T[erritory]
[early 1882]

Dear Sister,
 . . . I was Sorrow to Hear of My Mothers accident & of
Her Sickeness. I Hope You will Not let Such a thing occur again.
I Can Easily beleive My Mother is getting frail & it Needs Your
Care & watchfullness to prevent Such Accident. You ought Not to
allow Her to be rushing around falling over Carpets & Such like.
Pardon Me for Scolding You. I feel out of Sorts tonight. I Hope
My Mother will be well & enjoying good Health long Ere this
reaches You.
 I am glad to know that Sister Lizzie is at Home again. You
Say She wants to know How Much wages I am going to give Her.
You Can tell Her that She wont get immensly wealthy with all She

---

[43] Given the family's apparent lack of real interest in Mormonism, this
seems a strange, if pragmatic, suggestion. He may mean, of course, that David
should form an association with Mormons because they operated one of the
most efficient immigration services.

gets but I will do the best I Can for all of You. I Hear that there is going to be A change where I am employed at present. The Owners are likely to Stop work I Hear, in which Case I am likely to be out of employment. But there is Nothing certain. If Such A thing does occur it will interfere with My arrangments for David & Family. It May be later on in the Season before I Can Send the Money if the rumor Should be true. When I Send the Money I will Send it to You & You Can take out of it what it will require to clothe the family & fix them up in decent Shape & See to that Yourself.

Johnnie Thomson Has got Here & is working in the Mine He is Sitting by Me just Now reading A Novel and deeply interested. My Partner Sam [Alger] is trying to cod [kid] Him (as He Expresses it) about His ironclads Shoes. He is telling Johnnie that there is No wonder that the Brittish Navy rules the Sea if the Ships are built as Strongly as Johnnies Shoes & as Commodious.

You would like Me to give You A description of this Place. Well I am Not an adept at that Sort of thing, but if You Can picture in Your Mind A Small town in the Highlands, population 1200, Mountains everywhere You look, then You Have it as Near as I Can describe it. There is A little More bustle & Stir than in Most Highland Towns of its Size. The Shops or Stores as they are called Here are Much the Same as at Home only there is this difference; they are Not So Exclusive in the Stock they Carry. For instance, a Grocer Here Sells ready Made Clothing, boots & Shoes, Hats, & Caps, crockery, Hardware. There is No Milliner or Dressmaker in town but the women Folks put on a Heap of Style in Dress wherever they get it from. The Laws of trade are Much the Same. There is Not So Much Credit Business done as at Home.

There is about one third of the population Mexicans but they are the poorest class Here & Have No Social Standing in the Community & do Not Mix with the white part of the population & generally live off in A part by themselves.[44]

I was glad to Hear of You Making Such A Signal Success on the occasion of your Debut in public but I do Hope You will

---

[44] Bancroft reports that there was considerable racism in Arizona and that often a clamor would rise for the expulsion of Mexicans from mining camps because of the acts of a few individuals. Bancroft, *History of Arizona*, 575.

Never be Necessitated to follow it as A Means of livelyHood.[45] I dont think that I would like the ideal of My Sister being in that role, but I suppose My ideas are behind the times. You See I Have been So long in the Mountains that I Suppose My ideas & thoughts or Mode of thinking partakes More or less of the Nature & aspects of My Surroundings which is Nature in its roughest form.

Well Sister when You get tired of that Country Come out Here & pay Me a visit. I will try & supply you with the Substancials any How. You will always be Sure of A Hearty Highland welcome.[46] Do Not under any circumstances try to get that Poetic Scribble that I sent you published. I Hope You will obey My behests in this Matter. Johnnie thinks paper must be Scarce where auntie Lizzie is. Give My Love to Mother & tell Her to take the wourld a little Easier than She Has been doing up [to] this time. . . . I am as ever, Your Loving Brother,

Jas. B. McNeill

James B. MacNeil to Ann MacNeil

Globe City
[Arizona Territory]
22 April 1882

Miss A. Mc Neill,
Dear Sister,

I got a letter from David today & I am Surprised at the content of Said letter. Not a little the idea of My Mother being in dire poverty didnt Hardly agree with My Notions of right. Why you Should allow Such a State of things to exist without stating the Case to Me is A puzzler to Me. If that is what you Call pride I think you Have very false notions of what Constitutes real pride.

---

[45] There is no suggestion as to what Ann's "debut" was; perhaps she had some poetry printed in a newspaper, or perhaps she performed in a concert for money. However, among the letters is a certificate awarded to Ann MacNeil in 1875 indicating that she had received training to teach music. As in other parts of these letters, the absence of the other side of the correspondence leaves numerous lacunae to tantalize the reader.

[46] James is using a phrase found in Burns's "A Highland Welcome": "When Death's dark stream I ferry o'er, / (A time that surely shall come), / In Heav'n itself I'll ask no more / Than just a Highland welcome."

I believe I told You to let Me know if you were in Need of any thing. It seems that you Have Not paid the slightest regard to my wishes. Well, all right Sis I Shall in future try to get My informatin from another Source.

I will Send You 20 pounds tomorrow & enclose the Check in this letter So You Can draw it as Soon as You get this letter. Now if Lizzie Means to write to Me She Had better Not do any More talking & Meditating about it but do it right away. I am in a Hurry just Now So please Excuse this brief Note My Love to Mother as usual & all inquiring Friends I am as Ever your Brother

J. B. Mc Neill

James B. MacNeil to David MacNeil

Globe City
[Gila Co]
[Arizona Territory]
23 April 1882

Dear Brother,

I received Your Note bearing Date March 26. I was glad to Hear from You but I Must Say that I was Very Much Surprised by what you Said in regard to My Mother. I Had Not the Slightest idea of Such A State of things Existing without Me being Made aware of it. I cannot be Expected to know How things is at Home if the people at Home are Not Candid in telling Me.

I am Very Anxious at present to get A little Money Ahead for I See that there is chances for Me doing well in My present position, but Dave [it] requires Money to Make Money in this Country. It is the Starting that is the worst, but a Man that dont do well after He gets a Start Here it is because He dont Have Brains Enough to take Care of it or Himself. But chances or No, I dont Care to know that My folks are in want while I Can assist them, & if they do want it is their own fault for Not Making it known.

It May be better for to write to John in regard to your going to Him. As far as I Myself am Concerned it wont Make any Difference to Me. You Shall use Your own judgement in that Matter, as I would wish to do in the pursuit of My individual Happiness. My action in advising You to Come Here Might be attributed to interested Motives to Serve My own purposes, whereas I Merely want to give You A chance of bettering Your Condition. You Can go to whatever part of the world you think will Suit You best. There is No Hurry. You Can take time to think over it & let Me know Your decision when You Have Satisfied Your Mind by inquiries. If You intended Coming Here it Might be quite as well to wait until fall any way, as this is a warmer Climate than You Have been accustomed to & you Might Not like it Coming Straight from Scotland into this Country at the Hottest time of the Year.[47] It is A very Healthy Climate & Suits Me first rate.

My partner & Myself Have taken a Contract Hauling Ore from one of the Mines to the Smelter & it May be that we will have to buy one More team to fill the Contract. If So it will detain Me in Sending the Money for Your passage & Equipment but Not later than fall anyway, that is if you wish to Come then. My partner runs the Team. I Have No practical Experience in teeming, So I leave that to Him.

In My present position I am Comfortable enough. Johnnie Thompson is working for Me in the Mine. He gets 4 Dollars per Day & He Has Never lost A Day Since He Started. He Seems to be Very well Satisfied & He ought to be. He lives with Me Here in My Cabin.

I will Send You one of the papers published in Globe. There is A Notice in it of the Mine that I am in Charge of, the Borva Copper Mine.

I Sent a little Money to Mother today. It was all I Had at the time. It will Maybe releive Her present wants. Write as often as you find it Convenient & give Me all the News You Can try & give Me an idea of the way Mother & Sisters get a living, How Much Stock in Trade they Have. Give Me an estimate of their present resources & income as Near as You Can.

I would like to See all My Folks Here in this Country as I think they Could do Much better, but they are their own Masters & presume to know best what they want. I am the youngest of the Family and it looks like presumpion in Me to advise those So Much My Seniors . . . as Ever Your Brother,

J. B. McNeil

---

[47] The average temperature in Scotland during summer may range from around 52° to 65° F; in Arizona, from 96° to 108° F.

James B. MacNeil to Ann MacNeil

Globe City
Gila Co
[Arizona Territory]
5 October 1882

Dear Sister,

You will be wondering why I dont write & let you know How I am Coming on. Well the truth of the Matter is this I Have been rather unsettled for the past 4 Months. The Company that I am Employed by Stopped work on the first of June pending arrang-Ments for Consolidating with another Company. I am told However that they will begin again Soon. I Have Not done Much work for the past 4 Months although I Have done Very well what little I did do. I told I beleive in one of My letters that I Had taken a Contract at one of the Mines, Hauling ore to the furnace. Well I Had to buy another team to fill the Contract & Now I will Have to buy Still another & it keeps the Treasury pretty Low. However there is every likelyHood of My doing well. When I get fixed a little I intended Sending the Money for David this fall, but owing to My Having to buy More Teams I was Not able. But it will all Come right. Just Have a little patience. I am doing all I Can & all for the best as My wisdom dictates.

David Sent Me Johns letter to Father & it Surprised Me Very Much that John dared to write that on paper: while I stayed around Him I was the Cause of His Non Success in life. But I am So far removed from Him Now that there is No likelyHood of any one beleiving Me the Cause of His trouble, So He Must Needs find another object to vent His Spleen upon. I just received a letter from Him yesterday but there was Not A word of the like in it & He wont, because He knows that I know better.[48]

He purposes Coming Here & He would do well Here. But I did Not advise Him to do So because it Might lead to Complications that I do Not wish to be Concerned in bringing about. John

---

[48] Why David, Jr., would choose to send such a contentious letter, and one that would stir up animosity between the two brothers, is difficult to understand. The tendency to be disputatious seems to be endemic in the family. It is little wonder that there was no agreement on religious matters, and that personality conflict always lay just under the surface of cordiality.

Has a chronic ulcer on His Stomach that Sticks to Him under all circumstances. It is generally termed dissatisfaction. Of Course, if He Comes Here I Must do the best that I Can for Him irrespective of His weak kneed course & that I will do.

Now Ann if You Should Need a little Money let Me know at once. Dont be in Need while there is a likelyHood of My getting it . . . remember me to all the Folks. As Ever Your Loving Brother,

James B. MacNeill

James B. MacNeil to Ann MacNeil

Globe City
Gila Co
[Arizona Territory]
[December 1882?]

Dear Sister,

I Have received Your Letter Bearing Date Aug 27 & was glad as usual to Hear from You & to Hear from Home. I Have been Dilatory in writing to You for Some time past but as I intend Staying Here for Some time You Can Expect More punctual Correspondence.

I Have Never received an answer Yet from David. If He Still wishes to Come out Here I want to Know it & I will bring Him out, but while I am Struggling to Help Him I will Not be treated with undeserved Contempt. The kicking & Cuffing Days are over with for me. The unlimited Sway that both of My Brothers Manipulated to My Sorrow in My Youth is at an end. That Conviction Has Dawned upon Johns Mind. I want to be kind to them & treat them as Brothers. In fact it is My ambition to become the Benefactor of all My family but My Early Memories are fraught with Scenes that I do not wish to See enacted again. There is Some of them where David & Myself were the principal Actors, which You Yourself witnessed. Well, that Bombast will Have to be dispensed with if He Comes Here. It brings A Shade of Sorrow to My Mind when I think of it. But Enough of this, they are unpleasant Memories but like Banquios Gohst they will Not Down.[49] You Can Consult Him & if He wishes to Come I will Send the Money in the Spring to bring Him. . . .

---

[49] "Banquo's ghost" appears in Shakespeare's *Macbeth*.

I Had A letter from John about a Month ago & as usual He was Hard up. I Expect Him Down Here Soon. He wrote Stating that He would try to Come Down if I Had any Encouragement to Give Him, Meaning Money I Suppose, but I Had None that particular time. But I wrote to Him stating that if He wished to Come Here that as long as I was Here He Could be Sure of work at 4 dollars a Day & My assistance to get Him into Something better. That is all that I could do for Him. I dont know Whether He will Come or No as it is quite a Tramp from where He lives to this place, being one thousand Miles & John is Not accustomed to travelling.

I am Doing Very well Here & Have every assurance of doing better in future. I get $150 per Month & If You dont think that I feel thankful to God for His kindness to Me You are Sadly Mistaken. I Have Had Many A Hard Scrabble Since I left Home but I Have faced the Music with a Determination to Succeed & I will Stay with it untill it & I part for good. I am A little Case Hardened & weather beaten but withal A Much better Man (or boy rather for I am Not Married Yet) than I would otherwise Have been.

In the Event of You being in Need of A few pounds dont be backward in letting Me know of it. You Can be Sure of Help while I am able to give it.

I am Sorry to Hear that Janet is going of to Sydney but I Suppose it is A Much better Country than Scotland for to Settle in.[50] But from what I Can learn it is a sickly place. I Hope She will be blessed with good Health. It is a priceless Blessing & we Cannot be to Careful of it.

I am glad to Hear that Lizzie will be at Home again, for I know that My Mother Needs Her Help & I would rather pay Her to Stay at Home than to Have Her away from Home. I realize that My Mother Must be getting feeble & in Need of Her Help.

I Suppose it is Cold weather Now in Scotland. It is just as warm Here Now as it is [in] Scotland in Midsummer. Birds Singing like Spring time at Home. . . . Your Brother,

Jamie [MacNeil]

---

[50] In 1882, Janet Thompson McLean, his half sister, was thirty-six years old and about to leave for Australia.

[PS] I wish You A Merry Christmas & A Happy New Year.

James B. MacNeil to Ann MacNeil, Sr., and Ann MacNeil, Jr.

Clifton
[Greenlee County]
[Arizona Territory]
2 March 1883

Dear Mother & Sister,

I Received Your ever welcome letter Just as I was leaving Globe a week ago. The reason of My Not writing Sooner was on account of My being undecided as to what I Should do. I told You I beleive in a former letter that I was Engaged [in] teaming. My partner & I Having a contract Delivering ore to one of the Smelters Here at Globe.[51] We invested $3500.00 in teams. Well we done very well for a time & then the Supt got opposed to us & would Not live up to His Contract So the Consequence is we lost over $1000 in 3 Months time. Then we quit & I think we will begin Farming for our Selves Now. I dont know Much about it Myself but I Can learn & it is time I was settling down Now anyHow, if I ever intend to do.

Johnnie Thomson is at Globe & is working steady. I Seen Him the evening before I left there. He did Not Have anything to Say. He Seldom Spoke of Home & I Never insisted. In fact No person would take us for Relations that did Not know the fact. I gave Him Lizzies letter to read So He knows that She wishes Him to write. I presume I Have Served His turn & He, I presume, wishes No further [contact]. I Myself will Never be likely to insist on our Mutual relations to Each other. I dont know that I will See Johnnie any More & I do Not wish the Subject renewed. If He wishes to istrange Him Self from Me He Shall Have His wishes followed to the letter.

In regard to John I Heard from Him about three Months ago & I Have Not answered His letter yet. I Had Nothing to write about that could encourage Him So Have kept Silent.

---

[51] Clifton is approximately ninety miles southeast of Globe. These two towns were the centers of mining activity in eastern Arizona.

I thank You for My part of the Neerday Bun. It showed to Me that you thought of Me at Your great Social gathering.[52]

I will write You again as Soon as I find what I [am] going to do & I [will] try & describe the place to you. I will also Send My photograph in return for the Cards of My 2 Nephews. I will go away from Here tomorrow. Please address to me at Safford, Graham Co. A. T. I will write again Soon. My love to all. Your Loving Jamie.

James B. MacNeil to Ann MacNeil

> Pima
> Graham Co
> Ariz.
> [June ? 1883]

Dear Sister,

I Have just received your welcome letter & was glad to Hear from You as usual & Now that I have Settled & can answer More punctualy I will endevor to do so.

My Partner & Myself Have bought A farm on the Gila River, Near to the Town of Thatcher. There is Not Much of a Town Yet, there being only three Familys living there but it was only laid out A Month ago.[53] We build a Town Here in this Country Very fast when once begun.

We Have A Farm of Two Hundred Acres of as fine land as there is in Country. The River Skirts our land on the North. It is about 2/3 the Size of the [River] Clyde at Overtown. Plenty of fish in it & I am Very well pleased with the place. We were too late

---

[52] His mother and sister had sent James some "black bun," a dark fruitcake traditionally used in celebrating New Year's Eve or "Hogmonay" in Scotland. The "bun" is wrapped in heavy pastry, and it is reasonable to assume that is would still be edible after crossing the Atlantic and the United States.

[53] The town of Thatcher was named for Mormon leader Moses Thatcher, who visited the area at Christmas 1882. Among the early settlers were the Moodys and the Cluffs, both of whom were involved in events concerning James. The Thatcher townsite was selected in May 1883 by an English pioneer, Christopher Layton. Another settler in the region was Ebenezer Bryce, a convert from Glasgow, who gave his name to Bryce Canyon in Utah. McClintock, *Mormon Settlement in Arizona*, 249, 262; see also the Biographical Sketch of Ebenezer Bryce in the Utah State Historical Society.

in getting Started on the farm this Season So we will only farm about 60 Acres this Season. Most of the Grain that is raised Here is put in in the fall & winter. But we Can raise 2 Crops per Year in these parts; raise a Crop of wheat & Harvest that about the beginning of June, then put in Corn on the Same ground & raise A Crop of Corn. I am plowing & putting in Corn as fast as I Can. The work is a Little strange to me but I am getting on quite well for a begginner & it is time I was Making a Home & Settling down any way.

Johnnie Thomson paid Me the Money that He owed Me.

Now in regard to David, I Can Not Assist Him at the present for I Have No Money, but I May be able to Send Him Money Enough in the fall to bring Him Here. But I Cannot bring His family.

I Have been knocked out of time in a manner but I am just as Confident of Sucess as Ever. I Must just do as Mother used to tell Me, put A Stoot Heart ta A Stae brae My Laddie [put a stout heart to a steep hill]. This is Not My first disappointment: the best laid plans of Mice and Men, gang aft agley.

I dont know when I May See Scotland but I May be Called to go there any time. In that case I expect to go.[54] I would like you to Send Me a Song. I think it is Called The Land where I was born. Johnnie used to sing it. . . . Your Affectionate Brother
James B. McNeill
Excuse Haste.

James B. MacNeil to Ann MacNeil

Pima
[Arizona]
3 October 1883

[Dear Sister,]

I received Your welcome letter Yesterday & as it is raining today I take the opportunity presented of answering. In the first

---

[54] James is referring to the possibility of receiving a call from the church leadership in Salt Lake City to serve as a Mormon missionary in Scotland. Unlike modern Mormon mission calls, which are generally well planned and take into consideration one's financial status and family condition, calls in the nineteenth century tended to be more spontaneous and were designed to serve the needs of the church even if it inconvenienced the individual.

place I am well as usual & things Have changed greatly with me since I wrote you.

My partner & I Have parted. I bought Him out & I now owe Him 850 Dollars which is due on the first of January 1884. I dont know whether I will be able to Meet it or Not but I will do My best then if I am not able to Meet it I wont have any regrets Having done My best.

I have just Commenced to Harvest My Corn. That will take me until the latter part of December then I will begin again putting in Small grain on the first of February & put in until august. So you See a Farmer Can keep busy in this Country if He wants to.

I Had a letter from John about 3 Months ago Stating that He would Start Down Here on the 1 of Sept but Have Not Heard from Him Since. So I dont know whether He Has Started or Not & to tell the truth I dont Care whether He comes or Not, as I want peace & content & I Never Had that around John. So I am Not anxious to renew our intimacy. But do Not think that I am at enmity with Him. No I will Help Him all I Can but I wish to avoid the petty annoyances that He Subjects Me to by His weak unstable Nature. When A person gets imbuid with a Spirit of fault finding with everybody & everything it Makes ones life a Misery to Him & all around Him.

Now in regard to David, it dont Seem possible that I can gather Money Sufficent to bring Him & all the Family untill I get better off. To Send Money to put into any Business I regard as folly.[55] The only permanent good that Can be accomplished for Him Must be by emigration. Let Him Come Here possessing the energy that You Say & in 10 Years time He will be independent & it is Not the good that it accomplishes for Him alone but it is the Benefits to His Family by pursuing Such a Course. What it may accomplish for Him as an individual is a Secondary Consideration in Comparison to the Chance it will leave His Family. As far as the results of My efforts are concerned that is no Criterion to judge from as I Could readily explain if I were by Your side for an Hour. A Married Man does far better in this Country than

---

[55] This may be the "funny business" mentioned in an earlier letter to David. Like their father, David may have been thinking of opening his own business, but it is difficult to determine what business.

a single Man. If He Has a wife that is good for anything she Can Make a good deal.

I Might Sell Horses to get the Money to send for David & Family but if I done so I could not work the farm.

You Must Not think that because I have No Money that I am distitute. I am a great deal better of than I would Have been if I Had Stayed at Home. I am wealthy in experience, which is better than being Rich, & if Nothing of A Serious Nature Happens to Me I will be in A position of Comparitive independence in the course of 5 years. You See Farming in this Country is a business that You dont Handle Much Money in but You gather property around you which is Not So easily Squandered as Money & is of infinatly More accumulative value than Money.

Now I am Much obliged to You for the Song. You are right in your premise that I dont Hear Much Music. Very little indeed & that little of a very Poor quality. I live alone & do My own Cooking & it releives the dull Monotony of My daily life to rip out a Song at times. I use it as a kind of Safety Valve for accumelated Devilishness. After I receive Lizzies letter I wrote an answer to it, closed it & Stamped it & laid it away to take to the P.O. when I got leisure. And the other Day I was looking through My Trunk & found the letter that I Had written 9 Months ago to Lizzie.

I am glad to Hear of Your getting along & keeping out of Debt. It is a bad Business getting into Debt.

I will Draw to A Close with kind Regards to Friends. Love to mother, Lizzie & Yourself. I remain Your Affectionate Brother,

James B. Mc Neill

Editor's Note: As far as is known, this letter is the last that James sent to his family in Scotland. The next item written about him was an entry in the autobiography and Journal of Francis W. Moody, for 17 and 18 March 1884:[56]

The 17th of March, Bishop Cluff, Hyrum Weech and James McNeil appraised my father's estate, which amounted to $2119. On the

---

[56] On 7 March Moody recorded that the "Gila River is Higher now than it has been for several years." Mr. William R. Ridgeway of Thatcher, Arizona, provided me with a typed excerpt from Moody's Autobiography and Journal. The orginal is in the LDS Historical Department.

18th of March 1884, James McNeil and Abraham Bomen [Bowman] were crossing the Gila River opposite the Graham Ward, when the team and James went down the river. He and the team were all drowned, however, Bro. Bomen escaped by swiming to the shore. bro McNeil in attempting to save the team lost his life. The team went down about a quarter of a mile. It lodged against some willows on a small island. We managed to get the wagon and harnesses by throwing a long rope out which caught on the wagon box. Then I went across by means of the rope and managed to get the horses loose from the wagon and we towed them in to the shore. On the 19th, Bishop Rogers, Hyrum Weech and myself and others have been trying to find his body but failed. June 1884. On the 7th, the body of James McNeil was found about four miles down the river, he had been missing over two and a half months. He had been found by a little boy while fishing. They took his remains and buried him in Pima.

Allen Hendry to Ann MacNeil

> Pima Post office
> Graham coy Ariz Try
> 19 March 1884

Miss A. McNiel
55 Victoria Buildings
Wishaw, Lanarkshire S.C.

Miss,

I wish to inform you what has happen to your Brother James B. McNeil. He has been Stoping with Me Since before Chrismas. He went last week to work on his farm & Started to cross the river with his horses & waggon & got washed down the river & horses & hemself got drown. There has been a lot of Men hunting for him ever Since But have not found him yet. But we will Keept on untle we do find him if it is posable.

James was a real good young Men & very Much respected by all the folks that new him. I will rite you & let you know when we find him. Write when this reaches you. Your Freand & wellwisher,

> Allen Hendry[57]

---

[57] When he was twelve, Allen Hendry sailed from Liverpool on the *William Stetson*, 26 April 1855, with his widowed mother, Isabella, and her six other children. Liverpool Emigration Records.

Editor's Note: On 28 March 1884, John MacNeil read the following report in the *Deseret News* and sent it to his father.[58]

DROWNED
James B. McNeal Lost in the Gila River

The sad intelligence comes from Smithville, Arizona of the death by drowning of a young man named James B. McNeal. The fatal event took place on the 18th inst., and is related to have occurred as follows: Brother McNeal, in company with a man named Bowman, was going across the Gila River with a wagon, at a crossing some five miles above Smithville, and opposite the Yorgan settlement, to which place they were going for seed grain. A brother named Yorganson was riding ahead of the team on horseback.

When they approached the shore Brother McNeal had fallen too low and horses and wagon had got into a deep hole. The man, A. Bowman, jumped out above the wagon and McNeal jumped out in front as if to assist the horses. Bowman was washed under the wagon and when he got out he found McNeal struggling, with his face very bloody, as though he had received some injury from the horses. He sank and disappeared.

Bishop Rogers and twenty or twenty-five men were out hunting the body all next day, besides, many hunted the evening of the accident, but had failed to find anything but the drowned man's hat. The horses, large, fine animals were both drowned and lodged against drift wood. Brother McNeal was from Utah and it is said he has a brother in Davis County, in this Territory. We learn the above by letter from Brother E. W. East.

John MacNeil to David MacNeil

> Bountiful,
> Davis Co
> 1 April 1884

Dear Father,

It is with Sorrow I am Necessitated to write to You on Such an Unpleasant Subject but it Must be done by Somebody. The truth is My Brother James is No More. He was accidently Drowned in the River Gila in Arizona while trying to Cross. I have wrote to the party who put the Letter in the Deseret News but it will take

---

[58] *Deseret News*, 26 March 1884, in *Journal History* of same date. LDS Archives.

Sometime to get any answer because it is 12 hundred Miles from here. I will Send You a Copy of the paper with the Letter in it, giving all that I know as Yet about it. In haste.

This Leaves us all well and hope this will find You well also. I would Like to have Daves adress and Anns Address, because he has Left Some property which Must be Looked after and it May be Necessary for Me to get a power of Atorney from You and the rest of the family, to act in Your behalf. All property Left Intestate or without a will Passes into Cort and is Probated or divided between the Ayres. I dont know what he has Yet, or Much about it. Look Out for the paper which will give You the account of it as I have it. As Ever Your Loving Son and Daughter,

John *and* Annie MacNeil

[PS] Write soon again please.

He was Drowned on the 18th of March

Allen Hendry to Ann MacNeil

Pima Post office
Graham coy T. A
25 April 1884

Dear Madam,

Your deted the 8th is at hand So I take the earleyes appurtunity to reply. I am very Sorrow to inform you that we have never found him yet. The river was higher then it was ever Knowen before, So there was So Much Sand wishing down that he Must have got covered up. There has been a great dell of hunting for him.

When I first heard of it I thought it could not be possible But it is two true. There was a young Men with him when he drove in the river But he jumped out & got out & another one a horse back. But James was So anxious to Save his team & trying to Save them the horses Must have Struck him with there feet. They were a good pare of horses, well worth foure hundred dollars. He has property hear to the amount of Eight $8.00 Hundred dollars if it is Handle right. The bishop is loking after it. We got out the horses & waggons. The horses drowend.

The last letter I new of him geting was one a Silk andKerchief was in. His trunk is hear & a lot of old letters & liknesses. What

Shell I do with his trunk & what is in? Kept them till I have a chance to Sand them to his Brother John or have them Sold for Mony? I had a letter from John in Utah.

I have been acquinted with [him] over eight years. We first Meat at cottenwood & we meat has Brothers that had not Seen each other for a long time. I was only two days with him their But we had a good time together. For a year or two we rote to one another. But Since then I heve never heard of him till we Meat acceidently hear on the Gilly. So for a year now we have been together nearly all the time.

Please rite & Say what your Father & Mother wants don with his property. He has got one fift intres in a Saw Mill worth five $5.00 hundred dolars. He has got one Hundred achers of firming land worth foure $4.00 hundred dolars, a good waggon, one $100 dolars, a colt worth one $1.00 Hundred dolars & I think he ows about $2.00 Hundred. Thit is his nigh his [that is as near as] I can Say, gesing at it. He has Some horses at St Gorge.

If you had any noshen of coming to this country this would be good Property to come to, if you had the Mens to come with. It would be Sold it a Sacrafise to get the Money. So you can tell Me what you want don & I will tell the bishop. There is a great Many folks coming from Utah to this place. You can come on the rail road hear. It is no trouble for Me to rite So anything you wish to Know & I will take pleasure to tell you. I am a very pore ritter & spiler. I have been in Wishaw when I was about eight years old. My Mothes folks comes from there. There names is Mark. My Mother has got a Sister around there. Her name is Ellen. Excuse Me. Yours with Respect,

Allen Hendry

Ann MacNeil to David MacNeil, Jr., and Mary MacNeil

[Wishaw, Lanarkshire, Scotland]
[c. April 1884]

Dear Brother & Sister,

We got both of these letters in the beggining of the week but we are so pushed with work that I could not get copying this letter and you could hardly have made it out so I had to wait till to-day.[59] Mother is wondering why you have not written. What do you think we should advise John to do? Mother is afraid of him taking the journey seeing the state he is in and having nothing to go with.

And another thing, I think he supposes that there is far more left than there really is. There seems to be about 160 pounds worth and if it is sold it might draw far less. As the man says it would be sold at a sacrifice and it would take 30 pounds for John to go if he had it. So what would you advise in the matter?

I have not answered Johns letter till you write, so Write immediately as Mother is wondering if anything is wrong. Mother is keeping a good deal better and we are very busy. . . . Your afft sister,

Ann

[PS] I forgot to tell you that I wrote to the man telling him to send us Jamies letters & likenesses and that John would look after the rest.

John MacNeil to Ann MacNeil

Park City
Summit Coy
[Utah]
28 April 1884

Dear Sister Ann,

I Just recd Your welcome Note and hasten to answer it. There is No doubt about the fate of Our Brother James. And the Cause is Recklessness or rather Over anxiety. He Undertook to Cross the River when it was Not fit to be Crossed but he was doing So well and was in Such high hopes of accomplishing Some good for his folks that he took to driving Circumstances. He had arranged with Me to fetch Dave and family if I would try and fetch Father this Season and he Said he Wouldnt Marry until he gave all a Chance that wanted to Come here. Last Letter I had from him he was feeling Uplifted and Confident of accomplishing his purpose. He was Interested in a Saw Mill and Owns a farm. His team, which Means two horses, were drowned with him. That

---

[59] An apparent reference to Allen Hendry's letter of 25 April 1884.

is One Cause of his death. They were as fine animals as were in the Country and he was built up in them and See they was going to drown and [he] Jumped Out in the water ahead of the horses to try and assist them and they Struck him with there feet in their Efforts to get Out and the water being So Strong washed him among their feet. He thought if that team was Lost, he Might as well be (to Much Determination of purpose).[60] I have Nearly Sacrificed My Life in the Same way Several times Since Ive been in this Country.

I am going down to See after him and his Effects as Soon as I Can. He is Eleven Hundred Miles from here and it will Cost More than I Could Come and See You for. It will Cost One hundred & fifty $150 doller to go and Come and I have Only Earned fifty $50 dollers in the Last Eleven Months. Ive been Criple with rheumatics and there is Eight of us to keep. So You Can tell how well prepared I am to go any where. But Im going if I foot it Every inch.

Every person who knew him here are parilized with greef. He was well thought of Everywhere. My wife is feeling as bad Over it as if It had been Me. My Wife is a Mormon and So was Jim and there was a good deal of Sympathy between them.[61]

They havent found his Body Yet the Last account I had. The rivers there are Mostly Moving quick Sand and he May get Covered up in Some hole and Never be found.

If You knew all I know Annie, You would have No room for Your Silly pride and independance. I am Not Necessarily Evil because I differ in Opinion to You in Some things. I always thought You got that Letter and told My wife So.

My Only Friend in this Country is gone Now with the Exception of My wife. Jim & her New My heart but the Majority of the people here are Religious Bigots and have No Sympathy with any person who dont think as they do. To have the Only

---

[60] John is of course making some conjectural leaps; James no doubt wanted to do all he could to save his animals, but he probably did not consider that if they drowned so might he. John's interpretation, however, fits his tendency to be negative in his assessment of the actions of others.

[61] From the context it would appear that John no longer considers himself a member of the church.

Friends I had in the world go back on Me it Made Me a Little Calleous I Own.[62]

I Must tell You that Me and James has Suffered both hunger and Cold to try and help Our Folks and I dont want You to take My word for it Either. There is plenty of Living witnesses here. I am Sick and at work Just Now Strugling to get Enough to go down there. I will Not be able to go Until Sometime in June. I would like to have Davids Adress so I Could write him. I have wrote to My Father.

You Learned of it as Soon as I did Nearly. I didnt know Until the 28th of March and he was drowned on the 18th of March. I will write You More Soon. Comfort My Old Mother as Much as You Can, for her Lot Like James has been a hard One in this world. I have to go to work. So goodby this time From Your Loving Brother,

John H. MacNeil

Allen Hendry to Ann MacNeil

Pima
Graham coy
A.T.
16 June 1884

Dear Madam,
Yours deted May 19th is come to hand. I am Pleased to tell you that we found his body on the 7th of June & buried him Respectfully. He loked real well to have la[i]d in the watter So long. . . .

He felt real well & hearty & was in good Spirets all the time he Stop with us & [talked] often about you & his Mother to us, also about his Father. That he was a Smart Man had he used it for good. . . .

I was well accquiented with Sam Alger, his partner. He has gone to Utah now but I expect he will be back. But I am accqueanted with there bisness. James bought his partners shire

---

[62] It is unclear what John means by the reference to his only friends going back on him, but from the letters that went to Scotland it is evident that there was no love lost between them, despite John's praise of James after his

of everything they had. The land cost $850 dollars & they had a pare of horses worth $400 dolars & a waggon that cost $180 dolars & thay had a corn crop of growing that was reconed $400 dollars. So James agreed to give him $900 dollars for his Shire in everything. That was last Spring a year ago but James had till last January to pay hime. So he Sold two thirds of his land for $800 dolars & during the Summer he let Sam work the horses & he Ridd one. So Sam payed him $200 dolars for it. So when James Sold part of his land he Settle up with Sam & James Still has one third of the land & it is recond worth $400 dolars.

When John Comes hear I can nearly tell him everything what James had. The land that James had at Salt River he give up. Sam Spent his Money very free & did not Make Much, So thay bouth thought that it would [be] better to part. So thay parted good frends. James was the Man that he bought the Shire in the Saw Mill. $80 dollars & one Store bill $70 dollars & another Store $50 dolars & a few Smill bills. His land is about 7 Mills from our house. There was a Small house on his land when he bought it. This Men Bowman had just Started to work for him.

I am Pleased to answere all the questions you wish to aske. I am a very pore writer & dont prictice any carsely So I cannot think of anything to tell you In Such a case has this. I have heard of this Men that is the administrator going to Send Money to fetch his father to this country. John asked Me to see the probate Judge, So I have rode 12 Mils to See him to day But he was gon from home, So I will go toMorrow again. I want to See him before I answer Johns letter. So I Must close, Hoping to hear from you again.

Your last letter was a long time a coming. James used to till Me he was going to Scotland to ore three times yet. I have often thought I would like real well to see it. I was only about ten years old when I left there. So very little I know about it. Your Freand & well wisher,

Allen Hendry

---

death. John frequently raises the issue of freedom of thought, and this streak of independent thinking probably combined with his conflicts with James, his Mormon neighbors, and even his wife, to alienate him from the church.

John MacNeil to David MacNeil, Sr.

Bountiful
Davis Coy
August [1884]

Dear Father,

I have Just been talking with the Probate Judge of this County and he Says the best and only right way to do about Jameses property is for Me to get a power of Attorney to go down there and take it Out of there hands altogether and Settle Everything Myself.

Annie and Dave wrote to Me Letters Certifying they was willing I Should have there Share of Jameses Property. Little did they know that they Couldnt give Me a Cent of it Unles they done it Lawfully. I have wrote to Sister Annie telling her the proper Process; that is, to Send Me a power of Atorney Sworn to and Signed by all of You. Then I Can do Something in the Matter. They Apprized his property at twelve hundred and Ninty Six and fifty Cents $1296&50. If this thing is Sent Me quick I have a Chance to go down with Jameses partner Sam Alger and it will Cost Me Nothing to go. He knows More about Jameses affairs than any person.

Probably Annie will have the paper Made and Sent to You for You to Sign and Swear to before Some proper Officer of the Law who is authorized to Swear People. I Cant do Nothing if One Objects to this and it will be all Stolen in the Shape of Expences. This is the Experience of a probate Judge on this Matter. Your Son, and Daughter,

Jno and Annie MacNeil

John MacNeil to Ann MacNeil

Pima
Graham Coy
Arizona Ter[ritory]
[October? 1884]

Dear Sister Annie,

I thought I would Drop You a few Lines to Let You know I have arrived in Arizona on the Sene of My Brothers Misfortune. I travelled it in 18 days with a horse but it has Nearly Used it up. 1000 Miles in Eighteen days with One horse—it was a rough trip. I travelled hundreds of Miles and Never See a person Except an Indian Once in a while and would Not See water for 40 or 50 Miles at a time.

I have been to Jameses Grave and the place he was drowned and See his dead horses and the Man that Cross the river ahead of him. And also the Man that was in the wagon with him whoes Name is Bowman. I have also See the Administrator Joseph Cluff and I Can tell You I Just Arrived in time to Stop Every thing from being Stole.[63] I dont believe I Can Make My Expences but I am Not Sorrow I Come Now.

I Stood the trip very well but I Little thought I would have to play the part of a detective to recover My dead Brothers bed Clothing and Other things from his Brethern in the Church. Even a Man he fed and had in his Employ Stole his blankets—the Same Man Bowman who was in the wagon with him. But I found him Out and Made him glad to fetch the blankets to Me and beg for Mercy. This Cluff is also No Friend of James. Jim hated him whilest alive worse than a dog and he knowed it but he thought he See a good Chance to Steel so to get even on him. But I have petitioned the Court to have his Letters revoked and I will then be appointed Myself. But the process will Nearly Consume what there is. The Cort fees are So high and I dont believe I Can Sell anything for a Sixteenth part of its value. There is No Money in the place. They are Mostly all Farmers and as poor as Jobs turkey. Cluff Lent his horse harness to a party going to Mexico. Thought he would Never [be] Called in question about it. It wont be back for Sometime but I will hold his bondsmen Until Everything is replaced. James has a Colt, a gun, & pistol his bed and trunk and books I will Endever to retain if I Can Sell the Other property for

---

[63] Joseph Cluff was bishop of the Central Ward, St. Joseph Stake, Arizona, 1883–85. In the late 1880s he was involved in a dispute over buying and selling among the members of the ward, and a "Bishop's Court" (a Mormon ecclesiastical tribunal often used to settle disputes among Mormons) decided that Cluff should pay money and apologize for "scandalizing" a Brother Bigler's "character." Historical Record of Central Ward, St. Joseph Stake, Arizona; also Jenson, *Latter-day Saint Biographical Encyclopedia*, 1:798. (Note: the records of the LDS congregation with which James probably affiliated [Central Ward] did not begin until March 1885, a year after James's death.)

Enough to Meet the Expenses but I will write again Soon. . . .
Your Loving Bro,

John H. MacNeil

[PS] The Estate Cant be Settled up Until in April Sometime, ten
Months from the Ishuing of the Letters to Creditors which will
Cause Me to wait here, and I dont know how My family will get
along. I thought it Could be Settled Sooner.

John MacNeil to Elizabeth Thompson

> Pima. P. Office
> Graham Coy
> Arizona Ter[ritory]
> 29 December 1884

Dear Sister Elizabeth,

I thought I would Just take time whether I Could affort it
or Not to write You. I am here in Arizona on the Sene of Jamies
Misfortune, One thousand Miles from My family and among
Strangers and the principal part of them dont know the Meaning
of the word principal. You Can have a pretty good Idea what
kind of people they are when I tell My Experience among them.

I found the Man Bowman who was in the wagon with Jamie.
He told Me any amount of Lies about the thing. He was also
Staying with Jamie and working for him and when I asked him
about Jamies blankets and Little Effects he denied all knowledge
of them. I then had to play the part of detective and Succeded
very well So far. I Made him Own up to having the blankets and
fetch them to Me. He went down and begged for all was out that
I would have Mercy on him for his parents sake but I Expect to
punish him Yet. I have found More of his Stealing tricks Since
that which I Cant get Over.

I have also found Jamies presiding Bishop Out in Stealing
to. His Name is Bishop Joseph Cluff. He is or was administrator
for James Estate but I have had his letters revoked Since I got
here. He had things fixed up to Steal the whole thing had I Not
happened here as I did. He didnt know I was Coming. I wrote
and told him I wasnt in Circumstances So I Could Come and it
threw him of his guard. He thought he had it all his Own way.

But while I am Streightening those Matters time is flying and I am Not Earning a doller to help My family and they May be Suffering with Cold Now for all I know. I Left them with Just about Enough fire wood to do them a Month Expecting I Could get a Littel work here to help Me but it will take Me all My time to run around after the d — d Lying thieves. I dont think I Could get a days work anyhow without going Nearly a hundred Miles from here and I Couldnt tend to the Estate So far away. I am Adminstrator Myself Now. I Cant Settle the business up Until Sometime in March. The Law requires it Shall run ten Months from the Ishuing of Letters to Creditors So it will throw Me in Spring Coming home and the rivers are all Swollen at that time and dangerous to Cross. Theres No bridges in this Country.

I am Staying at Allan Hendrys. Johnie Thompson worked for Jamie at Globe while Jamie was boss of a Mine there but he got So Much Money for his work that it took away his brains. He got to fast, Made Jamie ashamed of him and offended him pretty bad through keeping Company with a public Hore and Eventually Marrying her. Jamie was glad to get away from there on account of him because people knew they was Connected. This whore Lived with him (Johnie) Until her and her Mother got things in Shape. So they got up One Early Morning bundled up and Left poor Jack with Nothing but his working Clothes. They were gone when he Came from work. So Johnie Left to and I dont know where he is. Jamie didnt know they played him So before he died.[64]

Write to Me and Let me know how Janet and Johnie McLean are getting along, also Bob and Maggie Paterson and Dave and family. I am Not a very good writer or I would write You all Oftener I am so Slow at it. . . .

Wishing You all a happy New Year I will draw to a Close this time. I havent herd from My family Since I have been here Now two Months. . . . Your Loving Brother,

John H. MacNeil

---

[64] John Thompson, a nephew of the MacNeils, had married Mary E. Scott, a daughter of Scottish immigrants, at Globe, Arizona, on 11 March 1883. She may indeed have been a "public hore" as John claims, but John's tendency to see the worst in a situation should be remembered. John Thompson to Ann MacNeil, 12 March 1883, Special Collections, Marriott Library, University of Utah.

John MacNeil to Ann MacNeil

Pima P.O.
[Arizona Territory]
20 January 1885

Dear Sister Ann

I recd Yours of Nov 7th all right. Was Sorry to hear that Mother was Suffering. I Can Sympathize with her very Much because I Suffer daily Myself with Rheumatics & Lumbago. I am almost Cripple with My back Just Now. The water here is Not good.

I wrote You as Soon as I arrived here and Seen how Matters Stood. I hope you recd it. I have had a terrible time with Unmitegated thieves of the Lowest Stripe. I have Everything in My Own hands Now but I Cant Sell Nothing as Yet. There is No Money in this Country to buy Nothing. Ill Soon be flying in rags and bare foot and Nothing to replace them and Cant Sell Nothing to rais a doller and 1000 Miles from Home. Every person that had any dealings with Jamie Stole all they Could.

I am afraid I have in My anxiety to do all I Could in this Matter reached to far I dont know how to get back home Unles I Can Sell Something. And that rascle Bishop Joseph Cluff has pushed it into as Much Expence as possible. He was a bitter Enemy of Jamies and thought to Swallow the whole thing. I am Living with Allan Hendry. He Owns himself that Jamie was the best friend he Ever Met and Yet with all he is Like the rest. Every few days his wife fetches Out Something belonging to Jamie and Say "Oh, heres Something belonging [to] Jamie." . . . and they told Me destinctly they gave Everything to Cluff when I first Come here. I treat them So kind and respectfull that there Conscience Checks them Ignorant as they are. The Mormons as a Class are the Scum of Creation thats Sure.

There is No work I Can get here at present to help Out. The Mines are all Shutting down (Stopping work) and I dont think I Could do Much if I had work to do with My back, and getting worse all the time. I thought it was well when I left Utah.

I will Endivor to fix a fence round Jamies grave and put up a Stone before I leave here. I will have to Cut the Stone Myself and Mark it.

I dont think I Can possibly Sell the Mill Intrest at present for anything and that is the Most Money. There is Six hundred and forty five dollers $645 in it belonging [to] James. I Expect I will have to Leave that in Care of Some Person Until times are a Little More Prosperous. There is No Use giving it away for Nothing.

I Expect this Matter will burst Me up. I gave a Mortgage on My Cow and a Colt for fifty $50 dollers when I Left to Come here with. It Looks rather Cloudy with Me Just Now. I dont know how it will all turn Out. My family are all well Last News. Expect Dave thinks I Slight him Not writing him but I have So Much running around to do. Write Soon, Your Loving Bro.

John H. MacNeil

John MacNeil to Ann MacNeil

Bountiful
David Coy
23 April 1885

Dear Sister Annie,

I have Just got Home. I was detained Longer than I Expected to be on the road Home through One of My Horses kicking the Other and Laming him. So I Could Not travel for two weeks. I had a rough trip of it. I Couldnt Come the way I went. There was to Much Snow that rout, So had to take a Strange road I New Nothing of. I got Meny a wetting which gave Me reumatics very bad. I Could Hardly get in and Out of the wagon I was So bad, but I feel a Little better Now I am home.

I Managed to Sell the Mill Intrest at the Last Minute for five Hundred dollars $500. Jamie had payed for it $746 dollers, but that was the best I Could do and I Only got the party who bought to assume the debts, or Claims against the Estate and pay them. I had a Scratch to get thirty dollers $30 in Money Out of it to take Me home. The bills and Intrest on them, and Court Expenses and My board bill while I was there, and Several Other bills for which I will Send Father receipts as Soon as I get them.[65]

---

[65] John may have been glad that he saw to his brother's affairs. From a practical perspective, perhaps he should have heeded Ann's caution in her letter

Tell Mother I Fixed Jamies Grave up Nice. I Cut a Stone Myself and fenced it with Nice plained pickets. I Cut the Letters out Nice. I also Cut a Scotch thissel on it.[66] I done it so Nice that I got a Job from another party to fix One for them. It is the Most respectable thing of the kind down in that Country, but it has put My affairs at home in a bad fix being So Long away and Not getting home in time to put My Crops in. I am Nearly a Month to Late. but it is the Last Service I will Need to render him and there will be Some way Out of My difficulties.

That Cluff the Administrator and Bishop, was a thief and Scoundrel. Also Allen Hendry was another, and Every One that had anything to do with him, with but One Exception. Thank god My Family have all kept well considering. I Could Sell Nothing but the Mill Intrest So I fetched the wagon and his Colt home with Me. His farm I left in Care of a party to Sell when times got a Little better [and] there was a doller in the Country to buy with. There was None when I was there. I Offered things for half there Value and Couldnt get an offer.

I got home Night before Last and I wrote Father Yesterday. I will write again Soon. I am in Misery at present with rheumatics So will Cut it Short. Hoping this will find You & Mother & Lizzie and all of You well as it Leaves us Comparitively well, Except me. Weather here is Cold and against My rheumatics very Much. Your Loving Bro & Son,

John H. MacNeil

[PS] Write Soon please.

---

of c. April 1884 to David, Jr. She feared that John "supposed there is far more left than there really is."

[66] According to William R. Ridgeway of Thatcher, Arizona, no tombstone for James MacNeil exists in the Pima area. The graveyard was abandoned in 1895 when the "rail-road obtained a right-of-way through this property." Letter to author, 24 August 1984.

6

"Times Are So Dull Here"

Letters from John MacNeil, Janet MacNeil,
David MacNeil, Sr., Annie E. MacNeil
1885–1904

After John Thompson and James MacNeil died and David MacNeil, Sr., separated from his wife, the flow of letters to Scotland decreased — although some of the gaps may be due to letters being destroyed over the years. John MacNeil also gives the impression that he doesn't want to trouble his family with a recitation of his difficulties. In 1887 his mother, Ann Boggie MacNeil, died, and in 1889 David MacNeil, Sr., came to Utah, which further reduced the motivation to write to Scotland.

The excitement of hoping to bring the family to the United States gave way, in this period, to the need to support a growing family — although by 1896 half of John's ten children had died. John persisted in his efforts to make his ranch in Bountiful a success. A major part of his work consisted of boarding and tending the cattle of neighbors during the winter. However, economic necessity and the long-lasting effects of the depression of 1893 dictated that he spend considerable time in other areas, notably in the coal fields of Rock Springs, Wyoming, and in the silver mines of Eureka and Silver City, Tintic County, in central Utah. He was also employed in the Daly West silver mine in Park City. His travels in search of employment and his wife's poor health meant that the family was often separated for long periods of time.

When the patriarch of the family, David MacNeil, Sr., finally came to America in 1889, he was sixty years old. There is good reason to believe that by this time he was only nominally a member of the church. His grandchildren in Utah were unaware that he had ever been a Mormon. His experience was basically separate from the pioneer era in territorial Utah, and for this reason only one of his seven letters has been included in the present collection.

John had his daughters, Annie and Janet, write to their Aunt Ann in Scotland, and it is obvious that he had the usual parental pride in seeing them grow and develop their talents. However, by the turn of the century there is also increasing alienation between John and his children as they sought to establish their individual identities. Of course, some conflict between generations is almost inevitable. But given John's tendency to suspect the motives of others, he may have read more into the difficulties he had with his children than the situation warranted. His oldest daughter, Annie, accompanied him to Park City shortly before his death and helped set up his home there, which indicates some family unity.

John MacNeil apparently did not consider himself a member of the Mormon Church in the last years of his life, and it is possible that his name may have been removed from the records. Although the five children and a stepdaughter are listed in the Census of 1900 for Silver City, Juab County, only the names of his wife and their oldest daughter, Annie, appear on the Record of Members of the Silver City Ward. Perhaps indicative of the relationship between John and Annie is the fact that although they had been married since 1874, on the ward record in 1900 Annie MacNeil was listed as married to William Warrilow. He was actually her first husband and the one to whom she had been sealed "for time and all eternity" in 1869.[1] John's pessimistic view of his family life in his final letters adds to the foreboding which is finally realized in 1903. John MacNeil died in November of that year, and the dream of the "good time coming" vanished forever. Within a year, David MacNeil, Sr., who had begun this Mormon odyssey in 1848, was also dead.

---

[1] Microfilm copies of the Census of 1900 and the Record of Members for the Silver City Ward were examined in the Family History Library, Salt Lake City. I was unable to locate the MacNeils in the ward records of the Bountiful area.

John MacNeil to Ann MacNeil

Bountiful,
Davis Coy.
28 November 1885

Dear Sister,

I take My pen in hand Once More to Let You know how things are in My world. I Expect You thought I had forgot You but I have Not but I was Sick with Catarrh in My head for Over two Months. I Could do Nothing. I am well Now but I have Some kind of a gathering on My Neck Now. Some Say it is a Cancer but I dont know. I havent seen a doctor Yet. It Costs $25 dollers to Speak to a docter and $50 to Speak to a Lawyer here.

I have been trying Farming Since I Come home but it wasnt very Successful because I wasnt well Enough to tend to the Crops.[2] Still, we Live. There has been to or three of My family very Sick this Season. I had a Letter recently From the probate Judge in Arizona requesting I should Send him thirteen $13 dollers for rectifying a Mistake of his own. They have got all poor Jamie had Nearly and Now they want to get a Little Out of Me. But they Cant get it because I havent got it. I payed them all for their Services before I Left. Give kind Love to Mother and Lizzie and all the rest for I havent forgot One of You and accept the Same Yourself. Your Loving Brother,

John H. MacNeil

[PS] Write Soon please and tell Me how Mother Stands it. I Many time think how I Should Like to See her Once More but when I Look at the Crowd of Young Ones around Me I Lose hope. You will forgive Me for Not writing You More and telling You all My

---

[2] By this time John and Annie MacNeil had apparently moved to a larger ranch of some 100 acres which probably straddled the boundary between Davis and Salt Lake County. In 1889 John transferred the title of this land to Annie, perhaps to protect it from lawsuits. It was transferred back to him after her death in 1903. Grantee and Grantor Index, Davis County, Utah, Recorder's Office. The record book containing an exact description of the ranch is missing at the Salt Lake County Recorder's Office, but John and Annie MacNeil are listed as landowners in the Index to Names in Salt Lake County. According to family recollections, the property was located east of Beck Hot Springs on a plateau near the Monroc Gravel Pit.

troubles but I am a Man and Never Can do it, because I know You have Enough of Your Own. Your Brother,

John [MacNeil]

John MacNeil to Ann MacNeil

Rock Springs
Sweetwater Coy.
[Wyoming Territory]
14 February 1886

Dear Sister,

It is a Long time since I wrote you Last but as I told You, I Never forget altogether. But I have Lots of trouble, More than I wish Everybody to know about, because they Couldn't help Me No Matter how well they wished Me. Looking after Jamies affairs burst Me up in this Country. I morgaged My home to get Means to go with and I am afraid I Never Can Lift it. Work is so Scarce and wages so Low and My family so big and Not big Enough to work to help Me any.

I Never get any answer to My Last Yet. I Hope Everything is Well with You all.

You May See by My Letter I am at Rock Springs [Wyoming]. That is a Little town on the Side of the Union Pacific Railway. It's three Hundred Miles from My home and family. I am digging Coal there. We have to dig all day and when we come home wash and go to work Cooking Our Own Supper. No women here. Costs to Much to fetch them here. Railway travel is so high here and the work so uncertain. It May run a Month and it May Not. It is Just according to the demand for Coal.

My health isnt as good as it used to be Either. I am troubled with Lumbago and rheumatics Considerable Now. I am going grey fast Now Annie, I dont Suppose You would know Me Now if you See Me. The last five years has Made an awful difference in Me.

I have four children alive besides the two My wife had when I Married her. They are grown up Young women.[3] One is Nearly

---

[3] He is referring to Elizabeth and Amberzine Warrilow, his foster daughters. According to John's granddaughter, Mrs. Gladys H. Thorne, John was

Nineteen, One Seventeen. I have One, My Oldest, Named after You and Mother, Annie; One after Janet. One boy David, One Cloyde.

I will have the Little girls write You. They are at School.[4] One, Annie is twelve, Nettie or Janet is ten past. Annie isnt a very Stout Child but Nettie is. Annie had a Severe Sick Spell when She was a baby and it Left Some drag to her health. But She is a bright Young One and Likes Study better than Nettie. . . . Your Loving Brother,

John H. MacNeil

[PS] Adress as before to Bountiful, write soon.

John MacNeil to Ann MacNeil

Bountiful
Davis Coy
19 March 1886

Dear Sister,

I recd Your welcome Letter all right. Was glad to hear from You Once More. That Cancer turned Out to be a blind boil and it is all well Now.

I have Just got Home from the Coal beds at rock Springs. I Stayed there three Months but I didnt Make Much. The work didnt run Steady. Times are duller here the Last two Years than was Ever Known before. Business is Nearly at a Stand Still and Nobody knows the Cause. Times are Just about the Same as You describe them to be there. I have felt better in health Ever Since that boil burst. I have felt better in health this winter than I have done for Several Years. I found My family all well in health when

very attached to these girls and treated them as his own children, giving them opportunities for schooling and the study of music.

[4] According to Mrs. Thorne, her mother, Annie MacNeil, attended a Congregational Church school in Bountiful. The "hidden curriculum" of these schools was to help "Christianize" the children of Mormon parents. However, even faithful Mormons sent their children to such institutions because they offered an education superior to the Mormon-run public schools. For a discussion of this phase of educational history in Utah see Buchanan, "Faith in Schooling," 154-67.

I come home but My wife was Sick. Nearly all the time I was gone. She suffers greatly with Neuralgia.

You think You wouldnt have done very well in this Country but women do far better than Men and there is always plenty of work for women here. My girls Can get work all the time but Men Cant. I am Out of work Now and Cant get None in the Country. Just Living and hoping for better times. Still we get Enough to Eat. If My health Keeps well and times Changes I May do better Yet. It will Not be Many Years before I have a boy big Enough to help Me a Little.

Annie and Janettie are going to write You a little Letter. They talk Lots about their Aunt Annie and how they would Like to See her and also their Scotch grandma. My Oldest is Annie Eleven, Next is Janettie, 9 past. Next is David 6 Years. Next is Cloyde or the baby who is three Years Old. My wife has two girls of her Own, Eldest is Ambroizine Worrilow. And Elizabeth Worrilow. Ambrozine is Nineteen. Lizzie is 17.

I dont get No word from arizona Lately. The Indians are raising thunder down there.[5] I am afraid I will Never realize Nothing from what is Left but thank goodness I done My duty and I feel Content it will all Come right Sometime. My Wife and Family Join in Sending there regards. Ask David to write Me a few Lines and Let me know how he gets along. . . . Your Loving Brother,

John and Annie MacNeil

P.S. You will See by the Papers No doubt How the Goverment is dealing with Polygamy here. That is Halping to Make times worse also.[6]

---

[5] The Indians were of course "raising thunder" because of the continual intrusion of whites on their lands. Conflicts between Apaches and Mormon settlers in the Gila Valley led to a number of deaths in 1885 and 1886, according to McClintock, *Mormon Settlement in Arizona*, 254.

[6] The federal campaign against polygamy had driven many Mormon leaders and businessmen into hiding by the end of 1886, thus contributing to economic instability in Utah. Arrington notes that "with almost all leaders of Latter-day Saint communities in prison or in hiding, business establishments were abandoned, or were kept in operation by inexperienced wives and children." Arrington, *Great Basin Kingdom*, 360. For a detailed analysis and account of the federal drive against polygamy, see chapters 4 through 10 of Larson, *The "Americanization" of Utah for Statehood*.

Janet MacNeil to Ann MacNeil

Bountiful
29 March 1886

Dear aunt Annie,

I thought I would write a few lines to you all hoping to find you all well. I wish I could write as good as you could.

I go to school now and have good times. The teacher is a good teacher. We had good times on Christmas and New years. We had a christmas tree here. The card is for grandma.

We read in the fourth reader and the fourth Geography in the third Arithmac and the first Grammer. I cannot write good enough to write to strangers. I close with kind love to all from Miss Nettie MacNeil.[7]

Annie E. MacNeil to Ann MacNeil

Bountiful
28 March 1886

Dear aunt Annie,

I thought I would write to you and grandma and Aunt Lizzie, just to show you I can write a little. I often wish I could write like you, then I would write you a long letter and ask you lots of funy questions.

I would like to no how old grandma is and when her birthday is. I often think I would like to see her and you and all of you. I think I could ask you questions enough to tire you all out ansering them.

I think if you was here I would have you make me a hat. I hope this will find you all well. From Miss Annie MacNeil.[8]

---

[7] Janet MacNeil was ten years old when she wrote this letter. She died of diphtheria in 1891 at the age of fifteen.

[8] Ann MacNeil was twelve years old in 1886.

John MacNeil to Ann MacNeil

Bountiful
13 December 1886

Dear Sister Annie,

I Just recd Your welcome Letter. Was glad to hear from You Once More. I had began to think Something was wrong that You didnt write. I Just recd a Letter from Father along with Yours. He also hasnt wrote for a Long time before. That Made Me think Something Must be wrong, but I am glad You are all alive. As for Me I am pretty well at present and So also is My family. My wife is pretty well as regards Neuralgia but is troubled Considerable with her breath. It is very Like Asthma Only it Comes and goes. She feels Stifled up.

Since I wrote before we have had an Increase on the Ninth of August in Our family, a boy Now 4 Months Old and doing well. His Name is Roy MacNeil.

I have been trying to farm this Summer but have Made Nothing. Times are So dull here that produce is worth Nothing So I Cant Say I have Earned anything Much Since Last winter. Only I rais My vegetables and Such for Our Own Living and also Our own Meat and Eggs and we raised a Little fruit this Season. Our Orchard is Just beginning to bear. That is Considerable help to a family here. I also Milk three Cows but butter Isnt worth Much, Only twenty five Cents per pound, and twenty five Cents in this Country is Just about Equivolent to two pence in Scotland. You get as much for two pence.

I turned Stone Mason this Summer and built Me a rock foundation for a house. I purpose trying to build the House Next Season Myself. It will be thirty feet Long by fourteen wide. There will be two rooms, One 15 x 14; the Other will be 14 x 14 and two rooms up Stairs for bed rooms. I will do it all Myself. Men here has to do Every thing themselves of that kind and almost Every other Kind.

The government is going after the Mormons here pretty Lively about polygamy. There determined to put it down. That is One Cause of the depression here. The Mormons is flying in all directions from the wrath to Come. They havent as Much faith in their god as You Could put in a Midges Eye but it [is] Making busines of all kinds dull until the trouble is Settled One way or tother.

I will [come] home after Christmas and hunt work Somewhere to get My flour and Some Clothing.⁹ I will draw to a Close this time by wishing You a Merry Christmas and a Happy New Year Give. My Love to Mother and Lizy and all the rest and accept the Same YourSelf. From Your Loving Brother *and* Sister,

Jno *and* Annie MacNeil

John MacNeil to Ann MacNeil

Bountiful
Davis County
2 August 1887

Dear Sister,

I Just recd Your Letter Last Night. Was Sorrow to hear of Mothers Death although I Cant say the Sad News was unexpected. I Looked for it Sometime. Your Mothers Birth day was the 17th of July. Nine days More would Made her 73 Years Old.¹⁰

I Expect You will feel Lonesome without her for Sometime but You Must brace up and Still Hope for brighter days. She Could Not Live always unles in Our Memorys. I Cant write Much this time but I will Send You a Little practicle Help. I will Send you a Little Money by post office Order. We are all well Unles Me. I am Lame by gitting kicked with a horse on the Leg. It is getting better though. Love to Lizzie YourSelf and all of You Let Me know where Mother is burried. No More this time From Your Loving Brother,

John MacNeil

[PS] Write again please

---

⁹ John is working at the Rock Springs, Wyoming, coal mines at this time.

¹⁰ Ann Boggie MacNeil died 8 July 1887 at Wishaw, Lanarkshire. Her age was recorded as seventy, but she was actually almost seventy-six, having been born 17 July 1811. When she joined the Mormon Church she gave her birth year as 1814, perhaps to reduce the eighteen-year gap between her age and that of her husband. David, incidentally, *increased* his age at that time and said he was born in 1827 instead of 1829. Airdrie Branch Record of Members.

John MacNeil to Ann MacNeil

Bountiful,
Davis Coy
29 January 1888

Dear Sister Annie,

It is Sometime Since I wrote You before but I have recd No answer to My Last as Yet. I wrote the Same Night I recd Intimation of Mothers Death and also Sent You fifteen dollers in the Shape of a post office Order. I have been anxious for Sometime to know if You got it all right. . . . I also recd One from Bro David at the Same time but have Not answered that as Yet. I had Occasion to go of to work away from home One Hundred and twenty five Miles . . . and I forgot Davids Letter in My Hurry going of and My folks Couldnt find it as Yet.

I am at present digging Coal in a place Called Pleasant Valley[11] but I think will Soon be home again to My family in Bountiful. Work in this Country is Not Steady Like it is in the Old Country. It will probably run two or three Months and then Shut Down. My health has been very good the Last Year and also My familys health with the Exeption of My wife who Suffers a great deal from Neuralgia. She is at present pretty Sick with a Sore throat the Last Letter I recd from them Intimated. . . . I would Like to know whether or Not You recd the Money. I would also Like to hear if You are all well and how You are getting along. . . .

I built Me a house this Summer Myself on My own Land with four rooms. I was busy doing that when I got Your Letter Stating Mother was dead. My Family So far as I know are Comparitively well at present. . . . Your Affectionate Bro,

Jno H. MacNeil

---

[11] A coal mining area then in Emery County, Utah, also known as Winter Quarters. Now in Carbon County.

John MacNeil to Ann MacNeil

Scofield[12]
Emery Coy
[Utah]
16 March 1888

Dear Sister,

I recd Your Welcome Letter all right. Was glad to hear from You Once More but am sorrow to think You feel So Lonely Since Mother died. I am glad You got that few dollers I Sent for I begin to get Uneasy about it and also about You. I thought Something Else Must be rong with You.

You Say I write Strange about Mothers Death. Well I will tell You I dreamed So frequently of her that I Nearly Expected the News. But I want You to Cheer up and Not Sink Under the affliction. There May be bright days in Store for You Yet. Have You Ever any Notion of Coming to America to visit Me. It Might do You good A trip across the Sea.

You asked a question about how women were paid in this Country. Well I Just tell You it is the best place in the world for girls. They Can double discount a Man at getting along. They get good Wages and plenty Employnent but it is hard for Men to get Sufficient. Girls gets from two dollers and a half to four dollers per week.

My wife Still Suffers from Neuralgia I havent been home for three Month. I am about one hundred and twenty five Miles from home. I will go home a few days Next Month. I am Sinking a pit for Coal.

Does David have No Notion of Coming to this Country? Now I would Like very Much to have the Means to Spare to Come and See You all. I Could go and Come for one hundred and forty dollers Now this Season but I have been building Me a house and it Costs a deal of Money hear for Lumber or boards are so dear.

I will write Dave Soon. Give Love to all Our folks and accept the Same for Yourself. Your Loving Bro,

John H. MacNeil

---

[12] In Carbon County since 1894.

John MacNeil to Ann MacNeil and Elizabeth Thompson

> [c/o Mrs MacDuff
> Hotsprings]
> Salt Lake City
> 1 December 1895

Dear Sister,

. . . I hate to write to anyone because I am So Subject to writing Just as I happen to feel and so I keep putting it of. I would rather Not Complain.

My Kind of Independance Seems to be different to Fathers. His kind of Independance is a humbug, a fraud; he Never knew what Independance Meant. His Independance has been Lazyness or an Excuse to throw up any work he Might get to do to Earn a Living, No Matter how Light, No Matter how Well Addapted to his Strength. He is down as Low as Old Mary Clark Ever was as a City Dodger and he is Set and determined to do it and disgrace us where ever we are or Else we must keep him in Spending Money and gambling Money.

He hunts up all My acquaintances and Jameses and Sponges & Milks them for all they will Stand. Then when they will do No More for him and have found him a Lazy Imposter he Calls them daft. Everybody is daft that will Not let him Impose on them and at the Same time abuse them. My Wife is a Hore, Mrs Marshall is a whore, all women are whores with him Now. And he is bound to treat them as Such in the face of there trying to Clean his filth and No person will Stand it.

No doubt he is pulling a poor Mouth to You and Dave Just as he did to Me while in the Old Country. I have a parcel of his poverty Stricken Letters kept to prove it to You if I Ever See You.[13] Then I take of My Means to fetch him to this Country and the first thing he does is to Commence ridiculing the Country and

---

[13] Unfortunately, none of the letters that David MacNeil, Sr., wrote to his family in Utah have survived. According to Mrs. Gladys Thorne, after John's death thieves broke into the family home in Bountiful and pilfered John's possessions. The letters he refers to may have disappeared at that time. It is possible, too, that the family may have discarded them as trash in later years. Presumably James MacNeil's surviving letters (which John brought from Arizona) were kept with John's.

telling My Connexions he Never See the day in the Old Country he hadnt a pound to put on a horse race. And My Wife gets to know it all and tells Me Ive Lied about him. I Used to tell her he was Such a perticular person about his Looks and Everything Else and then for him to turn Out directly the Opposite. It has given My Wife grounds for Saying things I will Never Forgive Worlds without End.

If I could Sell Out My property I would have Left before Now. But things are in Such a Condition in America Just Now You Cant Sell Nothing. Values are taken away from Everything through a financial Goverment Gamble.[14] So Much So the Country is Nearly Bankrupt. Both of My Oldest boys Left Me this Season, One 12 the Other 15 years Old.[15] They found Out they Could work a little and wanted to do it for themselves or in Other words they got to big for their Clothes.

My Wife is also Sick all the time in the Summer, Ever Since Janettie Died and Collin. Which is four Years Now.[16] It Costs all I Can Earn and More to Doctor her. Doctors here Charges 25 dollers for Looking at Your tongue. We are all More or Less troubled with Milaria or Fever and Ague in the Summer and It is getting a Hold on Me this Last two Years So My Health is giving way Considerably Lately. My Son David is a bigger Man than Me and They Could help Me Considerable, but in this Country they dont believe in it. If we had been raised here Father Never Could have done as he was with us. It is rightly Named Free America.

I do Not put to Much Stress on Fathers poverty Stricken Letters because he will always Squeel in time. I am terribly disapointed in Father. I Cant See how I didnt find him Out Sooner but he Must have Showed it up blunter after I Left the house.

There is No work for Men in this Country Just Now Everything is at a stand Still. Thousands of Men idel all Over the Country and the American people are finding Out that they are Not

---

[14] John may be referring to the repeal of the Sherman Silver Purchase Act in 1893, which relieved the federal government of the obligation to buy silver from American mines. Although repeal of the act contributed to financial stability in the East, it was highly unpopular in the western mining communities.

[15] Clouide James MacNeil and David William MacNeil.

[16] Colin (aged two years) died 9 September 1891, and Janet (aged fifteen years) died three days later, 12 September 1891, both of diphtheria.

Such a great people as they thought they were.[17] . . . Hoping to hear from you Soon and that You are all well I will Close this time by wishing You a Happy Christmas and a happy New Year. Your Loving Brother,

Jno H. MacNeil

P.S. the Child You was Curious about is a Little girl belonging to the Owner of the Lodging House in which he Stays and where he used to work and Might have been working Yet. The Child is attached to him greatly. He nursed and plays with her a good deal and She would rather go to him than its Mother.

John MacNeil to Ann MacNeil and Elizabeth Thompson

[c/o Mrs MacDuff
Becks Hotsprings]
Salt Lake City
9 March 1903

Dear Sisters,

I recd Yours of Feb 8th all right Yesterday. The Other MacNeils in Bountiful packed it around in their Pockets a week before giving it up. Had Lots of trouble with those Parties over My Mail. Theyr Mean Irish.

Now to Business. My Honest reasons for Not writing was this. I am given to writing as I feel very Much and I didnt want You to Shoulder any troubles of Mine. I thought Your Own would be Enough. Ive had a great deal of Sad Experience Since I wrote You Last. I have Burried five of My Children and have five Left and am Sorry I didnt burry them also.[18] Theyr Not worth Owning.

---

[17] During the years from 1893 until after 1900 the United States suffered one of its most severe economic depressions. Twenty percent of nonagricultural workers were unemployed, 800 banks failed, 156 railroad companies went bankrupt. At the beginning of the "Cleveland depression" there was a 64 percent drop in new stock issues in the stock exchange and farm prices dropped to their lowest point in thirty years. Utah's economy, based as it was on agriculture, mining, and transportation, was hard hit. John MacNeil was especially vulnerable because of his efforts to maintain his large family through farming *and* mining—the ardor of farmers had been dampened by the depression and mines were shutting down. Arrington, "Utah and the Depression of the 1890s," 3–18.

[18] If the surviving letters accurately reflect the actual correspondence between John and his sister, the last letter he wrote was in 1895. If this was

My Wifes been an Invalid Ever Since we Married Nearly. She is troubled with Asthma and Cant Live down in the valley any More. She is Living in the Mountains a Hundred Miles from Me, where I Used to work the Last Seven Years. I am on My Farm Now all alone. Cooking My Own Vitals but Not working the Farm. Just Staying On it trying to Sell it.

My boys that are Left Me Seems to be all thurily Lazy. They have taken after Father and My wifes People both. Never Nobody New them to work. Two of My boys are Over twenty and One 16 and they Hardly know what work is and Wont do it. The Effects of bad training by a too Indulgent Mother.

If I Should be fortunate Enough to Sell I Might Give You a Call Someday.

My Selection of a Partner wasnt very good. Ive realized the truth of the Song. Loves a riddle, and Marriage a Lottery and wives at the alter are Bought and Sold.[19] My wife has pulled at the Opposite End of the rope Ever Since we was Married and throw Cold water on My Enterprise Every Chance. My Wife is as Ignorant as a Stear Only in religious Matters. She is a Staunch Mormon. I have No use for religion whatever.[20] My troubles Have Made Me as grey as a rat, greyer than Father Lots.

I am Sorrow to tell You Annie but Father is playing You the Same as he did Me. I had a parcel of Poverty Stricken Letters I Preserved which he wrote Me from the Old Country which I Meant to be able to Show You before Now, but Circumstances Hasnt Permited. I think its a Shame You Should Sit up Nights Sowing Until You are Cripled to Earn Money to Send to a Man that will Put it to a bad Use.

---

indeed the case, then his account of the number of children buried since he last wrote is inaccurate. His children died as follows: John in 1879; James in 1882; Colin and Janet in 1891; Gladys in 1896. He had buried five children since 1879 but only one since 1895. Possibly there was a hiatus in writing between John and his sister, with most of the correspondence being between Ann and her father, David.

[19] Apparently a song of the period which I have not been able to identify.

[20] According to a strict Mormon interpretation of their marriage doctrine, the children his wife bore to him would in fact not be his, because he was never sealed to his wife for time and all eternity. She had already been sealed to her first husband on 2 February 1869, and she could not be sealed to John, too. If he realized this after being married and having children, it may have contributed to his alienation, although it was not the cause of it. Gladys H. Thorne to author, 10 March 1987.

He Says were aw [all] daft and Everybody Else that will tolerate him is daft also. He is fuller of tricks than Old Mary Clark Ever was.[21] If You give him a Shilling he will go to the gambling House right Straight and if he Makes it known to You he wants Some Money and You dont Shell Out he will go right before You to Shame You. [He will] go up to the Mayor of the City or the president of the bank and beg a few dollers. I Couldnt begin to tell You in a half dozen Letters of his tricks. He is as Clear heded today as he Ever was or Nearly So, but Scotch Independance he Never had None.

His Claim that his Scotch Independance was a bar to his Success was all My Eye. He Never had any. Laziness was the word as Mrs [Whasny?] Said about him. Everybody treats him to well. He Squeels in plenty good time, dont You forget it. He wont allow himself to be treated bad. He will find Some way to Make Someone wait on him and they will get No thanks after. Hees Liable to tell Someone theyr daft. I have No patience No More with it because it has ruined My Life. I worked, and My Brothers, to Support and Encourage a Lazy trickster, but we was taught it was rong to Suspect Your Parents. My Family have Inherited all of his traits with a dirtyer Streek added from the Other Side. So theyr No good.

I Could at One time have Sold My Home for thirteen thousand dollers. Now I am trying hard to get three thousand.[22] The Place has gone all to ruin through Leaving it to the Care of Strangers on account of her Asthma and Like Father, I get No thanks for that Sacrifice Either. So between One rascle and another I am Nearly ready to Sit down on the Lot.

I am all Over My Sickness Now and feel pretty good. Got Some flesh on My bones again. This has been a Long hard winter here and Still Snowing. To be Continued in My Next. Best wishes to all of You. . . . Your Loving Brother,

John MacNeil

Editor's Note: Around August of 1903 John MacNeil established another home in Park City where he was employed in the

---

[21] Mary Clark is mentioned as an example of an undesirable person who apparently lived near the MacNeils in Scotland.

[22] This was because of the depression's impact on land values.

Daly West silver mine. In September he was nominated as the Socialist Party candidate for Police Justice in Park City.[23] However, when his wife, Annie, died of pneumonia on 16 September 1903, he declined the nomination. Although many of John's sentiments about mine owners and "big wigs" in the Mormon Church reflect socialist orientation from the mid-1870s on, there is no evidence of his being affiliated with the movement until 1904. He may have first become acquainted with the movement during his sojourn c. 1902 in Eureka, Utah. It was in Eureka that the Socialist Party later had its greatest success in electing a socialist mayor and town administration.[24]

John MacNeil to Ann MacNeil and Elizabeth Thompson

> Daily West Mine
> [Park City, Utah]
> 5 October 1903

Dear Sisters,

It Seems as though I Cant write to You without it is a record of troubles. I have to tell You Now of the Death of My wife on the 16th of Last Month, but there is One thing I am thankful for that is the Children are all grown up. The Youngest is a Little girl Kattie Nearly 13 Years, Next is Roy 17 Years, Next is Clouide 20 Years. Next is David 23 Years, Next is Annie 28 Years. My wife Died of pneumonia in Park City, a Mining Camp 30 Miles from Salt Lake City. Me and Roy are working there Now. She had Just turned 55 Years. Had very poor Health all the time She Lived with Me. Was troubled with Asthma all the time and Other Complications. She took Colds Easy on Account of her Condition. Just a Change of bed gave her the Last Cold which Ended her Sufferings. I burried Her in Bountiful along Side 5 of Our Children.

It is Lots Cheeper to Live than to Die in this Country. It Cost 50 dollers for her Casket, 25 dollers for Embalming So I Could Ship her Home to Bountiful, 25 dollers for 3 visits of a

---

[23] The *Park City Record*, 12 September 1903.

[24] A relatively large number (more than 40 percent) of the Socialist Party members were also members of the LDS Church. Sillitoe and McCormick, "Socialist Saints," 121–31.

Doctor and so on all along the Line. But My Health is Comparitavely good and I wont give up Yet while that Lasts.

I See Father while down at the City. He Looked well but had the Usual Complaints to Make of Corse. He was Still Living in town but was talking of going to Springvalle about 56 Miles South of Salt Lake City. Some Scotchman of his acquaintance wanted him to go Live with them. I recd Your Photos all right. My wife Just got a Look at them before She Died.

You will have to address us at Park City until further Notified. We are all well at Present writing and hope You are also well. Will write You More Later on. My best regards to all at Present. Your Loving Brother,

John MacNeil

P.S. Put Daily west Mine acros the end of Envelop in Small writing.

Editor's Note: With this account of woe, John MacNeil's record of his attempts to establish a successful life in America came to an end. One month after John wrote this last letter to his sisters, his father picked up a copy of the *Salt Lake Tribune* for Sunday, 9 November 1903, and read there the following news item which he clipped and sent to his daughter Ann in Scotland.

TWO MINERS MEET DEATH BY CAVE-IN
Salt Lake Tribune
November 9, 1903
[TRIBUNE SPECIAL]

Park City, Utah, Nov. 9—John McNeil and Martin Powers were killed at 11:30 A.M. today by a cave-in at the Daly West mine. The victims of the accident were working in the face of a drift immediately above the 900-foot level when a slab of rock five feet long and a foot thick fell from overhead and crushed them.

BODIES ARE RECOVERED.

Carman Owen McGregor was standing near and the falling rock missed him by about two feet. The warning was passed to Shift Boss William Gray and the bodies were recovered from the debris in a few minutes. McNeil was dead and Powers expired on being let down to the 900-foot level.

The place of the accident is in a drift at the top of a raise and the ground was considered safe. The ore breaks off from the hanging wall, leaving a smooth, solid surface, called by miners "treacherous smooth." The workers took the usual precautions each day, so that the end came without a moment's warning. The men were both in a sitting posture engaged in drilling and the jar thus imparted to the rock brought the overhanging mass down.

BODIES TAKEN TO UNDERTAKERS.

Upon news of the accident the day shift of the Daly West was allowed to lay off for the rest of the day. The bodies were brought to Richardson's late this afternoon to await the wishes of the relatives.

POWERS AN OLD RESIDENT.

Mr. Powers is an old resident, having lived here nineteen years, and was 57 years old. He has a wife and three children in Butte, Mont., who have been apprised of the accident, but no message has yet been received from them. Mr Powers belonged to the Miners' union and will receive burial from that organization. He belongs to the order of Workmen and his family will receive $2000.

McNEIL FROM BOUNTIFUL.

Mr. McNeil was 55 years old, has a family of five children living, the youngest of whom is a 15-year old girl. Mr. McNeil came here from Bountiful about two months ago to work in the mine. Two weeks after this his wife died from pneumonia, so that the children are left without parents. Two of the boys are working in the Daly West and the family has just moved into a home together when the accident occurs.

DECLINES SOCIALIST NOMINATION.

Mr. McNeil was nominated by the Socialist party for the office of City Justice, but on account of his bereavement declined the nomination. He carried no insurance of any kind. His body will be shipped to Bountiful by his children tomorrow for burial. An inquest has not yet been decided upon.

David MacNeil to Ann MacNeil

> LINCOLN HOUSE
> 68 E. First South St.
> Salt Lake City, Utah
> Nov 9th 1903

Ann,

I enclose cutting from todays paper but must ask you to excuse me. I cant write. Four times I have undergone this kind of calamity, hand Shakes so much.[25]

I may steady further on.

Your Father D Mc Neil

(God preserve you)

*Annie E. MacNeil to Ann MacNeil
and Elizabeth Thomson*

[752 N. 2nd West]
Salt Lake City
20 April 1904.

Dear Aunties,

I have at last found time to answer your most kind & everso much welcome letter which I recd the latter part of March. You said Dear Auntie, I would wonder at you not writing sooner . . . I knew I should have written before but I knew that Grandpa would write & tell you about it all. And I was so bewildered & stunned at both Mamma and papa going so soon after the other that it very near drove me out of my mind & I have just began to feel that I must get along with[out] them.

Well Auntie you ask me where we was living when we left Bountiful. We went one-hundreed 100 Miles south to a mining place called Mammoth, where pa & the oldest boy was working in the mines. The other two boys were to yong, they went to school. We lived there 3 years. While we was living there we burried the baby. She was two years old when she died in Mammoth.

All the rest of the family was out there but my brother Clouide & I we were on the ranch in Bountiful. While my brother & I was on the ranch he took the Scarlet fever at the same time my two little sisters had it in Mammoth. The baby was so delicate she died but my brother & other little sister is still alive.

Pappa burried 5 children 2 two girls & three boys. There is 5 of us living, two girls three boys. Just the same amount living as

---

[25] The four calamities are probably the deaths of his stepson William Thompson in an industrial accident in Scotland in 1863, that of his stepson John Thompson in Illinois in 1874, the drowning of his youngest son, James, in Arizona in 1884, and now the accidental death of his oldest son, John, at Park City in 1903.

dead, but we have two half sisters that are married that are very good to us.

Dear Auntie after we had stayed in Mammoth for three years we then moved to Silver City 3 miles farther south where we stayed the remainder of the time untill one year ago last spring. Papa came back on to the ranch to prepare it for our coming back the following after. Then he went to Park City to work in the winter & left Mamma, my two Sisters & my yongest brother in Silver City. Then I came in here in the Spring to prepare for Mamma coming in the fall. When she come home she was only here about two days when she took sick again with her old complaint, the asthma. Then papa took her out to Park City with him. She was out there two days & felt fine when she took down with pneumonia and within 5 days we brought her corpse back. Then papa had me move out to [Park City] with him & the boys & my little sister went out to Mammoth with my married sister to go to school.

So I went up to Park City one sunday morning & papa met me at the depot, took me to the house he had rented and he told me to get the house fixed up and they would stay up to the bunk house untill I was ready for them. I got ready for them to come down Saturday. Papa stayed with us one night, went to work sunday morning, & at half past 4 oclock he was killed & never come home any more. They took him straight from the mine to the undertakers.

Dear Auntie I never got to see the mine that papa was killed in. The people would not let me go. They held me back & they wouldn't let me see him untill 7 oclock that night. Then he was all washed & dressed & he did look nice just like he had gone to sleep. He did have a pleasant look on his face. I thought he would be all crushed to pieces so that we would not know him, but not so. His arm was broken & his chest crushed and a little gash cut in his head. There was tuns & tuns of Rock fell on him they tell me, so I think he looked Nice to think his face & body was not mangled up any worse. We brought him home and burried him beside Mamma & the children.

Dear Auntie you ask me if the boys had work. No they have not had only two weeks work all winter. My oldest brother worked one week in Salt Lake City then he could not get any more work. Then he went to Eureka Mining Camp & he got one weeks work there. Papa had enough money to burry on & fix up the place just a little. We had to have something to live on so I had to get out to work, as the boys did not find work in the country. We are home now on the ranch.

Dear Auntie please do not address your letters to Bountiful anymore, as there is another McNeil in Bountiful. They get our mail & some time we do not get it for months, sometimes not at all.

Well Dear Auntie I will draw my letter to a close or you will never want me to write to you again. I hope you can read this. My pen was so poor that I could only scribble, and I have not got my nerves thurrly settled yet. Pleas do write soon & I will try & answer sooner. This is all this time. Good night from your sincer niece,

Annie E [MacNeil]

Editor's Note: In the next few years the stream of letters to the MacNeils, which began in 1853 with James Brady's description of life among the Saints six years after the Mormon entry to the Salt Lake Valley, dwindled to a mere trickle. After 1904 Ann MacNeil in Scotland and her niece, Annie MacNeil, in Utah exchanged only a few letters. Gone was the urgency and the conflict of the earlier years as a new generation, which had never known the call to gather to Zion or the struggle over religious commitment, began to build their own lives quite oblivious to the drama that had preceded them.

On 29 October 1904, the man who had forged the first links of the MacNeil family with Mormonism, David MacNeil, Sr., died of tuberculosis in St. Mark's Hospital.[26] On the same day he was buried in a pauper's grave in the Salt Lake City Cemetery. His grandchildren in Utah were unaware that he had died and his daughter, Ann, did not receive word of his death until almost nine months had elapsed. Nor were his kin in Utah aware that he had ever been a Mormon.[27]

---

[26] St. Mark's Hospital for many years functioned as the Salt Lake County Hospital and contracted to take care of indigents such as David MacNeil. Tuttle, *Reminiscences of a Missionary Bishop,* 403.

[27] Around 1911 Ann MacNeil revealed the extent to which the MacNeil family connection with Mormonism had faded over the years. Said she: "I have always meant to ask you if any of you belong to The Mormon Church. I know your father did not belong to it. I suppose there are all kinds of religion in the

David MacNeil's stepdaughter Elizabeth Thompson died in 1906 at Wishaw, Lanarkshire, at age sixty-three. In 1917, Ann MacNeil, Jr., who played such an important role in keeping the family in contact with each other and who apparently preserved the correspondence of fifty years, died in Wishaw at age sixty-four. She left instructions that a share of her estate be sent to her niece, Annie MacNeil Henkel, in Utah. However, the lawyers in Glasgow and Salt Lake City were unable to make contact with Annie and the money was divided among the cousins in Scotland.

When contacts were resumed in 1920, the MacNeils in Glasgow said they did not know the addresses of any of the family in Utah. Nor, ironically, did they know the whereabouts of the "American letters" which John and his brothers had sent from the United States over the years.[28] The last surviving son of David MacNeil and Ann Boggie Thompson MacNeil, David MacNeil, Jr., could not help his family in their search: he was senile and died at Glasgow 26 December 1922 at age seventy-two. Not until 1964, when the son of David, Jr., died in Ayr and the box of letters was discovered in his attic, did the MacNeils in Scotland become aware of the family's role as participants in the drama of the Mormon gathering to Utah.

City not like what it used to be. Are the Mormons allowed to rule, that is in the legislation of the Country [?] You will be amused at me asking these questions, but since your father died I hear so little." Ann MacNeil to Ann Eliza MacNeil Henkel, c. 1911. Special Collections, Marriott Library, University of Utah.

[28] David McNeill III to Ann MacNeil Henkel, October 7, 1920. Special Collections, Marriott Library, University of Utah.

Appendix A

Songs Requested by John and James MacNeil

The following are samples of some of the songs that John and James MacNeil asked their parents to send to them for entertainment while they were working in the mines at Almy, Wyoming, and Alta, Utah.

Pitty Paty
Thomas Augustine Arne
(1710–78)

One Morn eer sweet Peggy arose from her Bed,
I stole to the Chamber where lay the sweet Maid,
And op'ning the Curtain such Joy fill'd my Eye
That my Heart play'd a Tune that went Pitty Paty.

But finding she slept, O how great was my Bliss,
When on her sweet Lips I imprinted a Kiss;
The sight of her Bosom so fill'd me with Glee,
My Heart play'd a tune that went Pitty Paty.

Grown bold with success, I ventur'd to take
A second Salute, and sweet Peggy did wake.
Surpriz'd at my Presence she blush'd and cry'd Fie,
Tho' her Heart play'd a Tune that went Pitty Paty.

Callum-O'-Glen
James Hogg
1770–1835

Was every old warrior of suff'ring sae weary?
Was ever the wild beast sae bay'd in his den?
The Southron bloodhounds are kennel'd sae near me
That death would be welcome to Callum-O'-Glen.

My sons are all slain, and my daughters have left me,
Nae child to protect me where once I had ten;
My chief they have slain, and of stay have bereft me,
And woe to the grey hairs of Callum-O'-Glen.

The homes of my kinsmen are blazing to heaven,
The bright sun of morning has blush'd at the view,
The moon has stood still on the verge of the even
To wipe from her pale cheek the tint of the dew.
For the dew it lies red on the vales of Lochaber,
It sprinkles the cot and it flows in the pen;
The pride of my country is fallen for ever,
O, death! hast thou nae shaft for Callum-O'-Glen.

The sun in his glory hath look'd on our sorrow,
The stars have wep't blood over hamlet and lea,
O, is there no day star for Scotland, no morrow
Of bright renovation for souls of the free?
Yes! One above all has beheld our devotion,
Our valour and faith are not hid from His ken,
The day is abiding of stern retribution
On all the proud foemen of Callum-O'-Glen.

Appendix B

Life History of John Marshall

Editor's note: The following account was found in a journal of family records kept by John Marshall. Original spelling has been retained, but minor additions and deletions have been made and some punctuation and capitalization has been added for the sake of clarity.

    I John Marshall Born at No 40 Rottonrow Street Glasgow, County of Lanark, when eight year and six months old I Commenced to weave at factory. In Sept. 1837 I commenced my prenticeship at the old town head forge and Rolling Mill to [do] Iron Refining. On July 4th 1844 Commenced as Journyman Iron Refiner at Mossend Iron works, Bothwell parish Co. of Lanark Scotland. On Nov. 13th was married By Rev. peter Curry of Rope work entery of the free Church of Scotland.

    At 8.a.m. Jany 16th year 1850 By a Boiler explosion at the Mossend Iron works I was terrable scalded and also Burned with Melted Iron. Was in Bed for many weeks through this accedent. I at this time Betook myself to earnest prayer as I had Never Prayed Before. At all times while awaek I was in Commune with the god of heaven and earth through his son Jesus Christ. I Beged of god my eternal father to spare my life and at the same [time] I did promise him if . . . in and through his abundent mercey he would spare my life, and I Could But know how to serve him, I was willing to Be his obedient servant. At this time I . . . was an active member of the united preabteran Church of Scotland and had

Been for years. And Being a Constant Reader of scripture my mind became Confused. The reason Beign the written flowery Discourses of all the Sectarian *preachers* Discourses Did not in any way accord with Scripture [and] Did Confuse my mind.

On Thursday the first Thursday of June at half past 9. a.m. year 1850 while on my way to Church, it Being fast Day in Bothwell parish and County of lanark, all of a sudden a voice told me to go east from where I stood. . . . I had one mile west to go to the Church at this time. There were other people on the way to Church But No one Near me when the word of the voice of the Lord to me told me to go east. I stood still a few moments very much astonished and well I may. It Did not strick me then that it was the word of the Lord to me in answear to my prayers. But that [is] what it was. Haveing stood still a few moments I started again to Resume my Journy west, made But two steps when the voice of the Lord or his angel again told me to go east. Here was I in the Broad light of Day much astoneded. I then turned me around and went on the way east, I New not how far or where or the purpose.

I visited a friend of mine at Calder Iron works. Next I went from there to the whiflet Railway Staiston on the Caladonian Railway Staition a mile east of Coat-Bridge to take train home when the train Came up from glasgow. The staition house was Closed. I went into a house in the village to enquire when the trian would arive from glasgow. I found I had an hour and half to wait. I sat me Down By permission. I told the people I had used to frequent that house when Mrs. thomson lived in it. Mrs. thomson had Been remaried several years. The pepele told me Mrs. thomson had just Reurned to the village showing me where she lived. With much haste I hastened to the house where I found Mr. and Mrs [David] McNeil, the Now Mrs McNeil who was former Mrs thomson. They were latter Day Saints and here the New and everlasting gospel Door was thrown open to me. The train Came and went without me, had No use for it that day. At 12 o'Clock that night, two mile from there home, we stood on a Bridge where the luggie Brook empeyed into the River Calder Near Caranbrae Big house. After this Revelation to me I found what is true: that the thouhts and ways of man is not as the thoughts and ways of god. For the many years I had lived at Mossend one mile west of holytown where in the free Masons hall the Latter Day Saints had two meeting every Sunday and yet I had Never heard any one person utter the word latter Day Saint or Mormon Nor the Name of Joseph Smith the prophet of god arained [arrayed?] to the world the great last dispensation, of and through the mercy [of] god when the true and ever lasting gospel of Jesus Christ was Revealed to the human familey.

Now Dear friends I Bear and Record this tesimony to all people that the above is true and I make it in the Name of god the eternal father and his son Jesus, amen.

Signed By John Marshall at Pleasant View, Weber County, Utah in the year of hour Lord 1902.

Bibliography

Abbreviations
NA   National Archives, Washingtion, D.C.
UHi   Utah State Historical Society, Salt Lake City, Utah
ULA   Utah State University, Logan, Utah
USIC   Church Historical Department, Church of Jesus Christ of Latter-
            day Saints, Salt Lake City, Utah
USIGS   Family History Library, Church of Jesus Christ of Latter-day Saints,
            Salt Lake City, Utah

Airdrie Branch, Scotland. Record of Members 1841–54. USIC.
Alexander, Thomas G. "A Conflict of Perceptions: Ulysses S. Grant and the
    Mormons." *Grant Association Newsletter* 8 (1971): 36.
——. "Federal Authority versus Polygamic Theocracy: James McKean and the
    Mormons, 1870–75." *Dialogue: A Journal of Mormon Thought* 1 (1966):
    85–100.
——. "From Dearth to Deluge: Utah's Coal Industry." *Utah Historical Quar-
    terly* 31 (1963) 327–47.
——. *Mormonism in Transition: A History of the Latter-day Saints, 1890–1930.*
    Urbana and Chicago, 1986.
——. "The Word of Wisdom: From Principle to Requirement." *Dialogue: A
    Journal of Mormon Thought* 14 (1981): 78–88.
Allen, James B. *The Company Town in the American West.* Norman, Okla.,
    1966.
Allen, James B., and Thomas G. Alexander. *Mormons and Gentiles: A History
    of Salt Lake City.* Salt Lake City, 1982.
Allen, James B., and Glenn M. Leonard. *The Story of the Latter-day Saints.*
    Salt Lake City, 1976.
Anderson, Nels. *Desert Saints: The Mormon Frontier in Utah.* Chicago, 1966.
Armytage, W. H. G. *Heaven Below: Utopian Experience in England.* London,
    1961.
Arrington, Leonard J. "Abundance from the Earth: The Beginning of Commer-
    cial Mining in Utah." *Utah Historical Quarterly* 31 (1963): 192–219.
——. *The Changing Economic Structure of the Mountain West.* Logan, Utah,
    1963.

——. *Great Basin Kingdom: An Economic History of the Latter-day Saints, 1830-1900*. Cambridge, Mass., 1958.

——. "Utah and the Depression of the 1890s." *Utah Historical Quarterly* 29 (1961): 3-18.

Arrington, Leonard J., Feramorz Y. Fox, and Dean L. May. *Building the City of God: Community and Cooperation among the Mormons*. Salt Lake City, 1976.

Aspinwall, Bernard. "A Fertile Field: Scotland in the Days of the Early Missions." Paper presented at the annual meeting of the Mormon History Association, University of Oxford, 8 July 1987.

——. *Portable Utopia: Glasgow and the United States 1820-1920*. Aberdeen, 1984.

——. "The Scots in the United States." In *The Scots Abroad: Labour, Capital, Enterprise, 1750-1914*, edited by R. A. Gage. London, 1985.

Bancroft, Hubert Howe. *History of Arizona and New Mexico, 1530 to 1888*. San Francisco, 1889.

——. *History of Utah 1540-1884*. Las Vegas, Nev., 1982.

Belleville Weekly Advocate. Belleville, Ill.

Bennion, Lowell C. "The Incidence of Mormon Polygamy in 1880: 'Dixie' versus Davis Stake." *Journal of Mormon History* 11 (1984): 27-42.

Berry, Orville. "The Mormon Settlement in Illinois." *Transactions of the Illinois State Historical Society* 11 (1906): 88-102.

Book of the Dead. Sexton's Office, Salt Lake City Cemetery.

Brander, Michael. *The Emigrant Scots*. London, 1982.

Brodie, Fawn M. *No Man Knows My History*. New York, 1945.

Brooks, Juanita. *John Doyle Lee: Zealot, Pioneer, Builder, Scapegoat*. Glendale, Calif., 1972.

——. *The Mountain Meadows Massacre*. Rev. ed. Norman, Okla., 1962.

Brown, Callum G. *The Social History of Religion in Scotland since 1730*. London, 1987.

Bryce, Ebenezer. Biographical Sketch. MS. Works Progress Administration Project. UHi.

Buchanan, Frederick S. "The Ebb and Flow of the Mormon Church in Scotland, 1840-1900." *Brigham Young University Studies* 27 (Spring 1987): 27-52.

——. "Education among the Mormons: Brigham Young and the Schools of Utah." *History of Education Quarterly* 22 (1982): 435-59.

——. "The Emigration of Scottish Mormons to Utah, 1849-1900." Master's thesis, University of Utah, 1961.

——. "Faith in Schooling: Solving the Mormon Problem." *Review Journal of Philosophy and Social Science* 3 (1978) : 154-67.

——. "Imperial Zion: The British Occupation of Utah." In *The Peoples of Utah*, edited by Helen Z. Papanikolas. Salt Lake City, 1976.

Burns, Robert. *Poems and Songs of Robert Burns*. Edited by James Barke. London and Glasgow, 1962.

Byer, W. N., and John H. Kellom. *Hand Book to the Gold Fields of Nebraska and Kansas*. Chicago, 1859. Reprint. New York, 1973.

Campbell, Allen B. *The Lanarkshire Miners: A Social History of Their Trade Unions, 1775-1974*. Edinburgh, 1979.

Campbell, Eugene E., and Bruce L. Campbell. "Divorce among Mormon Polygamists: Extent and Explanations." *Utah Historical Quarterly* 46 (1978):4-23.

Cannon, Donald Q., and David J. Whitaker, eds. *Supporting Saints: Life Stories of Nineteenth-Century Mormons.* Provo, Utah, 1981.

Central Ward, Arizona. Historical Record. USIC.

Checkland, Sidney, and Olive Checkland. *Industry and Ethos: Scotland 1832–1914.* London, 1986.

Codman, John. *The Mormon Country: A Summer with the Latter-Day Saints.* New York, 1874.

[Coneybeare, William J.] "Mormonism." *Edinburgh Review* 99 (1854): 320–83.

Conley, Don C. "The Pioneer Chinese of Utah." In *The Peoples of Utah,* edited by Helen Z. Papanikolas. Salt Lake City, 1976.

Davenport, Rowland A. *Albury Apostles: The Story of the Body Known as the Catholic Apostolic Church (Sometimes Called the "Irvingites").* London, 1971.

Davis County, Utah. Censuses of 1870, 1880, 1890. USIGS.

——. Recorder's Office. Deeds and Tax Assessment Rolls. Farmington, Utah.

——. Grantee and Grantor Index. Farmington, Utah.

Deseret News. Salt Lake City, Utah.

Douglas, William M. Biography of William M. Douglas. Typescript, Special Collections, ULA.

Draper, William J. *History of the American Civil War.* New York, 1870.

Drummond, Andrew L., and James Bulloch. *The Church in Victorian Scotland 1843–1874.* Edinburgh, 1974.

Dunlop, Richard. *Doctors of the American Frontier.* New York, 1962.

Edinburgh Conference. Statistical Account, 1840–68. USIC.

Endowment House Records. USIGS.

Essholm, Frank. *Pioneers and Prominent Men of Utah.* Salt Lake City, 1913.

Family Group Records. USIGS.

Ferris, Benjamin. *Utah and the Mormons.* New York, 1856.

Fife, Austin. "The Legend of the Three Nephites Among the Mormons." *Journal of American Folklore* 53 (1940): 1–49.

Furniss, Norman F. *The Mormon Conflict, 1850–1859.* New Haven, Conn., 1960.

Gage, R. A., ed. *The Scots Abroad: Labour, Capital, Enterprise, 1750–1914.* London, 1985.

Gibson, William. Journal, 1841–70. USIC.

Glasgow Conference. Statistical Account, 1840–80. USIC.

Glasgow Herald. Glasgow, Scotland.

Hafen, LeRoy R., and Ann W. Hafen. *Handcarts to Zion.* Glendale, Calif., 1960.

Hamilton, Henry. Journal, 1831–1900. USIC.

Hammond, Bray. *Banks and Politics in America, from the Revolution to the Civil War.* Princeton, 1957.

Hartley, William B. "Edward Hunter: Pioneer Presiding Bishop." In *Supporting Saints: Life Stories of Nineteenth-Century Mormons,* edited by Donald Q. Cannon and David J. Whitaker. Provo, Utah, 1981.

Hicks, John D. *The American Nation.* 3d ed. Cambridge, Mass., 1955.

Hill, Marvin. "Mormon Religion in Nauvoo: Some Reflections." *Utah Historical Quarterly* 44 (1976): 172–74.

Holmes, Blair R., ed. Journal of James Sherlock Cantwell. Special Collections, ULA.

Jackson, W. Turrentine. *The Enterprising Scot: Investors After 1873.* Edinburgh, 1968.

306

Jenson, Andrew. *Encyclopedic History of the Church of Jesus Christ of Latter-day Saints.* Salt Lake City, 1941.
——. *Latter-day Saint Biographical Encyclopedia.* 4 vols. Salt Lake City, 1901–36.
Jessee, Dean C., ed. *Letters of Brigham Young to His Sons.* Salt Lake City, 1974.
Journal History of the Church. USIC.
Journal of Discourses. 26 vols. Liverpool, 1854–86.
Juab County, Utah. Censuses of 1870, 1880, 1900. USIGS.
Kearl, J. B., et al., comp. *Index to the 1850, 1860, 1870 Censuses of Utah.* Baltimore, 1981.
Lanarkshire, Scotland. Censuses of 1851, 1861, 1871. USIGS.
Larson, Gustive O. *The "Americanization" of Utah for Statehood.* San Marino, Calif., 1971.
——. *Outline History of Territorial Utah.* Provo, Utah, 1972.
——. "Utah and the Civil War." *Utah Historical Quarterly* 33 (1965): 55–77.
Launius, Roger D. "Joseph Smith III and the Mormon Succession Crisis, 1844–1846." *Western Illinois Regional Studies* 6 (1983): 5–22.
Lehman, William C. *Scottish and Scotch-Irish Contributions to Early American Life and Culture.* Port Washington, N.Y., 1978.
Liverpool Emigration Records. USIC.
Lyman, Edward Leo. *Political Deliverance: The Mormon Quest for Statehood.* Urbana and Chicago, 1986.
Lyon, John. *The Harp of Zion.* Liverpool, 1853.
Lyon, T. Edgar, and Glenn M. Leonard. "The Churches in the Territory." In *Utah's History*, edited by Richard D. Poll, et al. Provo, Utah, 1978.
Lyon, Thomas E., Jr. *John Lyon: Poet/Pioneer.* Salt Lake City, 1988.
McClintock, James J. *Mormon Settlement in Arizona.* Phoenix, Ariz., 1971.
McIntyre, Thomas. Journal. USIC.
MacKay, Charles. *Poetical Works of Charles MacKay.* London, 1876.
McLaws, Monte B. *Spokesman for the Kingdom.* Provo, Utah, 1977.
M'Neill, Peter. *Tranent and Its Surroundings: Historical, Ecclesiastical, and Traditional.* Edinburgh and Glasgow, 1883.
McNiff, William J. *Heaven on Earth: A Planned Mormon Society.* Oxford, Ohio, 1940.
McPhee, John. *The Crofter and the Laird.* New York, 1970.
Madison County, Illinois. *History.* Edwardsville, Ill., 1882.
Marshall, John. Autobiography of John Marshall. In possession of Cleone Marshall Wayment, North Ogden, Utah.
——. Life History of John Marshall. In possession of Dean L. Marshall, Modesto, California.
May, Dean L. "Towards a Dependent Commonwealth." In *Utah's History*, edited by Richard D. Poll, et al. Provo, Utah, 1978.
Miller, Harry Colin, arranger. *Forty-seven Popular Scottish Songs.* Second Series. Glasgow, 1915.
Military Service Record of John Thompson and Declaration for Widow's Pension submitted by Elizabeth Haig Thompson. NA.
Millennial Star, 1837–1900.
Moody, Francis W. Autobiography and Journal, 1881–1914. USIC.
Morrell, Lee W. P. *The Gold Rushes.* New York, 1941.
Mulder, William. *Homeward to Zion: The Mormon Migration from Scandinavia.* Minneapolis, Minn., 1958.

Mulder, William, and A. Russell Mortensen, eds. *Among the Mormons: Historic Accounts by Contemporary Observers*. New York, 1969.

Neff, Andrew Love. *History of Utah 1847 to 1869*. Edited and annotated by Leland H. Creer. Salt Lake City, 1940.

Newell, Linda King, and Valeen Tippetts Avery. *Mormon Enigma: Emma Hale Smith*. New York, 1984.

Nicol, John Murray, ed. *The James and Mary Murray Murdoch Family History*. Provo, Utah, 1982.

North Kanyon Ward, Bountiful, Utah. Children's Blessings, 1877–1900. USIGS.

Ordinance Gazetteer of Scotland. Edinburgh, 1885.

Papanikolas, Helen Z., ed. *The Peoples of Utah*. Salt Lake City, 1976.

Park City Record. Park City, Utah.

Peterson, Charles S. "The Limits of Learning in Pioneer Utah." *Journal of Mormon History* 10 (1983): 65–78.

———. "A Mighty Man was Brother Lot: A Portrait of Lot Smith — Mormon Frontiersman." *Western Historical Quarterly* 1 (Fall 1963) : 393–414.

———. *Take Up Your Mission: Mormon Colonizing along the Little Colorado River 1870–1900*. Tucson, 1973.

———. *Utah: A Bicentennial History*. New York, 1977.

Piercy, Frederick Hawkins. *Route from Liverpool to the Great Salt Lake*. Edited by Fawn M. Brodie. Cambridge, Mass., 1962.

Poll, Richard D., et al., eds. *Utah's History*. Provo, Utah, 1978.

Quinn, D. Michael. "Echoes and Foreshadowings: The Distinctiveness of the Mormon Community." *Sunstone* 3 (1978): 12–17.

———. "LDS Church Authority and New Plural Marriage, 1890–1904." *Dialogue: A Journal of Mormon Thought* 18 (1985): 9–105.

———. "The Mormon Succession Crisis of 1844." *Brigham Young University Studies* 16 (1976): 187–233.

———. The Practice of Rebaptism at Nauvoo." *Brigham Young University Studies* 18 (1978–79): 226–32.

Quorum of Seventy, Thirty-ninth. Minute Book. USIC.

———. Twenty-fifth. Minute Book. USIC.

Reorganized Church of Jesus Christ of Latter Day Saints. Archives. Independence, Mo.

Richards, Eric. *A History of the Highland Clearances: Agrarian Transformation and the Evictions 1746–1886*. London and Canberra, 1982.

Rowan, Matthew. Poetry Book. USIC.

Salt Lake County, Utah. Recorder's Office. Index to Names.

Salt Lake Tribune. Salt Lake City, Utah.

Scottish Conference. Statistical Account, 1880–99. USIC.

Sillito, John R., and John S. McCormick. "Socialist Saints: Mormons and the Socialist Party in Utah, 1900–1920." *Dialogue: A Journal of Mormon Thought* 18 (Spring 1985): 121–31.

Silver City Ward, Utah, Record of Members, 1897–1907. USIGS.

Sims, Ronald L. *History of Almy and the Church of Jesus Christ of Latter-day Saints*. N.p., c. 1978.

Slaven, Anthony. *Development of the West of Scotland: 1750–1960*. London and Boston, 1975.

Smith, Joseph. *A History of the Church of Jesus Christ of Latter-day Saints*. 7 vols. Salt Lake City, 1902–32.

Smith, Joseph Fielding, ed. *Teachings of the Prophet Joseph Smith*. Salt Lake City, 1951.

Smout, Christopher. *A Century of the Scottish People, 1830–1950*. New Haven, Conn., 1986.

Spencer, Clark C. *British Investments and the American Mining Frontier 1860–1901*. New York, 1958.

Taylor, Philip A. M. *The Distant Magnet: European Emigration to the U.S.A.* New York, 1971.

———. *Expectations Westward: The Mormons and the Emigration of Their British Converts in the Nineteenth Century*. Edinburgh and London, 1965.

———. "Why Did British Mormons Emigrate?" *Utah Historical Quarterly* 22 (1956): 249–70.

Thompson, Edward P. *The Making of the English Working Class*. New York, 1963.

Thorpe, Malcolm R. "The Religious Background of Mormon Converts in Britain, 1837–1852." *Journal of Mormon History* 4 (1977): 51–66.

Tullidge, Edward W. *History of Salt Lake City*. Salt Lake City, 1886.

Tuttle, D. S. *Reminiscences of a Missionary Bishop*. New York, 1906. Reprint. Helena, Mont., 1977; Salt Lake City, 1987.

Tyler, S. Lyman. "Indians in Utah Territory." In *Utah's History*, edited by Richard D. Poll, et al. Provo, Utah, 1978.

Walker, Henry P., and Don Bulkin. *Historical Atlas of Arizona*. Norman, Okla., 1979.

Walker, Ronald W. "The Commencement of the Godbeite Protest: Another View." *Utah Historical Quarterly* 42 (1974): 217–44.

Webster, David. *Scottish Highland Games*. Edinburgh, 1973.

Wilson, Alexander. *The Chartist Movement in Scotland*. New York, 1970.

Wilson, Gordon M. *Alexander McDonald: Leader of the Miners*. Aberdeen, 1982.

Young, Brigham. Letterpress Book. USIC.

Index